Matching the Gun
to the Game

MATCHING THE GUN TO THE GAME

Clair Rees

WINCHESTER PRESS

An Imprint of NEW CENTURY PUBLISHERS, INC.

Book design by Quentin Fiore

Printing code
11 12 13 14 15 16

Library of Congress Cataloging in Publication Data

Rees, Clair F.
    Matching the gun to the game.

    Includes index.
    1. Hunting guns.   I. Title
SK274.R43 1982   799.2'028'3   82-13375
ISBN 0-8329-3672-3

To the memories of
Francis D. Rees,
my father and shooting instructor;
and Stan Innes,
a fine sportsman and an inspiration

Contents

Introduction

Today's hunting sportsman is faced with a very real problem whenever he goes afield: which firearm, and what kind of ammunition to carry?

Nimrods living a century or so ago had a much easier time making this choice. The selection of gun types was considerably more limited than we have available today, and the muzzle-loading rifleman varied his ammunition primarily by using a little more—or less—powder behind his spherical lead ball. Black-powder shotgunners also manufactured their ammo on the spot, and terms like "magnum" or "field load" were all but unknown.

The modern rifleman has a long list of different calibers and cartridges to choose from, and each performs somewhat differently. For example, there are more than a dozen separate cartridge configurations available designed for .30-caliber projectiles. These range from the puny .30 Carbine on up to the potent .300 Weatherby and .308 Norma magnums. The first load is adequate for hunting rabbits and coyotes at relatively short range, while the big, belted magnums are capable of downing any game in North America and nearly everything Africa has to offer.

Once the caliber and cartridge are selected, the hunter still must choose the proper load for the game being hunted. Handloaders have a staggering number of options available, but even those who shoot factory ammunition exclusively have some decisions to make, chiefly with regard to bullet weight and construction. Sportsmen who own rifles chambered for the highly popular .30-06 cartridge can buy ammo over the counter loaded with saboted 55-grain .22-caliber slugs suitable only for the lightest-skinned varmints, as well as 110-, 125-, 150-, 165-, 180-, 200- and 220-grain bullets for considerably heavier game up to and including moose and grizzly. In that selection are included hollow-point, soft-point and a variety of controlled-expansion protected-point bullets, each featuring a somewhat different shape or construction.

Cartridge and bullet type aside, several different types of rifles are available from a number of different manufacturers. A deer hunter can choose from a bewildering array of bolt, autoloading, slide-action, single-shot and lever-action firearms. Which type is best? The correct choice depends on many factors, including range, the size of the animal being hunted (and therefore the accuracy level required), the need for rapid repeat shots, whether hand-loaded or factory-loaded ammo will be used, probable weather conditions and, finally, the personal taste and preference of the rifleman himself.

Shotgunners have only a half-dozen different gauges to make their selection from: 10, 12, 16, 20, 28 and .410. However, the variety of loads available for each gauge is large enough to confuse even experienced nimrods. If you own a 12-gauge shotgun with a 3-inch magnum chamber, it will digest factory ammunition including everything from full-length magnum shells containing 1⅜, 1⅝ or 1⅞ ounces of shot, 2¾-inch "baby magnums" containing 1½ ounces of pellets, long-range "Express" loads filled with 1¼ ounces of shot, or field loads throwing 1, 1⅛ or 1¼ ounces of shot. In addition there are special scatter loads available, as well as target loads featuring a 1⅛-ounce charge. You can also choose between steel, copper-plated, or soft-lead pellets, as well as from four different sizes of buckshot and a variety of rifled slugs. Standard "birdshot" is offered in BB, 2, 4, 5, 6, 7½, 8 and 9 sizes, to make things even more confusing.

Wingshooters, too, have a variety of different shotgun types available, and must also consider barrel length and choke, which is the amount of bore constriction at the muzzle end.

Hunting with a handgun is becoming increasingly popular in this country, and the sportsman who accepts this challenge has his own sizeable collection of calibers, gun types and loads to choose from. Again, some guns are better suited than others for hunting certain kinds of game.

Because there are so many different calibers, cartridges and gauges available in so many different firearms, today's hunter has a formidable task determining exactly which rifle, shotgun or handgun is the best possible choice for hunting a particular type of game. Where several different sizes of animal are to be hunted with a single firearm, what gun or rifle would be the best compromise? What kind of sights? Which variety of ammunition?

This book is intended to serve as a practical guide to matching both guns and ammunition to all North American game. It won't tell you precisely which make, model and caliber of rifle to buy for hunting a certain kind of game. Neither will the book reveal the one shotgun in the world that's best for you. There are simply too many variables, and too many excellent firearms available to narrow the choice to a single candidate.

The ultimate selection of a hunting firearm is a highly personal thing. Some riflemen like lever-operated carbines, while others prefer bolt-action repeaters. Still others opt for auto-loaders, slide-actions or single shots.

Similarly, a handgunner may favor single-action revolvers (that require thumb cocking before every shot) to the double-action variety, or be a fervent fan of the auto pistol. Conversely, he may shun repeaters altogether to hunt with a flat-shooting single shot that fires high-intensity rifle ammunition. It all depends on taste.

On the other hand, there are sometimes practical considerations that make one type of hunting rifle, or handgun, unsuited for a particular type of game. Your choice of action type may be limited when you intend to hunt large, dangerous game such as the Alaskan brown bear, as the rifles chambered for the potent, charge-stopping rounds recommended for these aggressive animals are generally available only in bolt-action and single-shot varieties. You can kill a big grizzly with a .30-06 Remington pump, but most Alaskan bear guides will be much happier if you show up in camp toting a .338 Winchester or .375 H&H magnum.

This book will provide a practical, easy-to-understand guide to selecting the firearms and loads needed to hunt different kinds of game. While it won't narrow the selection to a single, unique choice, it will tell you which combinations are the most suitable, and which should be dropped from consideration.

In addition to making recommendations regarding the combinations most suited to specific game animals or hunting conditions, it also discusses "all-around" rifles, shotguns or handguns that can be safely called upon to serve multiple duties afield. If you want to use the same rifle to hunt 2-pound prairie dogs at 300 yards as well as mountain muleys a hundred times heavier, some excellent choices are available that will do both jobs with equal ease. Similarly, the same scattergun can be used in the goose blind that you employed the day before to hunt close-flushing quail.

Making the *wrong* choice of firearm, sights or ammunition can prove costly. You may lose wounded game, destroy too much edible meat, or even find your own life endangered.

Choosing the wrong equipment is sure to lessen your enjoyment of a fine, healthy sport, and is likely to prove hard on the budget. Guns and accessories are relatively expensive items, and it only makes sense to protect your investment by choosing wisely in the first place.

Which rifle, shotgun or handgun do *you* need? Let's take a look and see.

Matching the Gun
to the Game

Deer Rifles and Guns 1

Of all the game animals hunted in this country, none have received more emphasis or attention than deer. Whether it be eastern whitetail, California blacktail or western mule deer, *Odocoileus* easily outranks all other four-footed game larger than rabbits or squirrels in terms of hunter popularity.

The vast majority of centerfire rifles sold to American sportsmen are purchased primarily with deer in mind. Similarly, many shotguns serve dual duty when deer season rolls around, and sales of ammo loaded with buckshot or rifled slugs soar in the fall and early winter months.

Handgunners also get their share of venison each year, and deer are the favorite target of those nostalgia-invoking riflemen who favor primitive muzzleloaders to newer, more modern armament.

So what is a "deer rifle"? Any rifle suitable for hunting deer would qualify, and some nimrods even refer to their slug-loaded shotguns as "deer rifles" because they throw rifled slugs.

Rifle Calibers and Cartridges

Many different calibers and cartridges are potent enough for use on deer, but some are much better than others. At the low end of the caliber scale, .22 centerfires such as the .223 and .22-250, and even the pipsqueak .17 Remington, have taken deer. For that matter, poachers have used the rimfire .22 long-rifle cartridge in deer woods with great success. Under ideal circumstances, deer can be killed with such cartridges, but that doesn't make them a good choice. A true sportsman owes it to his or her quarry to use a cartridge of adequate power to insure consistent, clean kills even when conditions aren't ideal.

In the hands of a skilled marksman with the patience and necessary woodsmanship to stalk his buck until the range is sure, a .22 centerfire will do the job. Unfortunately, most of us lack the skills and patience to get in close enough to place that tiny slug precisely, every time and without fail. Chances are, we'll be shooting at a running target, or one that's partly

Finnish Tikka chambered for 6mm Remington is a light, accurate deer rifle with low recoil. (Photo by Ken Turner.)

obscured by brush or branches. What's more, the range may be closer to 200 yards than 20, and a pounding heart and panting lungs are likely to be detracting from a rock-steady hold.

In other words, deer hunters need a cartridge with enough power to put a 150-pound (or heavier) animal down when it's hit somewhere in the chest cavity. The bullet must be heavy enough and tough enough to hold together and not simply fragment when it strikes a rib. At the same time, the bullet should be constructed to begin expanding on impact. A projectile that mushrooms to a larger diameter kills more effectively than one that simply passes through an animal unchanged.

Most hunting bullets must strike with a certain amount of force to expand and perform as designed. This means they must be traveling at high velocities. Since a bullet begins slowing down as it leaves the muzzle, you should choose a cartridge case capable of holding enough powder to provide sufficient speed at reasonable distances.

The bullet itself must be heavy enough to do the job. Light bullets shed velocity—and energy—relatively fast, making them poor choices for long-range work. All these facts argue against the use of any .22 centerfire for hunting deer. The lightly constructed 55-grain projectiles thrown by .222, .223 and .22-250 factory loads simply aren't designed for killing deer-size game, and even when heavier 70-grain slugs are substituted by handloaders, these .22's are at a ballistic disadvantage.

At the other end of the scale are those bigbore magnums designed for large, dangerous game. There's certainly nothing wrong with hunting deer with a .375 Holland & Holland Magnum or even a .458 Winchester. These cartridges are adequate—or more than adequate— for deer-size game, and from a "clean kill" standpoint they come highly recommended.

However, a rifle designed to stop a charging elephant or kill a half-ton grizzly is likely to generate more recoil than the average deer hunter will tolerate. In addition to being uncomfortable, sometimes bordering on downright unpleasant, heavy recoil promotes flinching and other bad habits not conducive to long-range accuracy.

To help compensate for recoil, rifles chambered for the large, magnum cartridges tend to be considerably heavier than most rifles favored for deer-woods use. This is another reason bigbore magnums aren't highly popular for hunting deer. No one enjoys toting more weight than necessary, and a 10½- or 11-pound scoped .375 H&H is simply too much rifle to lug around all day unless you're expecting an African lion or Cape buffalo to charge momentarily.

That brings us to the great "middle ground" of American hunting cartridges, rounds ideally suited for hunting deer-size game. This selection begins with the .243 Winchester and the 6mm Remington, rounds that are virtually identical in performance although Remington's 6mm holds slightly more powder and has the edge when handloaded. These two rounds are offered in factory loads with your choice of 80- or 100-grain weights. Handloaders

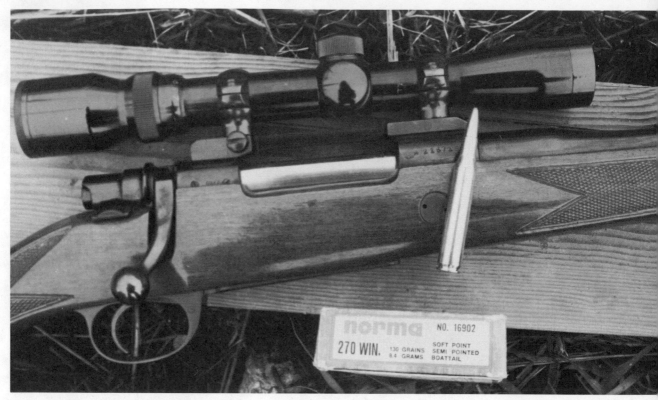

The .270 Winchester has long been a favorite cartridge for mule deer.

can choose among a variety of bullets weighing from 75 to 120 grains. For deer, stick with bullets weighing 100 grains or more, and leave the lighter stuff for shooting varmints.

With properly designed bullets, either the .243 Winchester or 6mm Remington make fine deer cartridges out to 250 yards. The trajectory is flat enough and many rifles chambered for these rounds are accurate enough to encourage shooting at even longer range, but they lack sufficient punch to be relied on much past that mark. These are multi-purpose cartridges that work equally well in the varmint field. They develop relatively little recoil, and are easy to shoot accurately. They fully deserve their great popularity.

The quarter bores offer similar versatility. The .25-06 Remington, .250 Savage and .257 Roberts all make fine combination varmint/deer rifle loads, as does Weatherby's .257 belted magnum. They throw slightly heavier (up to 125-grain) projectiles than either of the 6mm's, particularly if you limit your selection to factory fodder only. This makes them useful on even large deer, and many have used .25's on elk. The .257 Weatherby and .25-06 Remington are outstanding long-range cartridges for hunting deer and antelope, while the .250 Savage and .257 Roberts feature low recoil, and good effectiveness to 200 yards or so.

Winchester's .264 belted magnum ranks as a deer round, and it's capable of doing the job well past the 300-yard mark. It's a good, long-range cartridge for deer and even larger game, but it has the reputation of being a hard kicker and of burning up barrels. Based on the big .458 Winchester case, the .264 is an over-bore capacity round that is efficient only with slow-burning powders. This fast-stepping load, which throws a 100-grain bullet at around 3,700 feet per second (fps), enjoyed a certain amount of popularity in the 1960's. However, it's little used today. There are cartridges capable of delivering very similar performance without the same fuss and bother.

The .270 Winchester was introduced in 1925, and seems to become more popular every year. This is a highly versatile round considered by many to be ideal for hunting mountain muleys and other deer at longish ranges. It shoots flat, and has enough power to anchor elk, moose and other large game.

Because the .270 is so widely used, it is available in almost every bolt-action, single-shot or slide-action centerfire on the market. Bullets are offered in weights ranging from 100 to 180 grains, although the 130- and 140-grain projectiles seem to provide the best all-around performance on deer-size game.

The late Jack O'Connor did much to popularize the .270 during his long and prolific writing career. He used this cartridge to take a surprising variety of game all over the world. He and other experienced nimrods have used .270's to successfully hunt grizzlies and other dangerous beasts, although most experienced sportsmen would today consider that kind of armament decidedly on the light side for an Alaskan brown bear hunt.

The .270 has a well-earned reputation for accuracy, particularly when used in a properly tuned bolt rifle. It doesn't recoil as noticeably as its larger brother, the .30-06, and this hasn't hurt its popularity. Since the .270 Winchester is nothing more than the .30-06 cartridge necked down to accept a .277-inch projectile, it shares many of the dimensions *and* performance characteristics of that fine round.

Weatherby's .270 magnum pushes a 130-grain slug along some 200 to 250 fps faster than the standard .270, and so is even more potent. However, this (and most other) Weatherby magnum chamberings are offered only in Weatherby bolt rifles, which narrows your choice considerably.

The little 7x57mm Mauser makes an extremely fine deer round. Even though purposely underloaded by American ammo makers, the 7mm Mauser kills very well at any respectable range, and without producing much recoil.

While the 7mm Mauser is slightly less powerful than the popular .270 or Remington's 7mm Express, it has been used successfully on a surprising variety of game since its introduction in 1892. As a matter of fact, you'd be hard pressed to name a big game animal that hasn't been harvested with the 7x57, and that includes elephant. That doesn't make the 7mm Mauser (or *any* 7mm, for that matter) an elephant load, but it should bring pause to those magnum-minded nimrods who feel the little Mauser is too anemic to use on mule deer.

A number of different bullet types and weights are available, although domestic factory loads can be had only with 139-, 140- or 175-grain soft-point projectiles. Either the 139- or 140-grain loads make good deer medicine, while handloaders can use 130-, 140-, 145-, 154- or 160-grain bullets. Handloaders can also substantially better the 2,660-fps muzzle velocity delivered by 139-grain factory loads.

The new 7mm-08 Remington throws the same 7mm (.284-inch) bullets the 7mm Mauser digests, and has very nearly the same powder capacity. This means either round can be hand-loaded to about the same ballistics. However, Remington loads the 7mm-08 at an advertised 2,860 fps, 200 fps faster than the otherwise similar 139-grain 7mm Mauser factory load. Since the 7mm-08 is simply the popular .308 cartridge necked down, reloaders may tend to favor this newer number over the European Mauser. Non-handloaders will probably prefer it because of the higher velocities generated with over-the-counter ammunition. The 7mm-08 Remington fits in the same short-action rifles that take the .308 Winchester.

The .284 Winchester is another fine short-action 7mm that rivals the performance of the 7mm Mauser and 7mm-08 Remington. Unfortunately, this compact but potent round never enjoyed great popularity and is all but obsolete. At the moment, only custom rifles are being chambered for the .284 Winchester.

Remington's 7mm Express began life as the .280 Remington in 1957, and was renamed the 7mm Remington Express in 1979. This is a more potent cartridge than any of the above-named 7mm's, and is an excellent choice for deer. Its larger, heavier bullets make it a bit more powerful than the .270, but there's little to choose between these competing rounds as far as deer hunting is concerned. Like the .270, the 7mm Remington Express shoots flat enough and packs sufficient punch to be effective on deer out to and even beyond the 300-yard mark. The 150-grain factory load is a good choice for deer.

Even more potent is Remington's belted 7mm magnum. Some feel this round offers more punch than is really needed to do in a deer-size animal, and it does tend to recoil more sharply than the milder 7mm's. On the other side of the coin, the 7mm Remington Magnum has earned an enviable reputation as a long-range killer of deer and larger game.

As loaded by the factory, the 7mm Remington Magnum pushes a 150-grain slug out the bore some 140 fps faster than the beltless 7mm Remington Express, and that adds up to a somewhat flatter trajectory and more retained energy downrange. Basically, the 7mm Remington Magnum hits as hard at 400 yards as the 7mm Express does at 350. The tradeoffs are greater ammo costs, and increased recoil and muzzle blast.

The 7mm Weatherby Magnum is even more potent. Otherwise, the same comments apply. Either of the 7mm magnums will do a fine job on deer, particularly when the range is extreme. But they are more punishing to the shoulder. The 7mm magnums are good choices on one-rifle hunts where larger game like elk or moose may be taken, but beginning riflemen would likely be better off with something a bit milder.

Moving up to the .30 calibers, some sportsmen have attempted to use the .30 carbine as a deer rifle. This is a mistake, as the .30 carbine round is simply too puny and underpowered for the job. I'm not comfortable with any cartridge that won't deliver a bare minimum of 1,000 foot-pounds of energy at a range where the bullet goes to work. With a soft-nose 110-grain hunting bullet as loaded by the factory, the .30 carbine has only 950 foot-pounds of punch as it exits the bore, and just 575 foot-pounds 100 yards later.

The .30-30 Winchester is another story. This was introduced in 1895 as the first American smokeless-powder "small-bore" hunting round, and in the years since it has racked up a phe-

Western hunter totes .30-30 carbine into the deer woods. These light, handy rifles remain popular, although the .30-30 round is outclassed by many modern loads.

The .308 Winchester is a fine deer cartridge, but the right style and weight of bullet should always be used. This target shows the difference in bullet strike at a range of 200 yards when using 110-, 150- and 180-grain projectiles.

nomenal record in the deer woods. In all likelihood, more deer have been taken in North America with the .30-30 than with any other cartridge.

That record is less a tribute to the cartridge's overall effectiveness — which is limited to a range of about 150 yards — than to the vast number of light, handy, lever carbines in use that digest this round. The .30-30 remains highly popular today, and is a reasonably effective round in dense woods where shots are usually offered at close range. But many more-desirable deer cartridges are on the market. If you're a fan of the model 1894 Winchester or Marlin 336 saddle carbines, the .30-30 isn't a bad choice. You'll have to pass up long- or even medium-range shots, but for use in heavy timber it's okay.

The .35 Remington and the .375 Winchester Big Bore cartridges are designed for the same, basic type of lever-action carbines, but carry more punch than the .30-30. Because of their looping trajectories, they remain 150- to maybe 200-yard rounds. They're a better choice for deer-size game, but the vast majority of saddle guns sold continue to be chambered for the older, less potent .30-30. American deer hunters are a highly conservative lot, and many resist change with surprising stubbornness. "Both grandad and dad used a .30-30, and by gum they always brought home the venison," they say. "What was good enough for them is good enough for me!"

In truth, the only thing wrong with the .30-30 is that many better deer-hunting cartridges are available, modern cartridges that shoot flatter, farther and with more killing power. But don't ever let anyone tell you the .30-30 won't kill deer. It will! Just don't try any fancy long-range marksmanship when you're shooting one. Two hundred yards is a l-o-n-g shot for an open-sighted .30-30, and even adding a scope doesn't improve your chances much at that distance. Out there, the energy has fallen off below the 1,000 foot-pounds mark, and the bullet strikes about 9 inches below point of aim if the rifle is sighted for a 100-yard zero. Use the 170-grain flat-nose factory loads rather than the lighter 150-grain offerings, and if you handload don't try to boost velocities with heavy powder charges. The .30-30 cases, not to mention some of the rifles chambered for the round, simply aren't up to handling high pressures.

The .300 Savage is another aging .30-caliber deer round, but it's considerably more potent —and flatter shooting—than the .30-30. The only rifle still chambered for this load is the Savage model 99, and since this same lever gun is also available in .308 Winchester chambering there's little reason to choose a .300 Savage when buying a new deer rifle. This is still a good deer cartridge, but it's been upstaged by more modern loads.

My favorite .30-caliber deer load is the .308 Winchester. This stubby powerhouse is about a half-inch shorter than the .30-06, which allows it to be used in a variety of short-action rifles like the Browning BLR and Savage model 99 lever guns, in addition to any number of short-coupled bolt rifles that run several ounces lighter than the same firearms sporting full-length actions. Being naturally lazy, I'm partial to lightweight deer rifles, and the .308 provides plenty of power for the lightest of hunting centerfires.

As loaded by the factory, the .308 comes within 100 feet per second of equaling the velocities delivered by the larger .30-06, using the same bullet weights. The .30-06 cartridge case simply has greater powder capacity, so even careful handloading leaves a power gap. At the same time, the .308 is more than potent enough for the largest muley or whitetail buck, even at extreme ranges. Federal's Premium .308 Winchester load throwing a 165-grain boattail soft-point bullet produces 1,450 foot-pounds of punch clear out at 400 yards, and 1,230 foot-pounds at 500. And those are ranges no real sportsman will attempt to shoot deer at. Granted, game has been taken at 500 yards with a hunting rifle, but the most skilled marksman is more likely to wound than to kill cleanly at that distance. Even if the rifle is held perfectly still, a wind isn't blowing, and the crosshairs are held high enough to compensate for bullet drop, the rifle itself may not be capable of grouping shots inside a 2-inch circle at 100 yards. That means the bullet may strike as much as 10 inches off target at 500 yards, even if the rifleman does everything right.

I've killed several deer at 300 yards or so with the .308, and it does a fine job at that range. As I've pointed out, the right .308 load is capable of doing the job at much longer distances, but I don't encourage hunters to shoot at extreme range, regardless of the rifle and cartridge used.

A number of different bullet weights are available for the .308 Winchester, both in factory loads and as components for handloading. The deer hunter should stick with the 150-, 165- and 180-grain weights for best results. For years I enjoyed good success with pointed soft-point 150-grain projectiles, but I've now switched to 165-grain boattail bullets for the improved performance they provide at ranges past 200 yards.

Everything I've just said about the .308 Winchester applies to the .30-06 Springfield. This time-proven cartridge is the all-around hunter's favorite; the only round that could be credited with more deer kills in this country is the .30-30. As someone once said, "The .30-06 is never a mistake." That statement certainly holds true for North American game, although most experienced nimrods prefer something with a bit more oomph when hunting Alaskan brown bear. These big grizzlies have been killed with .30-06 rifles, and I once carried an '06 during a British Columbian grizzly hunt. But for tackling the oversize coastal bears the big magnums are a better choice.

For hunting deer, the 150- and 165-grain bullet weights are ideal in this caliber. Again, I prefer the 165-grain boattail bullets, available as factory loads from Frontier, and in Federal's Premium line. The 180-grain bullet weight is another good choice, although recoil is greater.

Because the .30-06 has a slight velocity edge over the .308, it's an even better cartridge for long-range shooting. The .308 offers an advantage only if you're weight conscious and a short action appeals, or if you want a lever-action rifle. If the rifle you'd like to buy is offered in only one action length that's used for both cartridges, choose the .30-06.

While the .30-06 is not a hard-kicking round, it does generate more recoil than most of the other cartridges mentioned so far in this chapter. The exceptions are the 7mm Remington and Weatherby belted magnums. Recoil sensitivity is largely a matter of mental conditioning, and most experienced riflemen have no trouble shooting a .30-06-class firearm accurately and without discomfort.

However, some riflemen (and women) find themselves flinching when shooting heavy loads in a .30-06. If recoil does bother you, you'd likely be better off with a .243 Winchester, 6mm Remington or a 7x57mm Mauser. These are all perfectly adequate deer rounds, and an accurately placed 100-grain 6mm slug does a much better job of anchoring game than a 180-grain .30-06 bullet that winds up a foot or more off target.

Another good deer load popular in Canada, though little used in the United States, is the .303 British. In this country, a single factory load is available. This pushes a 180-grain soft point along at 2,460 fps, and does a good job out to 250 yards. Handloaders should be aware that this caliber requires a .311-inch, and not a .308-inch diameter, bullet.

The .300 Winchester Magnum makes a fine, long-range deer cartridge, throwing a 180-grain bullet some 250 fps faster than the '06 does. The 150-grain factory load shoots flat enough to allow you to hold dead-on-target out to 350 yards when sighted to print 2½ inches high at 100.

Here's a lineup of top deer loads that can also be used for larger game.

Since the .300 magnum tends to jolt the shooter harder than the .30-06 does, it's generally avoided by recoil-shy riflemen. The cartridge *is* more powerful than really needed for use on deer, but it remains a perfectly reasonable choice. I've used the .300 Winchester on western mule deer, and it's always performed well. The 150-grain load is my first pick of the factory loads available, although I prefer a 165-grain Hornady, Nosler or Sierra boattail loaded to 3,150 feet per second for best results. There are several good handloads that will deliver this velocity and give fine accuracy.

The 8mm Mauser is another European military round that has seen wide use in the hunting field. Although it is much less popular than the 7x57mm Mauser, which is currently enjoying a resurgence of interest in this country, the 8x57mm is a good choice for deer even with anemic American factory loads that start a 170-grain slug at 2,360 fps. An 8x57mm rifle in good condition can safely digest much stiffer handloads to provide .30-06–class ballistics. Care should be taken that the rifle being used is the newer type designed to accept the .323-inch–diameter "JS" bullets, rather than the old "J" style bullets that mike .318 inch.

The .358 Winchester makes an excellent deer load, although it doesn't shoot flat enough for truly long-range marksmanship. With 200-grain factory loads, it's a fine choice out to 250 yards, though you have to hold the sights about a foot high at that distance. This is a fine woods round, but at this writing the only rifle still chambered for the .358 Winchester is Browning's BLR lever action. It still enjoys fair popularity in Europe.

A number of compact carbines are chambered for the .44 magnum handgun round. These combinations work well in dense woods where shots are likely to be this side of the 100-yard mark. Beyond that distance, the energy rapidly falls below the 1,000-foot-pound level.

The .444 Marlin throws the same 240-grain handgun bullet the .44 magnum handles, but pushes it out the muzzle some 600 fps faster. As a result, the .444 Marlin hits with the same force at 200 yards as the .44 magnum does at 100. Even so, the poor ballistic shape of the blunt handgun slug limits its usefulness to about that distance. Heavier 250-, 265- and 300-grain bullets are available to handloaders, and 265-grain factory loads are also available.

Many deer are still being taken every year by .45-70 rifles, primarily because this 110-year-old war horse has caught the fancy of nostalgia buffs. Both 300- and 405-grain factory loads are offered, and handloaders have a variety of .458-inch projectiles from which to choose. The .45-70 has a rainbow trajectory that limits its practical usefulness to about 150 yards.

A number of more potent rounds can be used in the deer woods, but there's really no need to carry a .338 Winchester or 8mm Remington magnum. These cartridges are for larger game, and generally speaking they're too uncomfortable for the average deer hunter to shoot well. Nothing is wrong with using a bigbore magnum to collect your annual venison supply, and many nimrods do just that. But in the strict sense of the word, the .338 Winchester, .358 Norma, .375 Holland & Holland and .378 Weatherby magnums aren't deer cartridges. They'll do the job, but with much more fuss and bother (recoil and muzzle blast) than necessary. They're also harder on the pocketbook than the rounds I've recommended.

Rifles and Scopes for Deer

What type of rifle is best for hunting deer? A complete discussion of the pros and cons of each rifle and action type appears in Chapter 14. Generally speaking, you don't need a barrel longer than 22 inches to get adequate performance from a typical "deer" cartridge, and stubby carbines 18 or 19 inches long usually do the job. Bolt rifles are generally preferred for long-range work, although a properly tuned single shot can also deliver excellent accuracy. Bolt-action rifles also offer some real advantages to the reloader, although lever, pump and autoloading firearms will digest properly assembled handloads.

Of course, some cartridges are available only in bolt rifle chambering, while others limit your choice to lever-action models. In the final analysis, the most important consideration is probably personal choice. Some riflemen use bolt-action models exclusively, while others use lever carbines or autoloaders with equal fervor. Within the range limitations I've listed, any of the cartridges recommended in this chapter will cleanly kill deer. Choose the bolt,

Bolt-action Savage 110 with 4X scope makes a fine combination for deer.

lever, pump, autoloader or single-shot model that best suits you, and if it digests one of these cartridges you'll have an effective deer rifle.

As far as sighting equipment is concerned, the vast majority of deer hunters these days use magnifying scope sights exclusively. Open iron sights are satisfactory on short-barrel saddle guns such as the model 94 Winchester and Marlin 336 lever carbines. For close-range use they can be faster than a scope, although the very fastest iron sight is a wide-aperture peep sight mounted close to the eye. Since the eye automatically centers the front sight bead when you look through the rear aperture, you needn't pay any conscious attention to that rear opening, much less try to focus on it. Just look through it, and put that front bead behind the deer's shoulder. Old-time woodsmen never used the small aperture disk that all peep sights come equipped with; they just unscrewed the disk and threw it away, using the threaded hole that remained as the rear sighting aperture. This is still the fastest sighting arrangement I know of for close-range rifle work.

If you own a Winchester model 94 lever gun, mounting a scope presents problems because the action ejects empty cases straight up through the top. This means the scope must be offset in a side mount. Too, a scope destroys the fast-handling balance of these fine little carbines. The side-ejecting Marlin lever rifles allow scopes to be mounted conventionally, but again the addition of a glass sight makes these carbines less handy to carry.

But as I've said, nearly everyone uses scope sights on deer rifles these days. And with good reason. In addition to offering a magnified image for more precise bullet placement, a good scope can add several minutes of hunting time to each day. The extra definition provided lets you see the target clearly under marginal light situations that would normally keep the animal hidden from eyesight. That means you can shoot earlier and later in the day.

Please note, I said a *good* scope. Many inexpensive, low-end models are available, but I advise any sportsman to buy the best riflescope he can afford. Stay with name brands: Leupold, Burris, Bushnell, Redfield, Lyman and Weaver. Zeiss and Leitz are also excellent choices, though these top-quality German brands tend to be costly.

Perhaps the most popular riflescope on the market today is the 3–9X variable. This is a good choice for dual varmint- and deer-hunting chores, but 9X magnification has little utility for the average deer hunter. These big variables are bulky, and heavy to boot. Nonetheless, 3–9X scopes abound, so you'll have lots of company if you select one for your pet deer dropper.

The 2–7X variables are somewhat smaller and lighter, and the power range makes more sense where deer hunting is concerned. An even better choice is the 1½–4½X variable. At the 1½X setting, this sight offers a very wide field of view for close shots at running game. When cranked up to the 4½X setting, it offers plenty of magnification for long-range shooting.

Fixed-power scopes have their advantages, too. They're easier to seal against moisture, and are more weatherproof than the variables. And since there are fewer adjustments to bother with, fewer problems develop. In short, fixed-power scopes tend to be sturdier and more trouble-free than the variable models. However, I've used variable-power scope sights on my rifles in the most miserable, wet, cold and nasty conditions imaginable without having a bit of trouble. The top-quality brands are highly reliable—variable- and fixed-power models alike.

From a practical point of view, many sportsmen would be every bit as well off with a fixed-power scope mounted on their rifles. Most variable scopes in use today are left on a 4X or 5X setting, which the hunter isn't likely to change when it's time to shoot. Too many other things command a rifleman's attention when game is in sight. I know I've shot deer at 350 yards with my sight set at 1½X. The last big muley buck I killed at approximately that distance spotted me the same instant I saw him. There simply wasn't time to fiddle with the scope's power setting. Such is typically the case when hunting deer, so the theoretical advantage offered by the variable-power scope remains largely that—theoretical.

Since fixed-power scopes are considerably less costly than comparable variable models, you can save yourself some money by opting for a good 2½X, 4X or 6X sight. A 4X scope handles most deer-hunting chores just fine.

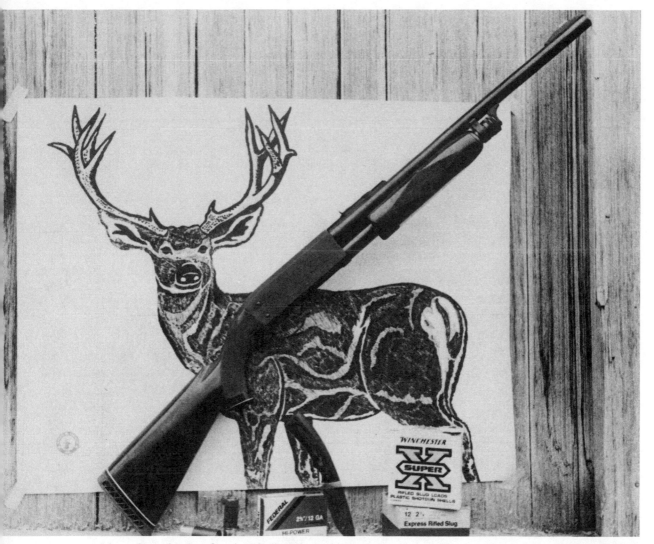

Ithaca Deerslayer is fitted with slug-choked barrel, complete with adjustable rifle-style sights for deer hunting.

Shotguns for Deer

In certain well-populated areas, shotguns are used in place of rifles for hunting deer. Either buckshot or rifled slugs will put a deer down at reasonable range, but the solid slugs are much more reliable. Actually, most rifled slugs aren't really solid, but cast in a hollow cone with one end closed. The bulk of the weight lies in the slug's nose, which makes it fly point forward. This stabilizes the slug's flight, *not* the "rifling" lands cast in its circumference.

While rifled slugs and buckshot can be used in any shotgun, these loads perform best in a straight cylinder-bore barrel. Shooting a soft, lead slug through a tight, full choke won't harm the barrel, but accuracy is apt to suffer. Too, putting a slug on target reliably calls for better sighting equipment than the single front bead most shotguns come equipped with.

For these reasons, most shotgun manufacturers offer special models with the deer hunter in mind. These are usually slide-action or autoloading guns fitted with a stubby 20- or 22-inch cylinder or improved-cylinder-choke barrel. These barrels feature adjustable rifle-type open sights, and you can mount 1½X or 2½X scopes on the receivers of most slug guns. Weaver's Qwik-Point receiver sight is also a good choice; it's fast, and very accurate out to 80 yards or so.

Double-barrel shotguns can be used with slugs, but the twin-tube arrangement makes accuracy difficult at anything but point-blank range. Usually, the two barrels won't shoot to

Shotgun slugs are accurate up to 100 yards, then begin to drop rapidly. This Marlin 120 pump is fitted with a long-eye-relief scope.

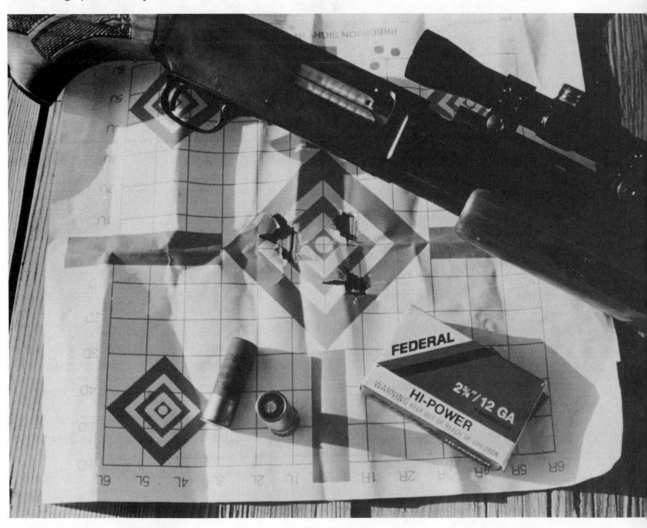

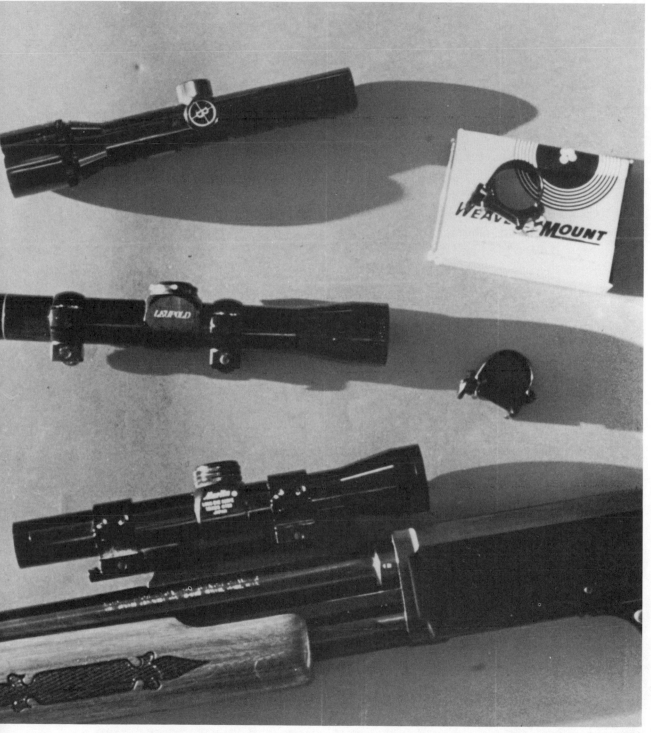

Telescopic sights help turn slug-shoting scatterguns into accurate "deer rifles." Scopes featuring long eye relief are recommended.

the same point of aim, and neither may print anywhere close to the mark provided by the simple bead sight. For that matter, many single-barrel guns group slugs poorly, and this can only be determined by shooting at paper targets. Most "slug guns"—shotguns fitted with rifle-sighted barrels designed specifically for slug use—produce 5-shot groups measuring no more than 6 or 8 inches across at 50 yards. That's sufficient accuracy for 70- or 80-yard shooting. Anything farther is a long shot with a slug gun. I've tested several slug guns that would print 2½–3-inch groups, and these guns would be effective out to 100 yards.

Buckshot is a different story. Precise sighting equipment offers little help here, as every buckshot load I've ever tested dispersed wildly beyond 40 yards. A standard 2¾-inch 12-gauge No. oo Buck load contains just 9 pellets, while the same length magnum shell holds 12. A 12-gauge 3-inch magnum hull carries 15 No. oo Buck pellets.

You can increase the density of your shot pattern by using smaller buckshot. For instance, the standard Express 12-gauge load, as I've already pointed out, holds nine No. oo Buck pellets. Switch to No. o Buck and the number of pellets increases to 12; or move down to No. 1 Buck to get 16 projectiles.

Both the "large shot, thin pattern" and "small shot, dense pattern" schools of thought have their adherents, but I'd be willing to bet more deer are taken with No. oo- and o-size buckshot than with smaller pellets. Whichever selection you make, your gun with buckshot is going to be largely ineffective beyond 50 yards.

Whether you opt for buckshot or slug loads for hunting deer, you should use a large-bore shotgun. In my opinion, the 16 gauge should be the smallest gauge considered, while the 12 is ideal. With buckshot, you want to throw as many pellets as possible, which means the 3-inch magnum 12 is the optimum choice. All the slug loads I'm aware of are offered in 2¾-inch loadings only, so a standard 12-gauge gun with a specially bored and sight-equipped slug barrel is your best bet.

At 50 yards, a 1-ounce 12-gauge rifled slug develops 1,340 foot-pounds of energy, and drops to 875 foot-pounds at 100 yards. A ⅘-ounce 16-gauge slug has 1,070 foot-pounds of hitting force at 50 yards, and 700 foot-pounds at 100. In contrast, the ⅝-ounce 20-gauge slug churns up only 840 foot-pounds of oomph at 50 yards, and 550 at 100. As far as the puny ⅕-ounce .410 slug is concerned, you can forget it for deer-woods use. At 50 yards it offers but 345 foot-pounds of energy, and 200 foot-pounds at 100 yards.

The 12-, 16- and 20-gauge slug loads sport very similar trajectories. All three drop 2.1 inches at 50 yards, and fall 10.4 inches at 100.

Handguns for Deer

Another type of firearm used for hunting deer is the handgun. Choosing a handgun for any type of hunting adds challenge to an already challenging sport, as most handguns are suitable for short-range shooting only. The development of long-eye-relief pistol scopes and modern, single-shot guns has made 150- to 200-yard kills possible, but as a general rule handgunners

The big .44 magnum is an ideal handgunning round for hunting deer.

should pass up most shots offered beyond the 50-yard mark. This means the handgunner must stalk within close range, which places him on a nearly equal footing with hunting archers.

Furthermore, before becoming proficient enough to hunt deer with any chance of success, the handgunner must spend a great deal more time at the practice range than the rifleman does. Compared to the modern rifle, the handgun is a pretty shaky instrument that's damnably difficult to shoot straight. Factory sighting equipment is coarse, and the slightest flinch or tremor throws a bullet way off course.

Nonetheless, deer are taken with handguns every year, and this is a sport that seems to be growing in popularity.

A number of different handgun calibers and loads can be relied on to kill deer in the hands of a skilled hunter and marksman. These start with the .38 Super ACP and 9mm Parabellum and range upwards. However, most states that allow the use of handguns for hunting deer specify cartridges at least as potent as the .357 magnum. As a matter of fact several states spell out the legal loads, limiting your selection to the .357 magnum, the .41 magnum and the .44 magnum specifically. Soft-nose bullets are also called for in most deer hunting proclamations.

If the state you plan to hunt in specifies the .357, .41 or .44 magnums, those are the calibers you must use in spite of the fact that there are even better, more potent choices available. For instance, the single-shot Thompson/Center Contender is available in .30-30 Winchester and .35 Remington rifle chambering, as well the hot .30 and .357 Herrett offerings. All of these outperform the .357 magnum by a substantial margin.

The .45 Colt is adequate for deer, and when used in strong, modern revolvers and single-shot pistols it can be handloaded to considerably greater potency. The .45 Winchester Magnum is a relative newcomer to the handgunning scene, and comes very close to duplicating .44 magnum ballistics.

Whichever cartridge you select, the handgun chosen should have adjustable sights and a reasonably long barrel. The 2- and 4-inch barrel lengths preferred for law enforcement purposes aren't suited for hunting deer. Most experienced handgunners consider a 6-inch barrel the minimum practical length for hunting medium or large game, and most prefer a 7½- or 8-inch barrel. The Thompson/Center Contender sports a 10-inch tube, and a 14-inch barrel is optional.

In states specifying the .357, .41 and .44 magnum calibers as the only legal choices for handgunning deer, you'll be forced to use either a revolver or single-shot pistol. Autoloaders aren't available in these chamberings, although the .45 Winchester Magnum is designed for auto pistol use. Chapter 18 deals more extensively with choosing a hunting handgun.

One more bit of advice regarding your deer-hunting handgun: remember that even the mighty .44 Remington Magnum develops less energy at the muzzle than the .30-30 Winchester rifle load does at 100 yards. In other words, use the heaviest caliber you can handle when using a handgun on deer-size or larger game.

Black-powder Guns for Deer

Still another type of firearm used in hunting deer is the muzzleloading rifle. These black-powder burners have become highly popular in the last decade or so, and some states even offer special hunting seasons for users of primitive firearms.

Modern replicas of the Hawken, Kentucky and other historical models are strong and accurate. What's more, within certain limitations, they can be fully as effective as cartridge rifles. The chief limitation is range, which shouldn't exceed 125 or 150 yards. That's a long shot for a muzzleloader, and most experienced black-powder hunters stalk much closer before attempting a shot. Another, more obvious limitation is the fact that you'd better make

Thompson/Center Renegade is an economy-priced yet high-quality percussion rifle available in .50 and .54 caliber. A flintlock version is also offered.

that first shot count. There are some double-barrel black-powder rifles on the market, but the vast majority of models sold are single shots. Since it takes a half minute or more to pour a fresh powder charge down the barrel, start and seat a patched ball or conical projectile, and reprime with a new percussion cap, you're not likely to get the chance to use a follow-up shot.

Muzzleloading rifles are available in several different calibers. In many states .45 caliber is the legal minimum in black-powder weaponry for hunting deer. That's probably the practical lower limit, too, as far as caliber is concerned. A good .45-caliber flintlock or percussion rifle throwing either a patched lead ball (.445-inch diameter) or a conical projectile such as the Thompson/Center Maxi-Ball is capable of killing deer cleanly as long as the range isn't stretched beyond 125 yards or so. The conical projectiles weigh more, and in my experience are more effective on medium-size or largish game. However, the spherical lead balls have been used for centuries and will certainly do the job.

My own preference is for a slightly larger caliber, and I lean towards either the .50- or .54-caliber rifles for hunting deer. The .58 is another good choice, although I generally reserve this caliber for even larger game.

As you can see, there is a large variety of firearm types and calibers that can be used in the deer woods, western mountains or deserts. Some have limited range, while others may produce objectionable recoil. But the large majority of choices listed could be called just about ideal for hunting deer. Make sure you use one of the recommended bullet types and weights listed for each cartridge, and you'll be well equipped for the hunt.

RECOMMENDED LOADS FOR DEER

(Courtesy Remington Arms Co., Inc., Federal Cartridge Corp., and Winchester Western)

CALIBERS	BULLET Wt.-Grs.	Style	VELOCITY FEET PER SECOND Muzzle	100 Yds.	200 Yds.	300 Yds.	400 Yds.	500 Yds.	ENERGY Muzzle	100 Yds.	200 Yds.
243 WIN.	100	Pointed Soft Point	2960	2697	2449	2215	1993	1786	1945	1615	1332
6mm REM.	100	Pointed Soft Point	3130	2857	2600	2357	2127	1911	2175	1812	1501
250 SAVAGE	100	Pointed	2820	2467	2140	1839	1569	1339	1765	1351	1017
257 ROBERTS	117	Pointed Soft Point	2650	2291	1961	1663	1404	1199	1824	1363	999
25-06 REM.	120	Pointed Soft Point	3010	2749	2502	2269	2048	1840	2414	2013	1668
6.5mm. REM. MAG.	120	Pointed Soft Point	3210	2905	2621	2353	2102	1867	2745	2245	1830
264 WIN. MAG.	140	Pointed Soft Point	3030	2782	2548	2326	2114	1914	2854	2406	2018
270 WIN.	130	Pointed Soft Point	3110	2823	2554	2300	2061	1837	2791	2300	1883
	130	Pointed	3110	2849	2604	2371	2150	1941	2791	2343	1957
	150	Soft Point	2900	2550	2225	1926	1653	1415	2801	2165	1649
7mm MAUSER	140	Pointed Soft Point	2660	2435	2221	2018	1827	1648	2199	1843	1533
7mm-08 REM.	140	Pointed Soft Point	2860	2625	2402	2189	1988	1798	2542	2142	1793
280 REM.	165	Soft Point	2820	2510	2220	1950	1701	1479	2913	2308	1805
7mm EXPRESS REM.	150	Pointed Soft Point	2970	2699	2444	2203	1975	1763	2937	2426	1989
284 WIN.	150	Pointed Soft Point	2860	2595	2344	2108	1886	1680	2724	2243	1830
7mm REM MAG.	150	Pointed Soft Point	3110	2830	2568	2320	2085	1866	3221	2667	2196
30 REM.	170	Soft Point	2120	1822	1555	1328	1153	1036	1696	1253	913
30-30 WIN.	150	Soft Point	2390	1973	1605	1303	1095	974	1902	1296	858
	170	Soft Point	2200	1895	1619	1381	1191	1061	1827	1355	989
	170	Hollow Point	2200	1895	1619	1381	1191	1061	1827	1355	989
30-06 SPRINGFIELD	150	Pointed Soft Point	2910	2617	2342	2083	1843	1622	2820	2281	1827
	150	Pointed	2910	2656	2416	2189	1974	1773	2820	2349	1944
	165	Pointed Soft Point	2800	2534	2283	2047	1825	1621	2872	2352	1909
	180	Soft Point	2700	2348	2023	1727	1466	1251	2913	2203	1635
	180	Pointed Soft Point	2700	2469	2250	2042	1846	1663	2913	2436	2023
30-40 KRAG	180	Pointed Soft Point	2430	2099	1795	1525	1298	1128	2360	1761	1288
	180	Pointed	2430	2213	2007	1813	1632	1468	2360	1957	1610
	220	Pointed	2160	1956	1765	1587	1427	1287	2279	1869	1522
300 WIN. MAG.	150	Pointed Soft Point	3290	2951	2636	2342	2068	1813	3605	2900	2314
	180	Pointed Soft Point	2960	2745	2540	2344	2157	1979	3501	3011	2578
	220	Pointed	2680	2448	2228	2020	1823	1640	3508	2927	2424
300 H. & H. MAG.	150	Pointed	2880	2640	2412	2196	1991	1798	3315	2785	2325
	180	Pointed	2580	2341	2114	1901	1702	1520	3251	2677	2183
300 SAVAGE	150	Pointed Soft Point	2630	2354	2095	1853	1631	1434	2303	1845	1462
	180	Pointed Soft Point	2350	2025	1728	1437	1252	1098	2207	1639	1193
	180	Pointed	2350	2137	1935	1745	1570	1416	2207	1825	1496
303 SAVAGE	190	Pointed	1940	1657	1410	1211	1073	982	1588	1158	839
303 BRITISH	180	Pointed Soft Point	2460	2233	2018	1816	1629	1459	2418	1993	1627
308 WIN.	150	Pointed Soft Point	2820	2533	2263	2009	1774	1560	2648	2137	1705
	180	Soft Point	2620	2274	1955	1666	1414	1212	2743	2066	1527
	180	Pointed Soft Point	2620	2393	2178	1974	1782	1604	2743	2288	1896
	165	Boat-tail Soft Point	2700	2520	2330	2160	1990	1830	2670	2310	1990
32 WIN. SPECIAL	170	Soft Point	2250	1921	1626	1372	1175	1044	1911	1395	998
8mm MAUSER	170	Soft Point	2360	1969	1622	1333	1123	997	2102	1463	993

FOOT-POUNDS			SHORT RANGE Bullet does not rise more than one inch above line of sight from muzzle to sighting in range.						LONG RANGE Bullet does not rise more than three inches above line of sight from muzzle to sighting in range.							BARREL LENGTH
300 Yds.	400 Yds.	500 Yds.	50 Yds.	100 Yds.	150 Yds.	200 Yds.	250 Yds.	300 Yds.	100 Yds	150 Yds.	200 Yds.	250 Yds.	300 Yds.	400 Yds.	500 Yds.	
1089	882	708	0.5	0.9	0.0	− 2.2	− 5.8	−11.0	1.9	1.6	0.0	− 3.1	− 7.8	− 22.6	− 46.3	24"
1233	1004	811	0.4	0.7	0.0	− 1.9	− 5.1	− 9.7	1.7	1.4	0.0	− 2.7	− 6.8	− 20.0	− 40.8	
751	547	398	0.2	0.0	− 1.6	− 4.9	−10.0	−17.4	2.4	2.0	0.0	− 3.9	−10.1	− 30.5	− 65.2	24"
718	512	373	0.3	0.0	− 1.9	− 5.8	−11.9	−20.7	2.9	2.4	0.0	− 4.7	−12.0	− 36.7	− 79.2	24"
1372	1117	902	0.5	0.8	0.0	− 2.1	− 5.5	−10.5	1.9	1.6	0.0	− 2.9	− 7.4	− 21.6	− 44.2	
1475	1177	929	0.4	0.7	0.0	− 1.8	− 4.9	− 9.5	2.7	3.0	2.1	0.0	− 3.5	− 15.5	− 35.3	24"
1682	1389	1139	0.5	0.8	0.0	− 2.0	− 5.4	−10.2	1.8	1.5	0.0	− 2.9	− 7.2	− 20.8	− 42.2	24"
1527	1226	974	0.4	0.8	0.0	− 2.0	− 5.3	−10.0	1.7	1.5	0.0	− 2.8	− 7.1	− 20.8	− 42.7	24"
1622	1334	1087	0.4	0.7	0.0	− 1.9	− 5.1	− 9.7	1.7	1.4	0.0	− 2.7	− 6.8	− 19.9	− 40.5	
1235	910	667	0.6	1.0	0.0	− 2.5	− 6.8	−13.1	2.2	1.9	0.0	− 3.6	− 9.3	− 28.1	− 59.7	
1266	1037	844	0.2	0.0	− 1.7	− 5.0	−10.0	−17.0	2.5	2.0	0.0	− 3.8	− 9.6	− 27.7	− 56.3	24"
1490	1228	1005	0.6	0.9	0.0	− 2.3	−6.11	−11.6	2.1	1.7	0.0	− 3.2	− 8.1	− 23.5	− 47.7	24"
1393	1060	801	0.2	0.0	− 1.5	− 4.6	− 9.5	−16.4	2.3	1.9	0.0	− 3.7	− 9.4	− 28.1	− 58.8	24"
1616	1299	1035	0.5	0.9	0.0	− 2.2	− 5.8	−11.0	1.9	1.6	0.0	− 3.1	− 7.8	− 22.8	− 46.7	24"
1480	1185	940	0.6	1.0	0.0	− 2.4	− 6.3	−12.1	2.1	1.8	0.0	− 3.4	− 8.5	− 24.8	− 51.0	24"
1792	1448	1160	0.4	0.8	0.0	− 1.9	− 5.2	− 9.9	1.7	1.5	0.0	− 2.8	− 7.0	− 20.5	− 42.1	24"
666	502	405	0.7	0.0	− 3.3	− 9.7	−19.6	−33.8	2.2	0.0	− 5.3	−14.1	−27.2	− 69.0	−136.9	24"
565	399	316	0.5	0.0	− 2.7	− 8.2	−17.0	−30.0	1.8	0.0	− 4.6	−12.5	−24.6	− 65.3	−134.9	
720	535	425	0.6	0.0	− 3.0	− 8.9	−18.0	−31.1	2.0	0.0	− 4.6	−13.0	−25.1	− 63.6	−126.7	24"
720	535	425	0.6	0.0	− 3.0	− 8.9	−18.0	−31.1	2.0	0.0	− 4.8	−13.0	−25.1	− 63.6	−126.7	
1445	1131	876	0.6	0.9	0.0	− 2.3	− 6.3	−12.0	2.1	1.8	0.0	− 3.3	− 8.5	− 25.0	− 51.8	
1596	1298	1047	0.6	0.9	0.0	− 2.2	− 6.0	−11.4	2.0	1.7	0.0	− 3.2	− 8.0	− 23.3	− 47.5	
1534	1220	963	0.7	1.0	0.0	− 2.5	− 6.7	12.7	2.3	1.9	0.0	− 3.6	− 9.0	− 26.3	− 54.1	24"
1192	859	625	0.2	0.0	− 1.8	− 5.5	−11.2	−19.5	2.7	2.3	0.0	− 4.4	−11.3	− 34.4	− 73.7	
1666	1362	1105	0.2	0.0	− 1.6	− 4.8	− 9.7	−16.5	2.4	2.0	0.0	− 3.7	− 9.3	− 27.0	− 54.9	
929	673	508	0.4	0.0	− 2.4	− 7.1	−14.5	−25.0	1.6	0.0	− 3.9	−10.5	−20.3	− 51.7	−103.9	
1314	1064	861	0.4	0.0	− 2.1	− 6.2	−12.5	−21.1	1.4	0.0	− 3.4	− 8.9	−16.8	− 40.9	− 78.1	
1230	995	809	0.6	0.0	− 2.9	− 8.2	−16.4	−27.6	1.9	0.0	− 4.4	−11.6	−21.9	− 53.3	−101.8	
1827	1424	1095	0.3	0.7	0.0	− 1.8	− 4.8	− 9.3	2.6	2.9	2.1	0.0	− 3.5	− 15.4	− 35.5	
2196	1859	1565	0.5	0.8	0.0	− 2.2	− 5.5	−10.4	1.9	1.6	0.0	− 2.9	− 7.3	− 20.9	− 41.9	
1993	623	1314	0.2	0.0	− 1.7	− 4.9	− 9.9	−16.9	2.5	2.0	0.0	− 3.8	− 9.5	− 27.5	− 56.1	
1927	584	1292	0.6	0.9	0.0	− 2.3	− 6.0	−11.5	2.1	1.7	0.0	− 3.2	− 8.0	− 23.3	− 47.4	
1765	415	1128	0.3	0.0	− 1.9	− 5.5	−11.0	−18.7	2.7	2.2	0.0	− 4.2	−10.5	− 30.7	− 53.0	
1143	886	685	0.3	0.0	− 1.8	− 5.4	−11.0	−18.8	2.7	2.2	0.0	− 4.2	−10.7	− 31.5	− 65.5	
860	625	482	0.5	0.0	− 2.6	− 7.7	−15.6	−27.1	1.7	0.0	− 4.2	−11.3	−21.9	− 55.8	−112.0	
1217	985	798	0.4	0.0	− 2.8	− 6.7	−13.5	−22.8	1.5	0.0	− 3.6	− 9.6	−18.2	− 41.1	− 84.2	
619	486	407	0.9	0.0	− 4.1	−11.9	−24.1	−41.4	2.7	0.0	− 6.4	−17.3	−33.2	− 33.7	−164.4	
1318	060	851	0.3	0.0	− 2.1	− 6.1	−12.2	−20.8	1.4	0.0	− 3.3	− 8.8	−16.6	− 40.4	− 77.4	
1344	1048	810	0.2	0.0	− 1.5	− 4.5	− 9.3	−15.9	2.3	1.9	0.0	− 3.6	− 9.1	− 26.9	− 55.7	
1109	799	587	0.3	0.0	− 2.0	− 5.9	−12.1	−20.9	2.9	2.4	0.0	− 4.7	−12.1	− 36.9	− 79.1	24"
1557	1269	1028	0.2	0.0	− 1.8	− 5.2	−10.4	−17.7	2.6	2.1	0.0	− 4.0	− 9.9	− 28.9	− 58.8	
1700	1450	1230	1.3	0.0	− 1.3	− 4.0	− 8.4	−14.4	2.0	1.7	0.0	− 3.3	− 8.4	− 24.3	− 48.9	
710	521	411	0.6	0.0	− 2.9	− 8.6	−17.6	−30.5	1.9	0.0	− 4.7	−12.7	−24.7	− 63.2	−126.9	24"
671	476	375	0.5	0.0	− 2.7	− 8.2	−17.0	−29.8	1.8	0.0	− 4.5	−12.4	−24.3	− 63.6	−130.7	24"

TRAJECTORY† 0.0 Indicates yardage at which rifle was sighted in.

CALIBERS	BULLET		VELOCITY FEET PER SECOND						ENERGY		
	Wt.-Grs.	Style	Muzzle	100 Yds.	200 Yds.	300 Yds.	400 Yds.	500 Yds.	Muzzle	100 Yds.	200 Yds.
35 REM.	150	Pointed Soft Point	2300	1874	1506	1218	1039	934	1762	1169	755
	200	Soft Point	2080	1698	1376	1140	1001	911	1921	1280	841
358 WIN.	200	Pointed	2490	2171	1876	1610	1379	1194	2753	2093	1563
	250	Pointed	2230	1988	1762	1557	1375	1224	2760	2194	1723
375 WIN.	200	Pointed Soft Point	2200	1841	1526	1268	1089	980	2150	1506	1034
	250	Pointed Soft Point	1900	1647	1424	1239	1103	1011	2005	1506	1126
44 REM. MAG.	240	Soft Point	1760	1380	1114	970	878	806	1650	1015	661
	240	Semi-Jacketed Hollow Point	1760	1380	1114	970	878	806	1650	1015	661
444 MAR.	240	Soft Point	2350	1815	1377	1087	941	846	2942	1755	1010
	265	Soft Point	2120	1733	1405	1160	1012	920	2644	1768	1162
45-70 GOVERNMENT	405	Soft Point	1330	1168	1055	977	918	869	1590	1227	1001

FOOT-POUNDS			TRAJECTORY† 0.0 Indicates yardage at which rifle was sighted in.													BARREL LENGTH
			SHORT RANGE Bullet does not rise more than one inch above line of sight from muzzle to sighting in range.						LONG RANGE Bullet does not rise more than three inches above line of sight from muzzle to sighting in range.							
300 Yds.	400 Yds.	500 Yds.	50 Yds.	100 Yds.	150 Yds.	200 Yds.	250 Yds.	300 Yds.	100 Yds	150 Yds.	200 Yds.	250 Yds.	300 Yds.	400 Yds.	500 Yds.	
494	3.9	291	0.6	0.0	−3.0	−9.2	−19.1	−33.9	2.0	0.0	−5.1	−4.1	−27.8	−74.0	−152.3	24"
577	445	369	0.8	0.0	−3.8	−11.3	−23.5	41.2	2.5	0.0	−6.3	−17.1	−33.6	−87.7	−176.4	
1151	844	633	0.4	0.0	−2.2	−6.5	−13.3	−23.0	1.5	0.0	−3.6	−9.7	−18.6	−47.2	−94.1	24"
1346	1049	832	0.5	0.0	−2.7	−7.9	−16.0	−27.1	1.8	0.0	−4.3	−11.4	−21.7	−53.5	−103.7	24"
714	527	427	0.6	0.0	−3.2	−9.5	−19.5	−33.8	2.1	0.0	−5.2	−14.1	−27.4	−70.1	−138.1	24"
852	676	568	0.9	0.0	−4.1	−12.0	−24.0	−40.9	2.7	0.0	−6.5	−17.2	−32.7	−80.6	−154.1	24"
501	411	346	0.0	−2.7	−10.0	−23.0	−43.0	−71.2	0.0	−5.9	−17.6	−36.3	−63.1	−145.5	−273.0	20"
501	411	346	0.0	−2.7	−10.0	−23.0	−43.0	−71.2	0.0	−5.9	−17.6	−36.3	−63.1	−145.5	−273.0	
630	472	381	0.6	0.0	−3.2	−9.9	−21.3	−38.5	2.1	0.0	−5.6	−15.9	−32.1	−87.8	−182.7	24"
791	603	498	0.7	0.0	−3.6	−10.8	−22.5	−39.5	2.4	0.0	−6.0	−16.4	−32.2	−84.3	−170.2	
858	758	679	0.0	−4.7	−15.8	−34.0	−60.0	−94.5	0.0	−8.7	−24.6	−48.2	−80.3	−172.4	−305.9	24"

Rifles for Moose and Elk 2

While even the largest members of the North American deer family aren't usually considered dangerous game, a big, bad-tempered, British Columbian bull moose came closer to settling my hash than any other animal I've ever hunted.

I was within 80 yards of the animal when I shot, but my view was obstructed by drizzling rain. That's my only excuse for not placing my first bullet exactly where it should have gone. When you're dealing with nearly ¾ of a ton of moose, that's always a mistake.

I saw water splash high on the bull's shoulder, then I quickly settled down and drove two follow-up slugs where the first shot belonged. They went behind the shoulder less than 2 inches apart, into the heart-lung area. The animal went down, and I could no longer see him in the high grass.

I was using a .30-06 Colt Sauer, loaded with Federal factory rounds throwing 180-grain soft-nose bullets. This rifle features a removeable 3-shot clip, and when the third shot drove home the magazine was dry. The Sauer is a fine, highly accurate firearm, but the clip in my rifle was so closely fitted that you had to f-e-e-l it back in after reloading. Until you felt the catch click into place, the magazine wasn't locked, and could easily fall out.

My guide, Ron Collingwood, and I circled so we didn't have to approach the downed animal from below, while I fed fresh loads into the Colt's clip. Ron wasn't carrying a rifle, and neither of us was expecting trouble.

Just as I felt the magazine catch engage, the bull churned out of the bush a good 40 yards from where we'd seen him last, and less than 10 yards from us. He paused long enough to throw his massive antlers up and give me a withering glare, then came for us.

By then I had my rifle up, and drove another 180-grain soft-point in where his neck met his chest. That staggered him for a second, and he turned just far enough to give me a clear neck shot. I missed the spine, and he again came directly for us. A third shot into his chest dropped him to his knees less than 2 yards from the Colt's muzzle.

Snorting blood that spattered my trousers, he heaved himself upright and tried to stagger forward. My magazine was again empty, and I just had time to throw another round into the

The author with a 56-inch British Columbian bull moose, which he took with a .30-06 Colt Sauer rifle shooting Federal 180-grain factory loads.

ejection port, close the bolt and put the seventh and last shot between his eyes. That did the trick and he expired, his forehead hairs singed by muzzle blast.

I learned a lesson that day. Properly hit with the first shot, a moose is fairly easy to kill. Bob Brister demonstrated that the very next day when a bull shot with his 7mm Remington Magnum dropped as if poleaxed. Even this animal required a follow-up shot, but he wasn't going anywhere. The first bullet had clipped the heart, torn open a lung, and finally lodged near the animal's spine.

But if that first slug doesn't go where it should, look out! Get a bull's attention and give his adrenaline a chance to start pumping, and the big critter takes an awful lot of killing before he finally gets the message. And never allow yourself to think that a moose—"only a big deer"—can't be dangerous! A big Alaskan bull can top 1,700 pounds, stand more than 7 feet high at the shoulder, and move surprisingly fast when angered.

What's more, a rutting bull may charge—anything—on sight and without provocation. Canadian moose have been known to take on railroad locomotives, and I know of at least one hapless hunter who was treed after angering an already irritated bull by shooting—and missing. He didn't pause for a second shot, but frantically started climbing. His guide went up another tree almost as fast, and the bull stood sentinel duty below the pair until nightfall.

While a bull elk is less likely to become pugnacious, a trophy animal can be almost as impressive. Few big bulls top 1,200 pounds, but their antlers tower far above them.

When hunting either moose or elk, you need a rifle with enough oomph to get the job done. That means small deer cartridges like the 6mm Remington and .243 Winchester should be passed up in favor of something more potent. Elk have been taken with 6mm's, but far better choices are available.

Some hunters use the quarter bores, or .25-caliber rifles on elk. I know of one Wyoming guide who swears by the .257 Roberts, and he's taken several wapiti with the cartridge. Another acquaintance uses a lever-action .250 Savage for everything, including western elk. In the right hands, these cartridges obviously will get the job done.

However, my own personal opinion is that the .25-caliber cartridges are decidedly on the light side for these magnificent animals. And yes, that indictment includes the .25-06 and .257 Weatherby Magnum, both of which are considerably more potent than the .257 Roberts or .250 Savage. None of these cartridges throws a bullet heavier than 117 grains factory loaded, and even handloaders can't top 125 grains for projectile weight. Even at the velocities at which the .25-06 Remington or the belted Weatherby magnum hustles these pills along, I'm simply in favor of throwing more lead when a half-ton animal is involved.

If pressed, I suppose I would use a .25-06 Remington or even one of the other .25's for hunting elk. But it sure wouldn't be my first, or even my fifth or sixth, choice. Too many other rounds are better suited for hunting these large deer.

Field & Stream Shooting Editor Bob Brister approaches Canadian moose downed with 7mm Remington Magnum. A wary approach is the right tactic; these animals can be dangerous as long as any life is left in them.

There's no way I'd even consider tackling a bull moose with a .25-caliber rifle. That's asking far too much for any quarter bore, and as I've said, a lot of really good choices are on the market. When you spend the time, money, planning and energy necessary to hunt trophy elk or moose, it makes little sense to go poorly equipped in the firearms department.

What are good moose and elk rounds? The .270 Winchester will work okay, as will the old 7x57mm Mauser and Remington's new 7mm-08. All three of these cartridges are adequate for hunting our largest deer.

The .270 Winchester earned its reputation with the 130-grain bullet weight, and if the projectile is properly constructed to hold together and penetrate, it will do a good job on elk. Again, I personally prefer a somewhat heavier slug like Hornady's 140-grain boattail spire point (available factory loaded in Hornady's Frontier ammo), or any good 150-grain slug. Barnes offers a 160-grain semi-spitzer soft point, and this could be an even better choice for handloaders.

As far as moose hunting is concerned, I'd be even more inclined to choose a heavier bullet. I'd consider the 140-grain Hornady the bare minimum here, and in typical moose country where shots aren't generally taken at extreme range, I'd give careful consideration to Barnes' big 180-grain round-nose slug.

Not that a 130-grain .270 bullet won't kill even a large moose with dispatch, provided you manage to slip it in between the ribs or behind the shoulder blade. The point is, a heavier slug, particularly one with heavy jacket walls and a soft, malleable core, will plow through more bone and meat to reach the vitals. It's just a matter of stacking the odds in your favor as much as possible. A moose is a big animal, and a real trophy bull is awesome in size. A properly placed shot that penetrates will put the largest *Alces alces* down in a hurry, but one that winds up in the wrong spot can give you big trouble, fast. Once his adrenaline starts pumping, a bull moose becomes surprisingly shock resistant. Never make the mistake of underestimating him.

I've mentioned the 7mm-08 Remington and the 7x57mm Mauser as suitable "big deer" rounds, but two larger 7mm's make even better choices. These are the 7mm Express Remington, which is nothing more than the old .280 Remington renamed, and the 7mm Remington Magnum. The 7mm Weatherby Magnum is even more potent than Remington's magnum.

The 7mm-08 Remington has the advantage of being usable in light, short-action rifles. In addition, it's a relatively soft-recoiling round. The 7mm Mauser is also easy on the shoulder, particularly when fed American factory loads. European fodder or good handloads provide much improved performance in this 90-plus-year-old war horse.

For the 7mm Express Remington — an excellent deer, elk and moose cartridge — Remington's factory .280 load (the same round, but with a different name, remember?) throwing a 165-grain bullet at 2,820 feet per second (fps) is a top choice. I'd use the 150-grain 7mm Remington Magnum factory load (or its handloaded equivalent) on elk, and move up to the 175-grain bullets for moose. These two larger-capacity cartridges (and the 7mm Weatherby Magnum) feature significantly more power than the smaller 7mm's mentioned earlier. If you want

A good, flat-shooting bolt rifle like this Ruger model 77 in 7mm Express Remington makes a fine all-around choice for North American big game.

more foot-pounds of striking force than the 7mm-08 or 7mm Mauser gives, but less recoil than the belted magnums produce, the 7mm Express Remington makes a fine compromise. It's one of my favorite all-around hunting cartridges, and will handle all North American game with the exception of the big, northern bears with power to spare.

The .284 Winchester is another good elk cartridge, but since no current factory rifles are chambered for this short-cased number, it's on the road to obsolescence.

Moving up to the .30 calibers, the old .300 Savage hangs on in the Savage model 99 lever rifle. This cartridge has taken its share of elk over the years, and if you have a vintage rifle in this chambering I wouldn't hesitate to use it. But since the more powerful .308 Winchester is also available in the Savage 99, there's little reason for any sportsman to purchase a new .300

Savage rifle today. Factory loads churn up about the same energy figures as those developed by the old, but reliable 7mm Mauser as loaded (or rather, underloaded) by American ammo makers.

By the same token, the .308 Winchester is a good elk round, and is adequate for moose. But the longer .30-06 packs more punch. If you prefer a short-action lever rifle, or a compact, lightweight bolt-action firearm, the .308 is a logical choice. But if you're buying a standard-length action that digests either round, the .30-06 is preferable.

Because the .30-06 has greater powder capacity and therefore higher velocity and energy potential, this round is effective with somewhat heavier projectiles than the .308 will handle. Winchester offers a 200-grain Silvertip factory load for the .308, while Remington's heaviest offering is a 180-grain Core-Lokt bullet. For the .30-06, Winchester manufactures both a soft point and Silvertip 220-grain loading. Remington sells a 220-grain soft-point combination.

For elk, I like either Frontier or Federal's 165-grain boattail soft-point .30-06 fodder, and have also had good luck with a variety of 180-grain loads. Moose are large enough critters to make 180-, 200 or even 220-grain bullets your best choice. Federal's Premium 200-grain boat-tail is just about ideal. Any of these loads shoot flat enough and carry enough power to kill even large animals well beyond the 250-yard mark, although longer shots should always be discouraged. Elk sometimes offer distant targets, but most moose are shot well this side of 200 yards.

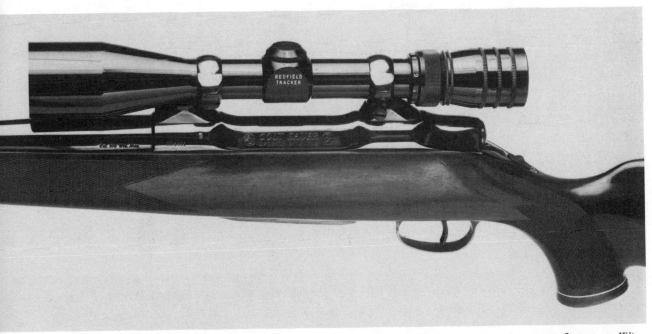

Colt Sauer with Redfield Tracker 3–9X variable scope makes a fine elk and moose rifle in .300 Winchester Magnum chambering.

If you expect to be doing much long-range shooting, the .300 Winchester Magnum (or Weatherby's potent belted .300) is a better choice than the .30-06. With the 180-grain loading most commonly used by hunters, .300 Winchester Magnum factory fodder actually shoots flatter than the lighter 150-grain .30-06 commercial ammo. It also strikes with more energy at 300 yards than the 180-grain '06 load does at 200. The .300 Winchester is an excellent elk and moose cartridge, offering plenty of anchoring power, excellent long-range trajectory and recoil that's really not all that objectionable. It does kick harder than a .308 or a .30-06, but anyone who can shoot an '06 without flinching should have little trouble moving up to the .300 Winchester Magnum. This is my first choice for moose and elk.

The old 8mm Mauser is badly underloaded by domestic ammo firms, but with Norma or

With either handloads or factory loads, the 8mm Remington Magnum is more than adequate for moose and elk.

other European loads it makes a fine moose and elk round. Handloads make it as potent as our popular .30-06, but if 170-grain American factory loads are used (the only bullet weight currently available) its use should be restricted to 150 yards or so. Handloaders have a variety of bullet styles to choose from, with weights ranging up to 250 grains. However, 220-grain projectiles are about as heavy as I'd recommend for this cartridge.

Remington's belted 8mm magnum is a very powerful, flat-shooting round that works very well for hunting elk and moose. As a matter of fact, I can't imagine hunting anything smaller with this potent cartridge, which was introduced in 1977.

The 8mm Remington Magnum 220-grain factory load starts out at more than 2,800 fps and produces nearly 2 tons of energy at the muzzle. The 185-grain load hustles along at some 3,080 fps, and isn't far behind the 220-grain ammo in terms of muzzle energy. Sighted to print 2 inches high at 100 yards, either load shoots flat enough to kill elk or moose at 300 yards without requiring any holdover. And at 300 yards, there's still a full ton of striking force left.

The inevitable price for this kind of potency is recoil, which can be downright unpleasant. In my experience, Remington's 8mm belted magnum is noticeably harder on the shoulder than the .300 Winchester Magnum, although recoil-resistant riflemen may not feel much difference. This is a fine choice for our largest deer, but only in the hands of experienced magnum shooters. A beginning rifleman will have trouble controlling this one.

The .338 Winchester and .340 Weatherby magnums fall into the same category. The .338 Winchester Magnum has been around since 1958, and has earned a real following among big-game hunters in this country. It's a popular choice among western elk hunters, and is widely used in Alaska. Like the 8mm Remington Magnum, the .338 Winchester shoots flat enough to make 300-plus-yard kills feasible even on large, tough animals, with power to spare.

Three different bullet weights are factory loaded: 200, 225 and 250 grains. The 200- and 225-grain soft points are the ones to choose for elk and moose, while the 250-grain Silvertip is best left to hunters of Alaskan brown bears. Again, this cartridge develops more recoil than the once-a-year hunter may want to put up with.

A much milder-recoiling round that throws an even larger bullet is the .358 Winchester. This is an excellent medium-range cartridge for both moose and elk, but it never achieved more than marginal popularity. Both Savage and Browning have offered lever rifles in this chambering, and a handful of bolt rifles were featured in this caliber. But .358 Winchester rifles are anything but plentiful. At ranges up to 200 yards, this is a fine choice for our biggest deer, but you'll be lucky to find a rifle chambered for this round in your dealer's gun rack.

Britain's .375 H&H Magnum is a potent number that has been used more than once on moose and elk. It's a fine round with good long-range ballistics, but it offers more power than an elk hunter really needs. The lightest factory load available throws a 270-grain slug, and when it's fired the results aren't kind to the shoulder. This is a fine load for those who can handle the recoil, and it is deadly on the largest moose that ever walked. But unless you also intend to hunt Alaskan bear or African game, I'd recommend something lighter and less punishing.

Rifles for Moose and Elk

In big elk country, a flat-shooting rifle with enough power to do the job at 200 yards is often needed.

The .444 Marlin and .45-70 Government cartridges will kill moose and elk, and these are available in Marlin's popular lever rifles. The .444 Marlin throws a relatively light 240-grain handgun bullet, and this limits its usefulness to ranges of 150 yards or so, as both energy and trajectory fall off fast. The .45-70 factory loads on the market are likewise too anemic for long-range use, although this cartridge can be handloaded to much greater potency in a strong bolt-action or single-shot rifle.

Much has been said regarding "brush rifles" and loads over the years, with pundits favoring large-caliber firearms lobbing relatively slow, heavy slugs for this kind of work. I don't much care for the term "brush gun," as I've found that *any* rifle projectile is easily deflected when fired through brush or twigs. Some nimrods use the .444 Marlin and .45-70 as "brush calibers," and I guess they work as well as anything else for this kind of duty. But don't count on them to "buck brush"; shoot only when you have a clear target, with an unobstructed bullet path. These rounds are best used at short "brush" ranges, however.

When hunting large animals such as moose and elk, bullet construction is of primary importance. Lightly constructed projectiles intended for 150- to 200-pound deer-size animals may be inadequate for a critter weighing five times as much. Whatever cartridge or caliber chosen (with the exception of the big 8mm, .338 and .375 magnums), only the larger, heavier bullets available should be used for best performance on trophy bulls. These bullets should be designed to penetrate deeply, and expand rather slowly when compared to deer and ultra-light varmint slugs. To perform properly, such projectiles must be driven at certain minimum velocities, and this is where cartridges with large powder capacities have the edge.

In areas where it's legal, you can hunt these large deer with handguns. Again, only the most powerful cartridges should be chosen, and these should be loaded with the heaviest bullets available. That pretty well limits your selection to the .41 and .44 Remington magnums in a revolver, or something like the .30 or .357 Herrett in the Thompson/Center Contender or other strong single shot.

Where muzzleloading rifles are concerned, I'd consider .50 caliber the absolute minimum — and would prefer a .54-caliber firearm shooting Maxi-Balls.

Although I advise any elk or moose hunter to use a rifle and cartridge combination adequate for the job at hand, it isn't a good idea to buy a big, booming magnum a week before the season begins. The magnums make fine "big deer" rifles, but take some getting used to. For that matter, some shooters never manage to master the recoil these cartridges produce. Getting used to even moderately stiff recoil takes patience and practice, and many sportsmen simply won't take the time to familiarize themselves thoroughly with a firearm before taking it afield. This results in clean misses, or worse — wounded animals that escape to die a lingering death.

A six-point bull makes his exit. You have to hunt long and hard to find real trophy animals.

If you can't, or won't, take the time to shoot up enough magnum ammo to accustom yourself to the recoil it generates, you'd be far better off with a 7mm Mauser, .270 Winchester or .30-06 that won't prove so punishing. You'll shoot better with a lighter-recoiling cartridge, and, as always, accurate bullet placement is far more important than sheer shocking power.

RECOMMENDED LOADS FOR MOOSE AND ELK

(Courtesy Remington Arms Co., Inc., Federal Cartridge Corp., and Winchester Western)

CALIBERS	BULLET		VELOCITY FEET PER SECOND						ENERGY		
	Wt.-Grs.	Style	Muzzle	100 Yds.	200 Yds.	300 Yds.	400 Yds.	500 Yds.	Muzzle	100 Yds.	200 Yds.
6.5mm REM. MAG.	120	Pointed Soft Point	3210	2905	2621	2353	2102	1867	2745	2248	1830
264 WIN. MAG.	140	Pointed Soft Point	3030	2782	2548	2326	2114	1914	2854	2406	2018
270 WIN.	130	Pointed Soft Point	3110	2823	2554	2300	2061	1837	2791	2300	1883
	130	Pointed	3110	2849	2604	2371	2150	1941	2791	2343	1957
	150	Soft Point	2900	2550	2225	1926	1653	1415	2801	2165	1649
7mm MAUSER	140	Pointed Soft Point	2660	2435	2221	2018	1827	1648	2199	1843	1533
7mm-08 REM.	140	Pointed Soft Point	2860	2625	2402	2189	1988	1798	2542	2142	1793
280 REM.	165	Soft Point	2820	2510	2220	1950	1701	1479	2913	2308	1805
7mm EXPRESS REM.	150	Pointed Soft Point	2970	2699	2444	2203	1975	1763	2937	2426	1989
284 WIN.	150	Pointed Soft Point	2860	2595	2344	2108	1886	1680	2724	2243	1830
7mm REM. MAG.	150	Pointed Soft Point	3110	2830	2568	2320	2085	1866	3221	2667	2196
	175	Pointed Soft Point	2860	2645	2440	2244	2057	1879	3178	2718	2313
30-06 SPRINGFIELD	165	Pointed Soft Point	2800	2534	2283	2047	1825	1621	2872	2352	1909
	180	Soft Point	2700	2348	2023	1727	1466	1251	2913	2203	1635
	180	Pointed Soft Point	2700	2469	2250	2042	1846	1663	2913	2436	2023
	180	Bronze Point	2700	2485	2280	2084	1899	1725	2913	2468	2077
	200	Boat-tail Soft Point	2550	2400	2260	2120	1990	1860	2890	2560	2270
	220	Soft Point	2410	2130	1870	1632	1422	1246	2837	2216	1708
30-40 KRAG	180	Pointed Soft Point	2430	2099	1795	1525	1298	1128	2360	1761	1288
	180	Pointed	2430	2213	2007	1813	1632	1468	2360	1957	1610
	220	Pointed	2160	1956	1765	1587	1427	1287	2279	1869	1522
300 WIN. MAG.	180	Pointed Soft Point	2960	2745	2540	2344	2157	1979	3501	3011	2578
	220	Pointed	2680	2448	2228	2020	1823	1640	3508	2927	2121
300 H.&H. MAG.	180	Pointed	2880	2640	2412	2196	1991	1798	3315	2785	2325
	220	Pointed	2580	2041	2114	1901	1702	1520	3251	2677	2183
300 SAVAGE	180	Pointed Soft Point	2350	2025	1728	1467	1252	1098	2207	1639	1193
	180	Pointed	2350	2137	1935	1745	1570	1413	2207	1825	1496
303 SAVAGE	190	Pointed	1940	1657	1410	1211	1073	982	1588	1158	839
303 BRITISH	180	Pointed Soft Point	2460	2233	2018	1816	1629	1459	2418	1993	1627
308 WIN.	180	Soft Point	2620	2274	1955	1666	1414	1212	2743	2066	1527
	180	Pointed Soft Point	2620	2393	2178	1974	1782	1604	2743	2283	1896
	165	Boat-tail Soft Point	2700	2520	2330	2160	1990	1830	2670	2310	1990
8mm MAUSER	170	Soft Point	2360	1969	1622	1333	1123	997	2102	1463	993
8mm REM. MAG.	185	Pointed Soft Point	3080	2761	2464	2186	1927	1688	3896	3131	2494
	220	Pointed Soft Point	2830	2581	2346	2123	1913	1716	3912	3254	2688
338 WIN. MAG.	200	Pointed Soft Point	2960	2658	2375	2110	1862	1635	3890	3137	2505
	225	Pointed Soft Point	2780	2572	2374	2184	2003	1832	3882	3305	2816
350 REM. MAG.	200	Pointed Soft Point	2710	2410	2130	1870	1631	1421	3261	2579	2014
358 WIN.	200	Pointed	2490	2171	1876	1610	1379	1194	2753	2093	1563
	250	Pointed	2230	1988	1762	1557	1375	1224	2760	2194	1723
444 MAR.	265	Soft Point	2120	1733	1405	1160	1012	920	2644	1768	1162
45-70 GOVERNMENT	405	Soft Point	1330	1168	1055	977	918	869	1590	1227	1001

FOOT-POUNDS			TRAJECTORY† 0.0 Indicates yardage at which rifle was sighted in.													BARREL LENGTH
			SHORT RANGE						LONG RANGE							
			Bullet does not rise more than one inch above line of sight from muzzle to sighting in range.						Bullet does not rise more than three inches above line of sight from muzzle to sighting in range.							
300 Yds.	400 Yds.	500 Yds.	50 Yds.	100 Yds.	150 Yds.	200 Yds.	250 Yds.	300 Yds.	100 Yds	150 Yds.	200 Yds.	250 Yds.	300 Yds.	400 Yds.	500 Yds.	
1475	1177	929	0.4	0.7	0.0	− 1.8	− 4.9	− 9.5	2.7	3.0	2.1	0.0	− 3.5	− 15.5	− 35.3	24"
1682	1389	1139	0.5	0.8	0.0	− 2.0	− 5.4	−10.2	1.8	1.5	0.0	− 2.9	− 7.2	− 20.8	− 42.2	24"
1527	1226	974	0.4	0.8	0.0	− 2.0	− 5.3	−10.0	1.7	1.5	0.0	− 2.8	− 7.1	− 20.8	− 42.7	24"
1622	1334	1087	0.4	0.7	0.0	− 1.9	− 5.1	− 9.7	1.7	1.4	0.0	− 2.7	− 6.8	− 19.9	− 40.5	
1235	910	667	0.6	1.0	0.0	− 2.5	− 6.8	−13.1	2.2	1.9	0.0	− 3.6	− 9.3	− 28.1	− 59.7	
1266	1037	844	0.2	0.0	− 1.7	− 5.0	−10.0	−17.0	2.5	2.0	0.0	− 3.8	− 9.6	− 27.7	− 56.3	24"
1490	1228	1005	0.6	0.9	0.0	− 2.3	−6.11	−11.6	2.1	1.7	0.0	− 3.2	− 8.1	− 23.5	− 47.7	24"
1393	1060	801	0.2	0.0	− 1.5	− 4.6	− 9.5	−16.4	2.3	1.9	0.0	− 3.7	− 9.4	− 28.1	− 58.8	24"
1616	1299	1035	0.5	0.9	0.0	− 2.2	− 5.8	−11.0	1.9	1.6	0.0	− 3.1	− 7.8	− 22.8	− 46.7	24"
1480	1185	940	0.6	1.0	0.0	− 2.4	− 6.3	−12.1	2.1	1.8	0.0	− 3.4	− 8.5	− 24.8	− 51.0	24"
1792	1448	1160	0.4	0.8	0.0	− 1.9	5.2	9.9	1.7	1.5	0.0	− 2.8	− 7.0	− 20.5	− 42.1	24"
1956	1644	1372	0.6	0.9	0.0	− 2.3	− 6.0	−11.3	2.0	1.7	0.0	− 3.2	− 7.9	− 22.7	− 45.8	24"
1534	1220	963	0.7	1.0	0.0	− 2.5	− 6.7	−12.7	2.3	1.9	0.0	− 3.6	− 9.0	− 26.3	− 54.1	24"
1192	859	625	0.2	0.0	− 1.8	− 5.5	−11.2	−19.5	2.7	2.3	0.0	− 4.4	−11.3	− 34.4	− 73.7	
1666	1362	1105	0.2	0.0	− 1.6	− 4.8	− 9.7	−16.5	2.4	2.0	0.0	− 3.7	− 9.3	− 27.0	− 54.9	
1736	1441	1189	0.2	0.0	− 1.6	− 4.7	− 9.6	−16.2	2.4	2.0	0.0	− 3.6	− 9.1	− 26.2	− 53.0	
2000	1760	1540	0.6	0.0	− 2.7	− 6.0	−12.4	−18.8	2.3	1.8	0.0	− 4.1	− 9.0	− 25.8	− 51.3	
1301	988	758	0.4	0.0	− 2.3	− 6.8	−13.8	−23.6	1.5	0.0	− 3.7	− 9.9	−19.0	− 47.4	− 93.1	
929	673	508	0.4	0.0	− 2.4	− 7.1	−14.5	−25.0	1.6	0.0	− 3.9	−10.5	−20.3	− 51.7	−103.9	
1314	1064	861	0.4	0.0	− 2.1	− 6.2	−12.5	−21.1	1.4	0.0	− 3.4	− 8.9	−16.8	− 40.9	− 78.1	
1230	995	809	0.6	0.0	− 2.9	− 8.2	−16.4	−27.6	1.9	0.0	− 4.4	−11.6	−21.9	− 53.3	−101.8	
2196	1859	1565	0.5	0.8	0.0	− 2.2	− 5.5	−10.4	1.9	1.6	0.0	− 2.9	− 7.3	− 20.9	− 41.9	24"
1993	1623	1314	0.2	0.0	− 1.7	− 4.9	− 9.9	−16.9	2.5	2.0	0.0	− 3.8	− 9.5	− 27.5	− 56.1	
1927	1584	1292	0.6	0.9	0.0	− 2.3	− 6.0	−11.5	2.1	1.7	0.0	− 3.2	− 8.0	− 23.3	− 47.4	24"
1765	1415	1128	0.3	0.0	− 1.9	− 5.5	−11.0	−18.7	2.7	2.2	0.0	− 4.2	−10.5	− 30.7	− 63.0	
860	626	482	0.5	0.0	− 2.6	− 7.7	−15.6	−27.1	1.7	0.0	− 4.2	−11.3	−21.9	− 55.8	−112.0	
1217	985	798	0.4	0.0	− 2.3	− 6.7	−13.5	−22.8	1.5	0.0	− 3.6	− 9.6	−18.2	− 44.1	− 84.2	
619	486	407	0.9	0.0	− 4.1	−11.9	−24.1	−41.4	2.7	0.0	− 6.4	−17.3	−33.2	− 83.7	−164.4	
1318	1060	851	0.3	0.0	− 2.1	− 6.1	−12.2	−20.8	1.4	0.0	− 3.3	− 8.8	−16.6	− 40.4	− 77.4	
1109	799	587	0.3	0.0	− 2.0	− 5.9	−12.1	−20.9	2.9	2.4	0.0	− 4.7	−12.1	− 36.9	− 79.1	24"
1557	1269	1028	0.2	0.0	− 1.8	− 5.2	−10.4	−17.7	2.6	2.1	0.0	− 4.0	− 9.9	− 28.9	− 58.8	
1700	1450	1230	1.3	0.0	− 1.3	− 4.0	− 8.4	−14.4	2.0	1.7	0.0	− 3.3	− 8.4	− 24.3	− 48.9	
671	476	375	0.5	0.0	− 2.7	− 8.2	−17.0	−29.8	1.8	0.0	− 4.5	−12.4	−24.3	− 63.8	−130.7	24"
1963	1525	1170	0.5	0.8	0.0	− 2.1	− 5.6	−10.7	1.8	1.6	0.0	− 3.0	− 7.6	− 22.5	− 46.8	
2201	1787	1438	0.6	1.0	0.0	− 2.4	− 6.4	−12.1	2.2	1.8	0.0	− 3.4	− 8.5	− 24.7	− 50.5	24"
1977	1539	1187	0.5	0.9	0.0	− 2.3	− 6.1	−11.6	2.0	1.7	0.0	− 3.2	− 8.2	− 24.3	− 50.4	
2384	2005	1677	1.2	1.3	0.0	− 2.7	− 7.1	−12.9	2.7	2.1	0.0	− 3.6	− 9.4	− 25.0	− 49.9	
1553	1181	897	0.2	0.0	− 1.7	− 5.1	−10.4	−17.9	2.6	2.1	0.0	− 4.0	−10.3	− 30.5	− 64.0	20"
1151	844	633	0.4	0.0	− 2.2	− 6.5	−13.3	−23.0	1.5	0.0	− 3.6	− 9.7	−18.6	− 47.2	− 94.1	24"
1346	1049	832	0.5	0.0	− 2.7	− 7.9	−16.0	−27.1	1.8	0.0	− 4.3	−11.4	−21.7	− 53.5	−103.7	24"
791	603	498	0.7	0.0	− 3.6	−10.8	−22.5	−39.5	2.4	0.0	− 6.0	−16.4	−32.2	− 84.3	−170.2	
858	758	679	0.0	−4.7	−15.8	−34.0	−60.0	−94.5	0.0	−8.7	−24.6	−48.2	−80.3	−172.4	−305.9	24"

Rifles for Caribou, Sheep and Mountain Goat 3

The first time I hunted caribou, I was surprised to find myself high atop a mountain in British Columbia's Skeena wilderness. The animal I was seeking was of the Osborn, or mountain, variety.

It was mid-September, and rutting season was underway. The animals weren't migrating in the huge herds I'd read about, but were scattered in passes and through high mountain valleys. As a matter of fact the caribou were living in such lofty country that the trophy bull I finally found was located while glassing for mountain goat. There were sheep in the area, too, and a hunter with the right license tags would have had little trouble bagging all three animals by simply walking a mile or two along the high ridge I was glassing from.

My caribou, a handsome, double-shovel bull carrying a live weight of some 500 pounds, was a good mile and a half distant when first spotted, and a two-hour stalk was required to get within shooting position. My guide, Reg Collingwood, and I kept the spine of a high ridge between us and the resting animal. This made it necessary for us to follow a circuitous, winding route that took us hurriedly across steep shale slides that terminated in a sheer dropoff into the valley far below. The scenery at that altitude was spectacular, but the air was just thin enough to make getting oxygen difficult while hurrying along the mountainside.

When we finally reached the bald knob that was our goal, I stopped to gulp deep lungfuls and give my pulse a chance to steady. While I was doing this, Reg popped up to the skyline for a brief look around, and slithered down with the welcome news that my bull was still where we'd seen him last. He was bedded down in a patch of snow with his harem of three cows, enjoying the coolness that helped keep the pesky black flies at bay.

"They're still there," he said with a happy grin. But his smile faded as he added, "I think there's something bothering them. One cow is on her feet, and another is looking nervous. I think you'd better get up there and pop that bull right now!"

I unbuckled my pack and, pushing it before me, bellied over the ridge. There was the bull, lurching to his feet some 300 yards below me. A long shot, but not from the prone position with the pack to serve as a rest. I quickly placed the fore end of the rifle on the pack, squirmed into position, and squeezed a shot off.

Sheep and goat terrain calls for lightweight but accurate, flat-shooting rifles — and stamina on the part of hunters. (Photos by Leonard Lee Rue III and Irene Vandermolen.)

By now the bull was standing, facing me almost directly. I held the crosshairs high on his chest as the rifle roared, and a second later the bull's knees buckled and he went down.

His cows were also on their feet, but surprisingly weren't even looking my way. Their attention was held by something down the valley. As I climbed to my feet and began sliding my way down the slope toward the fallen bull, the three cows were galvanized into action. The trio wheeled and broke into a high trot — straight toward me. They passed me on either side without so much as a second look, and disappeared over the ridge behind me.

When Reg and I reached my trophy, he was dead. We paused to admire his gracefully curving antlers, and I uncased my camera for the obligatory photo session that was to follow. I glanced up as I finished loading film in the camera, and movement caught my eye. Loping

59

up the slope less than 200 yards away, a pack of eight wolves were in hot, if distant, pursuit of the caribou cows.

I was surprised to see wolves this high in the mountains, well above timberline, but Reg assured me they were a common sight. He did point out that the pack's appearance would probably move the mountain goats we'd seen earlier that day to new territory. And that meant we'd be on a different mountain, ourselves, come morning. We still had goat tags to fill.

Cartridges and Calibers

Caribou, sheep and mountain goat are not difficult animals to kill, once you've managed to stalk within reasonable rifle range. The caribou is the largest of these highly desirable trophies, and a big Osborn bull may top 600 pounds. Barren-ground and woodland caribou are smaller, but even these varieties can weigh twice as much as a whitetail buck.

Both goats and Rocky Mountain bighorn may reach 300 pounds or more, while Dall and Stone sheep run about 100 pounds lighter. None of these animals, including the larger caribou, is particularly shock resistant, and most cartridges suitable for deer are potent enough to do the job.

However, since they're hunted in high, mountainous terrain, long shots may be called for. This possibility rules out lighter calibers such as the .243 Winchester and 6mm Remington. The .250 Savage and .257 Roberts are similarly marginal for long-range work. The only quarter bores I would even consider for mountain goat, sheep or caribou are the .257 Weatherby Magnum and the .25-06 Remington loaded with 117- or 120-grain bullets. Either of these will kill cleanly out to 350 yards as long as the rifleman does his job.

Remington's 6.5mm and Winchester's .264 magnums are both fine mountain cartridges, but these have fallen into disuse and rifles chambered for these numbers are no longer widely available.

One of the finest goat, sheep and caribou rounds is the old .270 Winchester. With properly constructed 130- or 140-grain projectiles, this is an excellent choice for long-range shooting. Sighted in to print 2½ inches high at the 100-yard mark, the 130-grain .270 factory load delivers flat enough trajectory to allow kills as far as 300 yards away without any holdover. Out at 400 yards, the projectile drops some 20 inches below the crosshairs, so some sight elevation is needed. But since it's usually possible to stalk within 250 yards or so even on mountain game, such super-long shots are seldom (if ever) advisable.

The .270 offers a fine balance of adequate power and flat trajectory without objectionable recoil. This means most riflemen have no trouble shooting accurately a properly stocked .270, and that's an important factor. The 130-grain soft-nose factory loads have long been favorites, but the factory combinations that get my vote for sheep and goat hunting are the Federal Premium fodder loaded with 130-grain Sierra boattails, and Frontier's load pushing a Hornady 140-grain boattail. These projectiles provide maximum performance for use on distant targets.

The 7mm-08 Remington is another mild-recoiling round capable of delivering good per-

Ruger's International model 77 Carbine in .308 Winchester is light, handy and potent enough for sheep, caribou and mountain goat.

formance on these animals. The 140-grain factory load works very well out to 350 yards, and rifles chambered for this number are available in short action lengths. Remington's 140-grain factory 7mm Mauser load is a bit less potent than the 7mm-08, but good handloads will turn the old 7x57 Mauser into a fine mountain-country round.

An even better 7mm for long-range work is the 7mm Express Remington (once known as the .280 Remington). As loaded by Remington, this round throws a 150-grain bullet at more than 2,950 feet per second (fps) with over 2,900 foot-pounds of muzzle energy. This shoots almost as flat as the .270 Winchester 130-grain load, and delivers about the same amount of energy on target. Because it throws a larger, slightly heavier bullet the 7mm Express Remington is favored by some nimrods over the .270 for taking largish game, but there's not enough difference between these two fine rounds to get excited about.

A highly popular 7mm cartridge for mountain use is the 7mm Remington Magnum. This pushes a 150-grain slug out the bore some 140 fps faster than does the 7mm Express Remington, giving the belted magnum even flatter trajectory and higher retained energy downrange. Weatherby's 7mm Magnum is even hotter. You pay a price for this added performance in terms of greater recoil and muzzle blast, but the 7mm magnums have a large and loyal following. Some hunters of Canadian and Alaskan game like the magnum's power margin because there's always a chance of encountering a grizzly. If you have a grizzly license in your pocket, the 7mm magnums make excellent sense.

The .308 Winchester makes a good goat and sheep round, but unless you're fond of short-action rifles (as I am), the .30-06 makes better sense. The .308 throwing a 150- or 165-grain slug, comes within 100 fps of the .30-06, but the '06 *does* have a bit of extra oomph, which makes it the cartridge of choice.

I might add that I own a couple of ultralight, fiberglass-stocked mountain rifles, and these are chambered for the .308 Winchester because of the weight advantage a shorter action provides. I happily use these flyweight firearms on caribou, sheep and goat, and they've given excellent performance.

Use the prone position when making long-range shots and place the rifle on some kind of rest if at all possible.

Both the .308 Winchester and .30-06 Springfield make good 300-plus-yard cartridges when used with 150- or 165-grain projectiles. Sight-in your rifle to shoot 2½ inches high at 100 yards, and you can use a dead-on hold out to 250 or 275 yards. Again, recoil isn't much of a problem with these .30-caliber rounds, although they can kick if the rifle stock isn't well designed. Ammo is available almost anywhere.

If recoil doesn't bother you, the .300 Winchester Magnum makes a superb long-distance killer. It shoots a 150-grain slug as flat as the 7mm Remington Magnum throws a 125-grain projectile, and delivers greater energy. Both of these popular magnums kick harder than a .270 or .30-06, but they're not really uncomfortable to shoot. Anyone who can handle .30-06 recoil can learn to handle a .300 magnum, but it does take time and a bit of practice.

Where you intend to use a single rifle on a Canadian or Alaskan hunt involving sheep or goats, along with larger game such as moose or grizzly, a .300 magnum makes a fine compromise.

Similarly, some mountain hunters tote either a .338 Winchester or 8mm Remington magnum on this kind of expedition, preferring the extra oomph these cartridges provide for the large coastal grizzlies. These magnums, too, make excellent long-range medicine for goat and sheep country. However, they're more powerful than really necessary for these animals, and recoil can be severe. Because they do have a hefty kick, few nimrods can shoot them with tack-driving accuracy over long distances. If you can handle their recoil without flinching, well and good.

As far as handguns are concerned, only the largest, flattest-shooting cartridges should be selected. Revolver buffs should stick with either the .41 or .44 magnums, while single-shot users can make good use of flatter-shooting numbers like the .30 and .357 Herrett rounds. Even with these fast-stepping wildcats, you must stalk long and carefully to get within realistic handgun range. The best of marksmen shouldn't attempt shots beyond 200 yards with a pistol or revolver, and I never shoot at game more than 100 yards away. This means the handgunning hunter of sheep and goats has his work cut out for him, and he can never hope for an easy hunt.

Bullet Design

Regardless of caliber and cartridge selected, it's important to choose the right bullet design. A too heavily constructed bullet may not expand as it should when used on medium-size game such as sheep or mountain goat. Conversely, a too-light projectile may not give adequate penetration. In either case, the animal may be wounded and possibly lost, even though the bullet isn't badly placed.

In addition, bullet shape is important. The ballistic coefficient of a bullet is the ratio of its sectional density to its coefficient of form. Without going into any complicated mathematical analyses, the fact is that a bullet with a relatively high ballistic coefficient travels through the air with less drag, or resistance. This means it travels faster, and shoots flatter, than a bullet of the same caliber with a lower ballistic coefficient. That's assuming both bullets start out at the same velocity.

Ballistic coefficient isn't awfully important at typical hunting range—up to 200 yards or so, but becomes a factor worth considering when long-range targets may be encountered.

Ballistic coefficients of different bullets are published in most handloading books and bullet-manufacturer tables. Generally speaking, pointed bullets have a higher ballistic coefficient than round- or flat-nose projectiles, and should be chosen over the blunter types for goat, sheep and caribou hunting. Boattail bullets also tend to create less drag than flat-based ones, and so have higher coefficients.

The bullets must be traveling fast enough to give proper expansion when they strike the target. A heavily constructed bullet with thick jacket walls requires more velocity to expand adequately than a thinner-walled projectile of the same size and weight does. This is one reason a fast-stepping combination is required for those 300-yard shots.

Handloaders should study bullet design with these criteria in mind before selecting the

Mountain caribou are found in the highest country, and getting a trophy back to civilization takes some work.

projectiles. If factory ammo is used, you should choose pointed, spitzer-shaped bullets of either flat-based or boattail design. Goat, sheep and caribou hunters should stick with the following bullet weights: .25 calibers—117 or 120 grains; .270 Winchester—130 or 140 grains; 7mm—139, 140, 150 or 154 grains; .30 caliber—150, 165 or 180 grains.

Choosing a Rifle and Scope

As far as rifle type is concerned, the vast majority of high-altitude hunters favor the bolt action. Bolt-action rifles are strong and reliable and have a well-deserved reputation for accuracy. You see a few high-quality single shots, but the bolt rifle is the hands-down favorite.

Weight is important when toting a rifle around in the rarefied atmosphere you find in the higher elevations, and savvy nimrods choose the lightest firearm they can find, provided it shoots accurately. There are several bolt-action sporters that weigh under 7½ pounds, and some shade that mark by a considerable margin. If you're really serious about shedding rifle weight, you can have an ultralight fiberglass stock fitted. These are available at reasonable cost from several manufacturers, who also offer finished custom rifles weighing 5 pounds or less.

As far as sighting equipment is concerned, a good, magnifying optical sight, or scope, is the only choice that makes sense. Select a top-quality glass by a well-known manufacturer: Zeiss, Leupold, Bushnell, Redfield, Burris or Weaver are all good choices, and other makers offer good optics, as well. A fixed 4X or, better yet, 6X sight will do the job, although an increasing number of riflemen are relying on 2–7X or 3–9X variables. Rangefinding scopes with dials to adjust for bullet drop provide a theoretical advantage, but from a strictly practical viewpoint you can probably do as well without them. By sighting-in any suitable caliber and bullet combination to print 2½ or 3 inches high at 100 yards, you'll be able to take your game with a "dead-on" hold out to 250 or even 300 yards. Beyond that range, a glance at the bullet trajectory tables at the end of the chapter will show you how much holdover is required. Since many hunters have difficulty estimating range accurately beyond 250 yards or so, it's best to limit your shooting to that distance if at all possible. At extended range, luck plays too large a factor for a real sportsman to be comfortable.

One way you can lean Lady Luck your direction is to use a solid rest whenever shooting at distant game. I've often used a backpack or rucksack as an improvised rest, and for the last few years have relied on a Harris bipod when hunting mountain game. This handy device can be quickly fitted to the front sling swivel stud, and the telescoping legs can be folded up against the fore end when not in use. Any shooting stick or walking staff can give added support to your rifle at that critical moment the game is in your crosshairs. The steadier your rifle is when you squeeze the trigger, the better your chances of taking that trophy home.

RECOMMENDED LOADS FOR CARIBOU, SHEEP, AND MOUNTAIN GOAT

(Courtesy Remington Arms Co., Inc., Federal Cartridge Corp., and Winchester Western)

CALIBERS	BULLET		VELOCITY FEET PER SECOND						ENERGY		
	Wt.-Grs.	Style	Muzzle	100 Yds.	200 Yds.	300 Yds.	400 Yds.	500 Yds.	Muzzle	100 Yds.	200 Yds.
25-06 REM.	120	Pointed Soft Point	3010	2749	2502	2269	2048	1840	2414	2013	1668
6.5mm REM. MAG.	120	Pointed Soft Point	3210	2905	2621	2353	2102	1867	2745	2248	1830
264 WIN. MAG.	140	Pointed Soft Point	3030	2782	2548	2326	2114	1914	2854	2406	2018
270 WIN.	130	Pointed Soft Point	3110	2823	2554	2300	2061	1837	2791	2300	1883
	130	Pointed	3110	2849	2604	2371	2150	1941	2791	2343	1957
	150	Soft Point	2900	2550	2225	1926	1653	1415	2801	2165	1649
7mm MAUSER	140	Pointed Soft Point	2660	2435	2221	2018	1827	1648	2199	1843	1533
7mm-08 REM.	140	Pointed Soft Point	2860	2625	2402	2189	1988	1798	2542	2142	1793
280 REM.	165	Soft Point	2820	2510	2220	1950	1701	1479	2913	2308	1805
7mm EXPRESS REM.	150	Pointed Soft Point	2970	2699	2444	2203	1975	1763	2937	2426	1989
284 WIN.	150	Pointed Soft Point	2860	2595	2344	2108	1886	1680	2724	2243	1830
7mm REM. MAG.	150	Pointed Soft Point	3110	2830	2568	2320	2085	1866	3221	2667	2196
30-06 SPRINGFIELD	150	Pointed Soft Point	2910	2617	2342	2083	1843	1622	2820	2281	1827
	150	Pointed	2910	2656	2416	2189	1974	1773	2820	2349	1944
	165	Pointed Soft Point	2800	2534	2283	2047	1825	1621	2872	2352	1909
	180	Soft Point	2700	2348	2023	1727	1466	2151	2913	2203	1635
	180	Pointed Soft Point	2700	2469	2250	2042	1846	1663	2913	2436	2023
300 WIN. MAG.	150	Pointed Soft Point	3290	2951	2636	2342	2068	1813	3605	2900	2314
	180	Pointed Soft Point	2960	2745	2540	2344	2157	1979	3501	3011	2578
300 H.&H. MAG.	150	Pointed	3130	2822	2534	2264	2011	1776	3262	2652	2138
	180	Pointed	2880	2640	2412	2196	1991	1796	3315	2785	2325
300 SAVAGE	150	Pointed Soft Point	2630	2311	2015	1743	1500	1295	2303	1779	1352
	150	Pointed	2630	2354	2095	1853	1631	1434	2303	1845	1462
308 WIN.	150	Pointed Soft Point	2820	2533	2263	2009	1774	1560	2648	2137	1705
	165	Boat-tail Soft Point	2700	2520	2330	2160	1990	1830	2670	2310	1990
8mm MAUSER	170	Soft Point	2360	1969	1622	1333	1123	997	2102	1463	993
8mm REM. MAG.	185	Pointed Soft Point	3080	2761	2464	2186	1927	1688	3896	3131	2494
338 WIN. MAG.	200	Pointed Soft Point	2960	2658	2375	2110	1862	1635	3890	3137	2505
	225	Pointed Soft Point	2780	2572	2374	2184	2003	1832	3862	3306	2816

FOOT-POUNDS			TRAJECTORY† 0.0 Indicates yardage at which rifle was sighted in. SHORT RANGE Bullet does not rise more than one inch above line of sight from muzzle to sighting in range.						LONG RANGE Bullet does not rise more than three inches above line of sight from muzzle to sighting in range.							BARREL LENGTH
300 Yds.	400 Yds.	500 Yds.	50 Yds.	100 Yds.	150 Yds.	200 Yds.	250 Yds.	300 Yds.	100 Yds	150 Yds.	200 Yds.	250 Yds.	300 Yds.	400 Yds.	500 Yds.	
1372	1117	902	0.5	0.8	0.0	− 2.1	− 5.5	−10.5	1.9	1.6	0.0	− 2.9	− 7.4	− 21.6	− 44.2	
1475	1177	929	0.4	0.7	0.0	− 1.8	− 4.9	− 9.5	2.7	3.0	2.1	0.0	− 3.5	− 15.5	− 35.3	24"
1682	1389	1139	0.5	0.8	0.0	− 2.0	− 5.4	−10.2	1.8	1.5	0.0	− 2.9	− 7.2	− 20.8	− 42.2	24"
1527	1226	974	0.4	0.8	0.0	− 2.0	− 5.3	−10.0	1.7	1.5	0.0	− 2.8	− 7.1	− 20.8	− 42.7	
1622	1334	1087	0.4	0.7	0.0	− 1.9	− 5.1	− 9.7	1.7	1.4	0.0	− 2.7	− 6.8	− 19.9	− 40.5	24"
1235	910	667	0.6	1.0	0.0	− 2.5	− 6.8	−13.1	2.2	1.9	0.0	− 3.6	− 9.3	− 28.1	− 59.7	
1266	1037	844	0.2	0.0	− 1.7	− 5.0	−10.0	−17.0	2.5	2.0	0.0	− 3.8	− 9.6	− 27.7	− 56.3	24"
1490	1228	1005	0.6	0.9	0.0	− 2.3	−6.11	−11.6	2.1	1.7	0.0	− 3.2	− 8.1	− 23.5	− 47.7	24"
1393	1060	801	0.2	0.0	− 1.5	− 4.6	− 9.5	−16.4	2.3	1.9	0.0	− 3.7	− 9.4	− 28.1	− 58.8	24"
1616	1299	1035	0.5	0.9	0.0	− 2.2	− 5.8	−11.0	1.9	1.6	0.0	− 3.1	− 7.8	− 22.8	− 46.7	24"
1480	1185	940	0.6	1.0	0.0	− 2.4	− 6.3	−12.1	2.1	1.8	0.0	− 3.4	− 8.5	− 24.8	− 51.0	24"
1792	1448	1160	0.4	0.8	0.0	− 1.9	− 5.2	− 9.9	1.7	1.5	0.0	− 2.3	− 7.0	− 20.5	− 42.1	24"
1445	1131	876	0.6	0.9	0.0	− 2.3	− 6.3	−12.0	2.1	1.8	0.0	− 3.3	− 8.5	− 25.0	− 51.8	
1596	1298	1047	0.6	0.9	0.0	− 2.2	− 6.0	−11.4	2.0	1.7	0.0	− 3.2	− 8.0	− 23.3	− 47.5	
1534	1220	963	0.7	1.0	0.0	− 2.5	− 6.7	−12.7	2.3	1.9	0.0	− 3.6	− 9.0	− 26.3	− 54.1	24"
1192	859	625	0.2	0.0	− 1.8	− 5.5	−11.2	−19.5	2.7	2.3	0.0	− 4.4	−11.3	− 34.4	− 73.7	
1666	1362	1105	0.2	0.0	− 1.6	− 4.8	− 9.7	−16.5	2.4	2.0	0.0	− 3.7	− 9.3	− 27.0	− 54.9	
1827	1424	1095	0.3	0.7	0.0	− 1.8	− 4.8	− 9.3	2.6	2.9	2.1	0.0	− 3.5	− 15.4	− 35.5	
2196	1859	1565	0.5	0.8	0.0	− 2.2	− 5.5	−10.4	1.9	1.6	0.0	− 2.9	− 7.3	− 20.9	− 41.9	
1707	1347	1050	0.4	0.8	0.0	− 2.0	− 5.3	−10.1	1.7	1.5	0.0	− 2.8	− 7.2	− 21.2	− 43.8	
1927	1584	1292	0.6	0.9	0.0	− 2.3	− 6.0	−11.5	2.1	1.7	0.0	− 3.2	− 8.0	− 23.3	− 47.4	
1012	749	558	0.3	0.0	− 1.9	− 5.7	−11.6	−19.9	2.8	2.3	0.0	− 4.5	−11.5	− 34.4	− 73.0	
1143	886	685	0.3	0.0	− 1.8	5.4	−11.0	−18.8	2.7	2.2	0.0	− 4.2	−10.7	− 31.5	− 65.5	
1344	1048	810	0.2	0.0	− 1.5	− 4.5	− 9.3	−15.9	2.3	1.9	0.0	− 3.6	− 9.1	− 26.9	− 55.7	
1700	1450	1230	1.3	0.0	− 1.3	− 4.0	− 8.4	−14.4	2.0	1.7	0.0	− 3.3	− 8.4	− 24.3	− 48.9	
671	476	375	0.5	0.0	− 2.7	− 8.2	−17.0	−29.8	1.8	0.0	− 4.5	−12.4	−24.3	− 63.8	−130.7	24"
1963	1525	1170	0.5	0.8	0.0	− 2.1	− 5.6	−10.7	1.8	1.6	0.0	− 3.0	− 7.6	− 22.5	− 46.8	24"
1977	1539	1187	0.5	0.9	0.0	− 2.3	− 6.1	−11.6	2.0	1.7	0.0	− 3.2	− 8.2	− 24.3	− 50.4	
2334	2005	1677	1.2	1.3	0.0	− 2.7	− 7.1	−12.9	2.7	2.1	0.0	− 3.6	− 9.4	− 25.0	− 49.9	

Armament for Bears, Large & Small 4

It was an arctic November morning. The thermometer registered 40 degrees of frost, and water splashed from the fast-running Gravina River rimed the tops of my hip boots in ice.

In spite of the subzero temperature, I was beginning to sweat under my wool shirt and down vest. Criss-crossing the hip-deep river was hard work, but its dense, brush-choked banks forced us to wade from sandbar to snow-covered sandbar as we picked our way downstream.

My guide, Ed Stevenson, and I were hunting the world's largest carnivores. The 14-inch-long tracks we were following belonged to an Alaskan brown bear boar we'd seen the day before. Ed judged he'd square 10 feet or better, and guessed his weight at well over 1,200 pounds.

Ed makes his living hunting these oversize grizzlies, and has his share of hair-raising tales about them. A few years earlier, a big boar had surprised him from behind while Ed and a sportsman he was guiding were approaching a downed bear the client had shot. They weren't aware of the second grizzly until a split-second before it grabbed Ed in his jaws and shook him like a giant terrier with an oversize rat. Ed's rifle was thrown from him in the process, and he was at the mercy of the bear until the dude showed enough presence of mind to put a .375 H&H Magnum slug in the animal's ear.

Ed's torso is still well-scarred from that incident, and he now packs a .44 magnum revolver in an under-arm shoulder holster in addition to his usual armament, which consists of either a battle-scarred, barrel-taped .375 H&H Winchester model 70 or an Ithaca model 37 riot gun loaded with 12-gauge Brenneke slugs.

Ed's son, Bill, relies on an open-sight .458 Winchester Magnum to keep disgruntled bears from chewing on him or his clients. Both guides need "stoppers"—rifles throwing a big, heavy slug with enough force to shatter bone and halt a charging grizzly in its tracks. A bear guide usually won't shoot until after the paying hunter has had his chance, but some encounters happen so fast and at such short range that such niceties can't be safely observed.

Because there's always the chance of meeting up with a big brownie at badminton range, Ed isn't much on rifles with only marginal stopping power. As a matter of fact he specifically

Bear guide Ed Stevenson packs a slug-loaded Ithaca riot gun as a charge-stopper. At close range, a 12-gauge slug is potent medicine.

requests his clients to bring nothing smaller than a .338 Winchester Magnum to bear camp. It's Ed's opinion that if you can't handle the recoil of a round that big, you have no business hunting the gargantuan grizzlies found along the Alaskan coast.

Other guides I've known are less fussy, and some take the attitude that you shouldn't bring a Big Bertha rifle unless you're sure you can shoot it well. One master guide who has since retired used to tell his clients to bring along the old '06 if that's the rifle they were used to. Of course, he carefully backed up those clients with his .375 Holland & Holland, and he shot well enough to keep his paying guests out of serious trouble.

I've hunted the behemoth bruins just enough to have tremendous respect for these mighty beasts. They're unbelievably strong, frighteningly fast and sometimes lack totally any fear of man. A mama bear with cubs is always bad news, and boars can be nasty just on general principles. The big grizzlies can be downright difficult to hunt, and can slip away through densely packed brush without a whisper of noise. What's more, they display remarkable cunning when stalked, and often double back on their trail to lie in wait for their pursuers. A set of tracks I once followed proved that I had unknowingly walked by within mere feet of my quarry, who simply lay hidden and watched as I hurried along his trail. Apparently, he was simply curious as to what kind of critter dared follow him. His curiosity satisfied, he strolled away with a ground-eating gait that soon left me in the distance. Other bears have been considerably less tolerant of their pursuers, and during hunting season Alaskan hospitals routinely stitch up survivors of the resulting encounters. And there are always a few who don't survive.

While the giant brown bears inhabiting Kodiak Island and the Alaskan coast are enormous, highly dangerous animals, the grizzlies found farther inland run considerably smaller in size. Black bears are smaller yet. All of these bears feature different color phases, with grizzlies running from dark, chocolate brown to almost beige. Black bears can appear either brown or black, and the rare glacier bear of Yakutat Bay sports a bluish-gray pelt. Of course the now-protected polar bear is white.

From a strictly practical viewpoint, there are three different kinds of bears: medium-size bears, big bears and HUGE bears. As far as a hunter facing one is concerned, there's really no such thing as a "small bear."

The black bear, or *Ursus americanus*, has the "medium bear" category all to itself. The average black bear tips the scales at around 225 pounds, and some adults may weigh but 150. These bears stand about 3 feet high at the shoulder, and measure between 4 and 5 feet in length. If that sounds puny, you've never seen what a black bear can do. These animals are enormously strong, and can be formidable opponents when cornered. If not quickly killed, a black bear that's been brought to bay can decimate a pack of costly hounds, and under those conditions, can be counted on to attack the hunter if he gets half a chance.

Some black bears edge their way into the "big bear" category. A few big boars top the 600-pound mark, and one outstanding specimen killed a century ago in Wisconsin scaled over 800 pounds. A 600-pound bear is a big animal, whether it be a boar blackie or a grizzly sow.

The grizzly, *Ursus arctos horribilis*, and the giant Alaskan brown bear, *Ursus arctos middendorffi*, are basically the same critter, differentiated primarily by location and size. It is believed the big, coastal grizzlies attain their awesome ¾-ton size through their salmon-rich diet. Grizzlies farther inland find fish less plentiful, and some mountain bruins get no heavier than 400 or 500 pounds.

Bear Rifles, Large and Small

Your choice of armament, of course, depends primarily on the size and kind of bear you're hunting.

Black bears have traditionally been taken with the full range of "deer rifle" calibers, from the .243 Winchester upwards in size. Many hunters who follow hounds after bears rely on handguns to dispatch the animals after they're treed, and under those conditions a carefully placed .357 magnum slug will do the job. A holstered handgun is easy to carry while the hunter runs through the woods in pursuit of his baying hounds, and once the bear is treed can be used at relatively close range.

If the bear bays on the ground where he can get his teeth and claws into any dog that ventures within reach, a hunter armed with a light handgun is at a real disadvantage. Precise bullet placement isn't easy when you're trying to pick your target through a whirling mass of bear and hounds. A .44 magnum shooting 240-grain soft-nose bullets is a better choice here, and a good rifle or carbine is better yet.

Black bears have been killed with buckshot and rifled slugs, and in swamp country where shots are offered at running animals at close range, either shotgun load can be effective. Most shotgun hunters use a 12-gauge gun and No. oo or No. ooo buckshot, unless rifled slugs are employed.

In some states, black bear are hunted pretty much like deer. Some parts of Idaho, for instance, sport sufficiently heavy populations of lightly hunted bear to give a sportsman who doesn't use dogs a good chance of scoring. Of course, having a lot of four-footed help always improves the odds.

Under normal circumstances, black bears aren't difficult to kill. Any rifle caliber suitable for hunting deer (see Chapter 1) is adequate for black bear. The same holds true for loads and bullet selection. If a relatively small caliber such as the .243 Winchester or 6mm Remington is used, only 100-grain or heavier bullets should be considered.

While bears have fallen to 6mm and .25-caliber slugs, and will continue to do so, I personally prefer bullets of greater size and weight. A 139- to 154-grain 7mm slug makes a good choice, as does the 130-, 140- or 150-grain .270 load. The .308 Winchester makes an excellent black-bear load with 150- to 180-grain projectiles.

Alaskan brown bears reach 1,500 pounds on their salmon-rich diets. Experienced hunters shoot to break one or both front shoulders since these big bruins can't move far with an injured front leg. (Photo by Leonard Lee Rue III.)

Some hunters go after black bears with handguns and hounds. A treed bear can be finished off with a well-placed .357 magnum slug, but if the bear bays on the ground a light handgun may be inadequate. (Photo by Charles G. Summers Jr., c/o Leonard Rue Enterprises.)

Countless bears have been taken with .30-30 saddle carbines, while the .35 Remington, .375 Winchester Big Bore and .444 Marlin cartridges are also available in handy lever-action rifles and carbines. Because I'm always hoping to run across an outsize blackie, I optimistically opt for one of these more potent killers. When hunting in the western states, I'm more apt to tote a 7mm Mauser or .308 Winchester than a stubby lever carbine shooting .30-30 cartridges. At 200 yards, these flatter-shooting rounds are much more effective.

At the same time, you don't really need anything more potent than a .30-06 for these ubiquitous bears. Use a bigbore magnum if you must, but don't kid yourself into thinking it's really necessary.

Grizzlies are another story. These magnificent beasts have succumbed to .270 Winchester and .30-06 wounds, and under the right circumstances these cartridges can be used on mountain grizzlies. By "right circumstances" I mean a situation where the hunter is shooting *downhill* at a range of 200 yards or so, and is backed up by a professional toting much more potent weaponry.

These four rounds have been used to kill our largest bears; most guides now recommend nothing smaller than .338 Winchester Magnum and 8mm Remington Magnum for Alaskan brown bears.

30-06 SPRG.   300 WIN.   338 WIN.   8mm REM.
                  MAGNUM   MAGNUM   MAGNUM

The .358 Norma Magnum and .375 Holland & Holland Magnum are top-rated cartridges for the largest bears.

Since, for most sportsmen, a grizzly is a once-in-a-lifetime trophy, I'd never recommend anything less powerful than a 7mm magnum or a .300 magnum. The 8mm Remington Magnum is even better, and the all-around favorite grizzly cartridge today is probably the .338 Winchester Magnum. With any of these cartridges, the heaviest bullet weights should be used.

Other excellent choices include the .340 Weatherby and .358 Norma magnums, and the venerable .375 Holland & Holland Magnum. Where the huge Alaskan brown bears are concerned, these and the .338 Winchester Magnum are the cartridges of choice.

Any of these magnums shoot flat enough to kill at ranges well beyond 200 yards, and with power to spare. They're particularly comforting to have on hand in close cover, where a bear may appear at 30 or 40 feet rather than 150 yards. At short range, you definitely need enough power to anchor a grizzly *right now!* A big bruin can be remarkably tenacious of life, and even a heart-shot grizzly is liable to live long enough to do interesting things to the hunter unlucky enough to be too close.

Because a grizzly or Alaskan brown bear is dangerous until it draws its last breath, the accepted technique is to shoot to break down one or both front shoulders. A big bear can't travel far without both front legs in working order, and the shock of having its shoulder shattered by a heavy, high-speed bullet may kill the animal outright. Conversely, breaking a rear leg buys you nothing but trouble. A grudge-holding grizzly can easily overhaul the fastest hunter, even with a hind leg out of action. If you're directly below the animal when you shoot, you may be unlucky enough to have it roll literally over you in its death throes. If the beast has any life left when it reaches you, you'll have an opportunity to regret shooting it in the first place.

That's another reason you need a magnum rifle throwing a large-caliber, heavily constructed bullet. Lighter, smaller-diameter slugs simply can't be relied on to smash through heavy bone. And that's what you may have to do to stop a grizzly. You need a rifle that will *anchor* game—not simply kill it.

Handguns and Muzzleloaders

A number of handgunners have taken big bears with magnum revolvers. If you bear in mind that even the big .44 magnum handgun cartridge generates no more energy than the anemic .30-30 rifle round, you have a better idea of the chore you're biting off when you try to get within handgun range of any grizzly. The majority of oversize bruins harvested with a handgun had a few other holes in them when they finally gave up the ghost. Holes that were made by the guide's .375 or .458 magnum rifle.

Because long shots of 100 yards or more may be offered, I'd never personally carry anything but a magnum rifle when hunting grizzlies. But for stopping a close-range charge, a 12-gauge shotgun slug does a fine job. By "close range," I mean 25 yards or less. At that distance, a ⅞- or 1-ounce rifled slug carries a lot of punch, and many Alaskan bear guides, and some BLM and Forest Service people, rely on slug-loaded riot guns for insurance.

Our pioneering forefathers killed bears with muzzleloaders, and modern black-powder buffs can do the same. Any .50-caliber or larger rifle is adequate for black bear, and many of these animals are taken by muzzleloaders each year.

Tackling a grizzly or Alaskan brown bear with a front-stuffing single shot is a different story. It *can* be done—and you should use a .54-, .58- or .60-caliber rifle packing the heaviest charge it will safely handle if you ever attempt this feat—but the dangers involved should be evident. Quite simply, you may need more than one shot to get the job done. Since a mayhem-minded grizzly can cover 100 feet in two seconds flat, your fingers need to be mighty nimble to get that rifle reloaded for a follow-up shot, if needed.

Like the daredevil handgunner, the muzzleloading rifleman who hunts grizzly should have a well-armed guide backing him up—and I *don't* mean with another muzzleloader!

Sights for Bear Rifles

Most serious grizzly and brown bear hunters rely on a modern, magnum repeater. This pretty much narrows the choice to a bolt-action firearm, and a perfectly satisfactory choice it is. Bolt-action rifles are strong, and most are highly dependable even under adverse weather conditions. And dependability is of utmost importance.

This brings up the matter of sight selection. Most riflemen today strongly favor magnifying optical scope sights, and these do offer several advantages over the best iron sights available. In the first place, a scope helps clarify distant targets, allowing you to shoot a little earlier —and later—in the day. The scope's crosshair reticule obscures little of the animal you're shooting at, and helps make precise bullet placement possible. Finally, many middle-aged nimrods aren't very eagle-eyed any more, and a scope provides welcome optical aid.

Looking at the other side of the coin, a scope can be rendered temporarily useless by rain or snow collecting on lens surfaces, and if the tube fails to remain perfectly sealed and vapor-tight the sight can fog up. For this reason, bear hunters should select only the highest-quality scopes for their rifles. Choosing a second-rate sight is the worst possible way to economize, particularly if you're planning a spring or fall bear hunt in Canada or Alaska.

Because bear are often hunted in dense, heavy brush where close encounters are probable, the high-magnification scopes with their narrow fields of view are best avoided. Leave that big 3–9X variable home. If a fixed-power scope is selected, it should have no more than 2X magnification for close-quarters work. Probably the favorite all-around optical sight among Alaskan bear hunters is the 1–4X or 1½–4½X variable. Cranked down to the lowest power level, this scope provides a comfortably large field of view for those tight situations where fast shooting is necessary. If a long shot is offered, it takes only a second to dial up 4X or 4½X magnification.

In my experience, those plastic-cap-on-a-rubber-band lens covers aren't very effective in the cold, wet north country. Moisture condenses on the lenses they cover, and they have a way of working off without your noticing. I usually carry my rifle with the scope uncovered, and stop every few minutes to make sure the lenses are still clear. I keep a few handfuls of toilet paper or paper napkins in a hip pocket for this chore (paper is more absorbent than a cloth handkerchief, and does a better job of sopping up moisture), and occasionally have to dig compacted snow from the forward part of the tube. If you cradle the rifle muzzle-downward in one arm, it's possible to keep the scope's eyepiece pressed against the inner part of your elbow. This does a fair job of keeping rain and snow off the lens.

Some guides stick with factory iron sights because they're less likely to be affected by inclement weather. At charge-stopping range, open sights are extremely fast, and they're the most reliable sighting equipment you can use. Unfortunately, they're not at their best at ranges much past 100 yards.

One alternative is to use a high-riding see-through scope mount that allows you to use the magnifying scope sight, or simply lower your head a bit and use the factory iron sights instead. Pachmayr makes an excellent mount that lets you pivot the scope to one side when

Bear country in late fall or early winter often means miserable weather and very close cover. Only a large-caliber stopper with a very low-powered scope or open sights will do here!

you'd prefer to use open sights. When you return the scope to its over-the-bore position, it retains its original zero.

Whatever size bear you hunt, it's well to remember that any bear can be dangerous. The black bear found throughout the United States is generally a timid soul, and almost always gives man a wide berth. But separate a mama blackie from her cubs, or corner a big boar, and these animals can become downright mean.

Similarly, most grizzlies will leave you strictly alone, but that's an attitude you can't always count on. And if *Ursus horribilis* decides to attack, the largest magnum won't feel like too much rifle.

When choosing armament for hunting bear, it's always best to make sure you're not going afield undergunned. Select a cartridge you know will do the job, and make sure it carries a heavily constructed bullet that will hold together and penetrate. Then become familiar enough with the rifle—*before* the hunt—to shoot it well.

RECOMMENDED LOADS FOR BROWN BEAR

(Courtesy Remington Arms Co., Inc., Federal Cartridge Corp., and Winchester-Western)

CALIBERS	BULLET		VELOCITY FEET PER SECOND						ENERGY		
	Wt.-Grs.	Style	Muzzle	100 Yds.	200 Yds.	300 Yds.	400 Yds.	500 Yds.	Muzzle	100 Yds.	200 Yds.
7mm REM. MAG.	175	Pointed Soft Point	2860	2645	2440	2244	2057	1879	3178	2718	2313
300 WIN. MAG.	220	Pointed	2680	2448	2228	2020	1823	1640	3508	2927	2424
300 H.&H. MAG.	220	Pointed	2580	2341	2114	1901	1702	1520	3251	2677	2183
8mm REM. MAG.	220	Pointed Soft Point	2830	2581	2346	2123	1913	1716	3912	3254	2688
	225	Pointed Soft Point	2780	2572	2374	2184	2003	1832	3862	3306	2816
338 WIN. MAG.	250	Pointed	2660	2395	2145	1910	1693	1497	3927	3184	2554
350 REM. MAG.	200	Pointed Soft Point	2710	2410	2130	1870	1631	1421	3251	2579	2014
358 WIN.	250	Pointed	2230	1968	1762	1557	1375	1224	2760	2194	1723
375 H.&H. MAG.	270	Soft Point	2690	2420	2166	1928	1707	1507	4337	3510	2812
458 WIN. MAG.	510	Soft Point	2040	1770	1527	1319	1157	1046	4712	3547	2640

RECOMMENDED LOADS FOR BLACK BEAR

(Courtesy Remington Arms Co., Inc., Federal Cartridge Corp., and Winchester-Western)

CALIBERS	BULLET		VELOCITY FEET PER SECOND						ENERGY		
	Wt.-Grs.	Style	Muzzle	100 Yds.	200 Yds.	300 Yds.	400 Yds.	500 Yds.	Muzzle	100 Yds.	200 Yds.
243 WIN.	100	Pointed Soft Point	2960	2697	2449	2215	1993	1786	1945	1615	1332
6mm REM.	100	Pointed Soft Point	3130	2857	2600	2357	2127	1911	2175	1812	1501
250 SAVAGE	100	Pointed	2820	2467	2140	1839	1569	1339	1765	1351	1017
257 ROBERTS	117	Pointed Soft Point	2650	2291	1961	1663	1404	1199	1824	1363	999
25-06 REM.	120	Pointed Soft Point	3010	2749	2502	2269	2048	1840	2414	2013	1668
6.5mm REM. MAG.	120	Pointed Soft Point	3210	2905	2621	2353	2102	1867	2745	2248	1830
264 WIN. MAG.	140	Pointed Soft Point	3030	2782	2548	2326	2114	1914	2854	2406	2018
270 WIN.	130	Pointed Soft Point	3110	2823	2554	2300	2061	1837	2791	2300	1883
	130	Pointed	3110	2849	2604	2371	2150	1941	2791	2343	1957
	150	Soft Point	2900	2550	2225	1926	1653	1415	2801	2165	1649
7mm MAUSER	140	Pointed Soft Point	2660	2435	2221	2018	1827	1648	2199	1843	1533
7mm-08 REM.	140	Pointed Soft Point	2860	2625	2402	2189	1988	1798	2542	2142	1793
280 REM.	165	Soft Point	2820	2510	2220	1950	1701	1479	2913	2308	1805
7mm EXPRESS REM.	150	Pointed Soft Point	2970	2699	2444	2203	1975	1763	2937	2426	1989
284 WIN.	150	Pointed Soft Point	2860	2595	2344	2108	1886	1680	2724	2243	1830
7mm REM MAG.	150	Pointed Soft Point	3110	2830	2568	2320	2085	1866	3221	2667	2196
30 REM.	170	Soft Point	2120	1822	1555	1328	1153	1036	1696	1253	913
30-30 WIN.	150	Soft Point	2390	1973	1605	1303	1095	974	1902	1296	858
	170	Soft Point	2200	1895	1619	1381	1191	1061	1827	1355	989
	170	Hollow Point	2200	1895	1619	1381	1191	1061	1827	1355	989
30-06 SPRINGFIELD	150	Pointed Soft Point	2910	2617	2342	2083	1843	1622	2820	2281	1827
	150	Pointed	2910	2656	2416	2189	1974	1773	2820	2349	1944
	165	Pointed Soft Point	2800	2534	2283	2047	1825	1621	2872	2352	1909

| FOOT-POUNDS | | | SHORT RANGE — Bullet does not rise more than one inch above line of sight from muzzle to sighting in range. | | | | | | LONG RANGE — Bullet does not rise more than three inches above line of sight from muzzle to sighting in range. | | | | | | | BARREL LENGTH |
300 Yds.	400 Yds.	500 Yds.	50 Yds.	100 Yds.	150 Yds.	200 Yds.	250 Yds.	300 Yds.	100 Yds	150 Yds.	200 Yds.	250 Yds.	300 Yds.	400 Yds.	500 Yds.	
1956	1644	1372	0.6	0.9	0.0	− 2.3	− 6.0	−11.3	2.0	1.7	0.0	− 3.2	− 7.9	− 22.7	− 45.8	24"
1993	1623	1314	0.2	0.0	− 1.7	− 4.9	− 9.9	−16.9	2.5	2.0	0.0	− 3.8	− 9.5	− 27.5	− 56.1	
1765	1415	1128	0.3	0.0	− 1.9	− 5.5	−11.0	−18.7	2.7	2.2	0.0	− 4.2	−10.5	− 30.7	− 63.0	
2201	1787	1438	0.6	1.0	0.0	− 2.4	− 6.4	−12.1	2.2	1.8	0.0	− 3.4	− 8.5	− 24.7	− 50.5	24"
2384	2005	1677	1.2	1.3	0.0	− 2.7	− 7.1	−12.9	2.7	2.1	0.0	− 3.6	− 9.4	− 25.0	− 49.9	
2025	1591	1244	0.2	0.0	− 1.7	− 5.2	−10.5	−18.0	2.6	2.1	0.0	− 1.0	−10.2	− 30.0	− 61.9	
1553	1181	897	0.2	0.0	− 1.7	− 5.1	−10.4	−17.9	2.6	2.1	0.0	− 4.0	−10.3	− 30.5	− 54.0	20"
1346	1049	832	0.5	0.0	− 2.7	− 7.9	−16.0	−27.1	1.8	0.0	− 4.3	−11.4	−21.7	− 53.5	−103.7	24"
2228	1747	1361	0.2	0.0	− 1.7	− 5.1	−10.3	−17.6	2.5	2.1	0.0	− 3.9	−10.0	− 29.4	− 60.7	
1970	1516	1239	0.8	0.0	− 3.5	−10.3	−20.8	−35.6	2.4	0.0	− 5.6	−14.9	−28.5	− 71.5	− 40.4	24"

TRAJECTORY† 0.0 Indicates yardage at which rifle was sighted in.

| FOOT-POUNDS | | | SHORT RANGE — Bullet does not rise more than one inch above line of sight from muzzle to sighting in range. | | | | | | LONG RANGE — Bullet does not rise more than three inches above line of sight from muzzle to sighting in range. | | | | | | | BARREL LENGTH |
300 Yds.	400 Yds.	500 Yds.	50 Yds.	100 Yds.	150 Yds.	200 Yds.	250 Yds.	300 Yds.	100 Yds	150 Yds.	200 Yds.	250 Yds.	300 Yds.	400 Yds.	500 Yds.	
1089	882	708	0.5	0.9	0.0	− 2.2	− 5.8	−11.0	1.9	1.6	0.0	− 3.1	− 7.8	− 22.6	− 46.3	24"
1233	1004	811	0.4	0.7	0.0	− 1.9	− 5.1	− 9.7	1.7	1.4	0.0	− 2.7	− 6.8	− 20.0	− 40.8	
751	547	398	0.2	0.0	− 1.6	− 4.9	−10.0	−17.4	2.4	2.0	0.0	− 3.9	−10.1	− 30.5	− 65.2	24"
718	512	373	0.3	0.0	− 1.9	− 5.8	−11.9	−20.7	2.9	2.4	0.0	− 4.7	−12.0	− 36.7	− 79.2	24"
1372	1117	902	0.5	0.8	0.0	− 2.1	− 5.5	−10.5	1.9	1.6	0.0	− 2.9	− 7.4	− 21.6	− 44.2	
1475	1177	929	0.4	0.7	0.0	− 1.8	− 4.9	− 9.5	2.7	3.0	2.1	0.0	− 3.5	− 15.5	− 35.3	24"
1682	1389	1139	0.5	0.8	0.0	− 2.0	− 5.4	−10.2	1.8	1.5	0.0	− 2.9	− 7.2	− 20.8	− 42.2	24"
1527	1226	974	0.4	0.8	0.0	− 2.0	− 5.3	−10.0	1.7	1.5	0.0	− 2.8	− 7.1	− 20.8	− 42.7	24"
1622	1334	1087	0.4	0.7	0.0	− 1.9	− 5.1	− 9.7	1.7	1.4	0.0	− 2.7	− 6.8	− 19.9	− 40.5	
1235	910	667	0.6	1.0	0.0	− 2.5	− 6.8	−13.1	2.2	1.9	0.0	− 3.6	− 9.3	− 28.1	− 59.7	
1266	1037	844	0.2	0.0	− 1.7	− 5.0	−10.0	−17.0	2.5	2.0	0.0	− 3.8	− 9.6	− 27.7	− 56.3	24"
1490	1228	1005	0.6	0.9	0.0	− 2.3	−6.11	−11.6	2.1	1.7	0.0	− 3.2	− 8.1	− 23.5	− 47.7	24"
1393	1060	801	0.2	0.0	− 1.5	− 4.6	− 9.5	−16.4	2.3	1.9	0.0	− 3.7	− 9.4	− 28.1	− 58.8	24"
1616	1299	1035	0.5	0.9	0.0	− 2.2	− 5.8	−11.0	1.9	1.6	0.0	− 3.1	− 7.8	− 22.8	− 46.7	24"
1480	1185	940	0.6	1.0	0.0	− 2.4	− 6.3	−12.1	2.1	1.8	0.0	− 3.4	− 8.5	− 24.8	− 51.0	24"
1792	1448	1160	0.4	0.8	0.0	− 1.9	− 5.2	− 9.9	1.7	1.5	0.0	− 2.8	− 7.0	− 20.5	− 42.1	24"
666	502	405	0.7	0.0	− 3.3	− 9.7	−19.6	−33.8	2.2	0.0	− 5.3	−14.1	−27.2	− 69.0	− 36.9	24"
565	399	316	0.5	0.0	− 2.7	− 8.2	−17.0	−30.0	1.8	0.0	− 4.6	−12.5	−24.6	− 65.3	− 34.9	
720	535	425	0.6	0.0	− 3.0	− 8.9	−18.0	−31.1	2.0	0.0	− 4.8	−13.0	−25.1	− 63.6	−126.7	24"
720	535	425	0.6	0.0	− 3.0	− 8.9	−18.0	−31.1	2.0	0.0	− 4.8	−13.0	−25.1	− 63.6	−126.7	
1445	1131	876	0.6	0.9	0.0	− 2.3	− 6.3	−12.0	2.1	1.8	0.0	− 3.3	− 8.5	− 25.0	− 51.8	
1596	1298	1047	0.6	0.9	0.0	− 2.2	− 6.0	−11.4	2.0	1.7	0.0	− 3.2	− 8.0	− 23.3	− 47.5	
1534	1220	963	0.7	1.0	0.0	− 2.5	− 6.7	−12.7	2.3	1.9	0.0	− 3.6	− 9.0	− 26.3	− 54.1	24"

CALIBERS	BULLET		VELOCITY FEET PER SECOND						ENERGY		
	Wt.-Grs.	Style	Muzzle	100 Yds.	200 Yds.	300 Yds.	400 Yds.	500 Yds.	Muzzle	100 Yds.	200 Yds.
	180	Soft Point	2700	2348	2023	1727	1466	1251	2913	2203	1635
	180	Pointed Soft Point	2700	2469	2250	2042	1846	1663	2913	2436	2023
30-40 KRAG	180	Pointed Soft Point	2430	2099	1795	1525	1298	1128	2360	1761	1288
	18C	Pointed	2430	2213	2007	1813	1632	1468	2360	1957	1610
	220	Pointed	2160	1956	1765	1587	1427	1287	2279	1869	1522
300 WIN. MAG.	150	Pointed Soft Point	3290	2951	2636	2342	2068	1813	3605	2900	2314
	180	Pointed Soft Point	2960	2745	2540	2344	2157	1979	3501	3011	2578
300 H.&H. MAG.	150	Pointed	2880	2640	2412	2196	1991	1798	3315	2785	2325
	180	Pointed	2580	2341	2114	1901	1702	1520	3251	2677	2183
300 SAVAGE	150	Pointed	2630	2354	2095	1853	1631	1434	2303	1845	1462
	180	Pointed Soft Point	2350	2025	1728	1467	1252	1098	2207	1639	1193
	180	Pointed	2350	2137	1935	1745	1570	1416	2207	1825	1496
303 SAVAGE	190	Pointed	1940	1657	1410	1211	1073	982	1588	1158	839
303 BRITISH	180	Pointed Soft Point	2460	2233	2018	1816	1629	1459	2418	1993	1627
308 WIN.	150	Pointed Soft Point	2820	2533	2263	2009	1774	1560	2648	2137	1705
	180	Soft Point	2620	2274	1955	1666	1414	1212	2743	2066	1527
	180	Pointed Soft Point	2620	2393	2178	1974	1782	1604	2743	2288	1896
	165	Boat-tail Soft Point	2700	2520	2330	2160	1990	1830	2670	2310	1990
32 WIN. SPECIAL	170	Soft Point	2250	1921	1626	1372	1175	1044	1911	1393	998
8mm MAUSER	170	Soft Point	2360	1969	1622	1333	1123	997	2102	1463	993
35 REM.	150	Pointed Soft Point	2300	1874	1506	1218	1039	934	1762	1169	753
	200	Soft Point	2080	1698	1376	1140	1001	911	1921	1280	841
358 WIN.	200	Pointed	2490	2171	1876	1610	1379	1194	2753	2093	1563
	250	Pointed	2230	1988	1762	1557	1375	1224	2760	2194	1723
375 WIN.	200	Pointed Soft Point	2200	1841	1526	1268	1089	980	2150	1506	1034
	250	Pointed Soft Point	1900	1647	1424	1239	1103	1011	2005	1506	1126
44 REM. MAG.	240	Soft Point	1760	1380	1114	970	878	806	1650	1015	661
	240	Semi-Jacketed Hollow Point	1760	1380	1114	970	878	806	1650	1015	661
444 MAR.	240	Soft Point	2350	1815	1377	1087	941	846	2942	1755	1010
	265	Soft Point	2120	1733	1405	1160	1012	920	2644	1768	1162
45-70 GOVERNMENT	405	Soft Point	1330	1168	1055	977	918	869	1590	1227	1001

FOOT-POUNDS			TRAJECTORY† 0.0 Indicates yardage at which rifle was sighted in. SHORT RANGE — Bullet does not rise more than one inch above line of sight from muzzle to sighting in range.						LONG RANGE — Bullet does not rise more than three inches above line of sight from muzzle to sighting in range.							BARREL LENGTH
300 Yds.	400 Yds.	500 Yds.	50 Yds.	100 Yds.	150 Yds.	200 Yds.	250 Yds.	300 Yds.	100 Yds	150 Yds.	200 Yds.	250 Yds.	300 Yds.	400 Yds.	500 Yds.	
1192	859	625	0.2	0.0	− 1.8	− 5.5	−11.2	−19.5	2.7	2.3	0.0	− 4.4	−11.3	− 34.4	− 73.7	
1666	1362	1105	0.2	0.0	− 1.6	− 4.8	− 9.7	−16.5	2.4	2.0	0.0	− 3.7	− 9.3	− 27.0	− 54.9	
929	673	508	0.4	0.0	− 2.4	− 7.1	−14.5	−25.0	1.6	0.0	− 3.9	−10.5	−20.3	− 51.7	−103.9	
1314	1064	861	0.4	0.0	− 2.1	− 6.2	−12.5	−21.1	1.4	0.0	− 3.4	− 8.9	−16.8	− 40.9	− 78.1	
1230	995	809	0.6	0.0	− 2.9	− 8.2	−16.4	−27.6	1.9	0.0	− 4.4	−11.6	−21.9	− 53.3	−101.8	
1827	1424	1095	0.3	0.7	0.0	− 1.8	− 4.8	− 9.3	2.6	2.9	2.1	0.0	− 3.5	− 15.4	− 35.5	
2196	1859	1565	0.5	0.8	0.0	− 2.2	− 5.5	−10.4	1.9	1.6	0.0	− 2.9	− 7.3	− 20.9	− 41.9	
1927	584	1292	0.6	0.9	0.0	− 2.3	− 6.0	−11.5	2.1	1.7	0.0	− 3.2	− 8.0	− 23.3	− 47.4	
1765	415	1128	0.3	0.0	− 1.9	− 5.5	−11.0	−18.7	2.7	2.2	0.0	− 4.2	−10.5	− 30.7	− 63.0	
1143	886	685	0.3	0.0	− 1.8	− 5.4	−11.0	−18.8	2.7	2.2	0.0	− 4.2	−10.7	− 31.5	− 65.5	
860	626	482	0.5	0.0	− 2.6	− 7.7	−15.6	−27.1	1.7	0.0	− 4.2	−11.3	−21.9	− 55.8	−112.0	
1217	985	798	0.4	0.0	− 2.8	− 6.7	−13.5	−22.8	1.5	0.0	− 3.6	− 9.6	−18.2	− 41.1	− 84.2	
619	486	407	0.9	0.0	− 4.1	−11.9	−24.1	−41.4	2.7	0.0	− 6.4	−17.3	−33.2	− 33.7	−164.4	
1318	060	851	0.3	0.0	− 2.1	− 6.1	−12.2	−20.8	1.4	0.0	− 3.3	− 8.8	−16.6	− 40.4	− 77.4	
1344	1048	810	0.2	0.0	− 1.5	− 4.5	− 9.3	−15.9	2.3	1.9	0.0	− 3.6	− 9.1	− 26.9	− 55.7	
1109	799	587	0.3	0.0	− 2.0	− 5.9	−12.1	−20.9	2.9	2.4	0.0	− 4.7	−12.1	− 36.9	− 79.1	24”
1557	1269	1028	0.2	0.0	− 1.8	− 5.2	−10.4	−17.7	2.6	2.1	0.0	− 4.0	− 9.9	− 28.9	− 58.8	
1700	1450	1230	1.3	0.0	− 1.3	− 4.0	− 8.4	−14.4	2.0	1.7	0.0	− 1.3	− 8.4	− 24.3	− 48.9	
710	521	411	0.6	0.0	− 2.9	− 8.6	−17.6	−30.5	1.9	0.0	− 4.7	−12.7	−24.7	− 63.2	− 26.9	24”
671	476	375	0.5	0.0	− 2.7	− 8.2	−17.0	−29.8	1.8	0.0	− 4.5	−12.4	−24.3	− 63.6	− 30.7	24”
494	359	291	0.6	0.0	− 3.0	− 9.2	−19.1	−33.9	2.0	0.0	− 5.1	− 4.1	−27.8	− 74.0	−152.3	24”
577	445	369	0.8	0.0	− 3.8	−11.3	−23.5	−41.2	2.5	0.0	− 6.3	−17.1	−33.6	− 87.7	−176.4	
1151	844	633	0.4	0.0	− 2.2	− 6.5	−13.3	−23.0	1.5	0.0	− 3.6	− 9.7	−18.6	− 47.2	− 94.1	24”
1346	1049	832	0.5	0.0	− 2.7	− 7.9	−16.0	−27.1	1.8	0.0	− 4.3	−11.4	−21.7	− 53.5	−103.7	24”
714	527	427	0.6	0.0	− 3.2	− 9.5	−19.5	−33.8	2.1	0.0	− 5.2	−14.1	−27.4	− 70.1	−138.1	24”
852	676	568	0.9	0.0	− 4.1	−12.0	−24.0	−40.9	2.7	0.0	− 6.5	−17.2	−32.7	− 80.6	−154.1	24”
501	411	346	0.0	−2.7	−10.0	−23.0	−43.0	−71.2	0.0	−5.9	−17.6	−36.3	−63.1	−145.5	−273.0	20”
501	411	346	0.0	−2.7	−10.0	−23.0	−43.0	−71.2	0.0	−5.9	−17.6	−36.3	−63.1	−145.5	−273.0	
630	472	381	0.6	0.0	− 3.2	− 9.9	−21.3	−38.5	2.1	0.0	− 5.6	−15.9	−32.1	− 87.8	−182.7	24”
791	603	498	0.7	0.0	− 3.6	−10.8	−22.5	−39.5	2.4	0.0	− 6.0	−16.4	−32.2	− 84.3	−170.2	
858	758	679	0.0	−4.7	−15.8	−34.0	−60.0	−94.5	0.0	−8.7	−24.6	−48.2	−80.3	−172.4	−305.9	24”

Pronghorn and 5
Desert Bighorn Rifles

The shimmering desert heat made the image of the distant pronghorns dance in the binoculars. Even through the powerful Zeiss 10x40 lenses, the animals looked tiny and far away.

The entire band had their eyes glued on Ken Turner's truck, parked off the Jeep trail a half-mile behind me. Twenty minutes earlier, Ken and I had spotted the animals resting far away at the base of a low knoll. The 30X spotting scope had shown at least one respectable buck in the group. I won the toss, and a few minutes of careful glassing disclosed a likely route for my stalk. If I could keep the rolling, sagebrush-dotted terrain between me and the antelope until I could work my way into decent rifle range, I stood a good chance of nailing the trophy.

Antilocapra americana, or American pronghorn, have amazing eyesight. They had spotted us long before we'd seen them, and every move we made was being noted from a full 2 miles. At that distance we represented no real threat, and the animals knew it. But they were keeping careful track of us, all the same.

After a hurried conference, I put the truck between myself and the antelope, then dropped into a gully that let me keep out of sight while I circled widely right. Ken stood by the truck, watching the band through the spotting scope. He moved around enough to keep the pronghorns' attention. All the same, if I accidentally showed myself before I was close enough to shoot, the game would be up.

Western deserts aren't perfectly flat, but consist of plains interspersed by low rises, draws and arroyos. Here and there, the sagebrush grows high enough and dense enough to provide good cover for a man crouched over. Otherwise, there's often enough low brush to hide a belly-crawling hunter.

My stalk took me through a dry watercourse, gouged from the parched ground by periodic thunderstorms, along a low ridge to an alkali-whitened hillock. A few sparse patches of sage at the top of the rise would mask my movements long enough for me to get into shooting position. It would be a long shot—more than 300 yards—but the hilltop was as close as I could hope to stalk undetected.

The sun was brushing the horizon as I finally wormed my way the last 30 yards through the pungent-smelling sagebrush. My knees were raw under my dirty jeans, and both elbows were scraped and smarting. My eyeglasses were muddied with sweat and dust.

I paused long enough to give their lenses a couple of swipes with a bandanna from my hip pocket. Then I rechecked the rifle and its 2–7X variable scope. Rolling to one side, I unhooked the Harris bipod from my belt. Using a coin as screwdriver, I quickly attached it to the front sling swivel. Then I lowered the spring-loaded legs and pushed forward, looking for a suitable opening in the brush.

After crawling another 10 feet, I could see the herd. The sagebrush petered out just ahead, and I was behind the last clump that provided decent cover. I was sure the animals hadn't seen me, but three doe were on their feet and the entire band was staring in my direction. Either a vagrant desert breeze had carried my scent, or my stalking skills needed work. The animals were alerted, and the whole band could take off any second, vanishing into the distance at 50 miles an hour.

Elbowing my way to one side of the sagebrush for a clear shot, I quickly settled behind the buttstock and centered the crosshairs on the large buck. His black horns had stood out clearly through the spotting scope, and at this distance looked downright massive.

My movement brought the entire herd to its feet, but I squeezed the shot off before it burst into flight. As the .270 bellowed, the buck stumbled and fell. The survivors literally melted into the sunset.

I counted 320 long paces as I walked to the downed animal. Allowing for the difference in elevation and the rough terrain, the actual range was probably a little shy of 300 yards. I'd overestimated and held about a half-foot high, but the error was negligible. The rifle was sighted to print its 130-grain soft point 2½ inches above the point of aim at 100 yards. That made it dead on at around 220, and about 6 inches low at 300. For all practical purposes, I could have held the crosshairs exactly where I wanted the bullet to go, and still killed cleanly even at that distance.

Distance is the key when hunting pronghorn, as it's difficult to sneak very close to these sharp-eyed animals. The available cover is usually sparse, and pronghorn can usually spot you a long way coming.

Another eagle-eyed desert denizen is *Ovis canadensis nelsoni*, or the desert bighorn. These

Desert bighorn sheep are found farther south and in drier, more desolate terrain than are pronghorn antelope. Both species can be hunted with the same firearms, although bighorns tend to weigh a little more than pronghorns. (Photo by Leonard Lee Rue III.)

animals typically haunt even more arid and forbidding terrain than antelope do, and live farther south than most pronghorn. A large desert ram may weigh 40 pounds more than an antelope buck, but the firearm requirements for the two animals are virtually the same.

Scopes and Trajectories

To hunt either of these desert-dwelling species successfully, your best armament is an exceptionally flat-shooting rifle with enough power to kill efficiently out to 400 yards or even more. Granted, the wise hunter tries to stalk within half that range, but the results of such maneuvers are always in doubt. Long shots are the rule, not the exception, when seeking a trophy buck or ram.

High-powered optics are also advisable. A good 2½X scope may be sufficient for hunting deer and elk, but provides only marginal magnification in the desert. The most popular choices are the 3–9X or 2–7X variables, although many sportsmen favor a straight 6X sight. A 4X glass will also do the job, but more magnification can be advantageous when shots are offered at extreme range.

A number of scope sight manufacturers offer rangefinding models and scopes with dials that can be adjusted to compensate for bullet drop when shooting at extended distances. The problem with most rangefinding scopes is that they must be adjusted to bracket the target animal from the top of its back to the bottom of its chest. In order for this method to give an accurate reading, the animal in question must measure 18 inches from back to brisket. That may be a fair average for a mule or whitetail deer, but sheep, antelope and other game have different physiques. Even deer vary in size.

In other words, these rangefinding scopes can be counted on to give "approximate" distance readings, at best. And that's always assuming the rifleman has time to twirl the adjusting knobs and take those readings at leisure. What's more, the fact that many such scopes blithely show readings out to 600 yards may tempt shooters into attempting to kill an animal at that distance.

The problem with the scopes with built-in trajectory-compensating scales is that their use is also dependent on more or less accurate range estimation. The pronghorn or desert-sheep hunter using a rangefinding sight to reckon distance isn't going to make a 100 percent accurate reading (unless his intended trophy carries those robust 18-inch measurements). And even experienced hunters are likely to be 50 yards (or more) off when eyeballing distances of more than 200 yards.

The crux of all this is that you're probably better off by simply choosing a cartridge and bullet weight that shoots flat enough to allow you to hold dead on target out to 275 or 300 yards with the proper zero. There are a number of cartridges that give you this option. The 130-grain .270 factory load, for instance, when sighted in to print 2 inches above the point of aim at 100 yards, is dead-on at 200, and drops less than 7 inches below the crosshair intersection at 300 yards. Since the vital area of a trophy ram or pronghorn buck is deeper than that,

Antelope country is open country. Binoculars, high-power riflescopes and flat-shooting rifles are necessary for pronghorn hunting.

This trophy pronghorn was shot with a .243 Winchester, a popular choice that can do double duty on deer and varmints, as well.

you should be able to anchor your trophy even at that extended range without raising your crosshairs at all.

At 400 yards that same cartridge and zero point puts the bullet 20 inches low, and out at 500 it drops more than 40 inches. You can see that accurate range estimation, along with a detailed knowledge of your load's trajectory, becomes critical. Which is yet another reason for any sportsman to avoid extreme-range marksmanship attempts in the hunting field. At anything beyond 300 yards, the odds for a misplaced bullet skyrocket.

Another point for long-range addicts to ponder: many hunting rifles simply aren't capable of keeping all their shots within a 2-inch circle at 100 yards, regardless of how skilled the shooter is. That means even a fine shot could miss his intended mark by 3 or 4 inches at 200, and out at 400 yards the margin grows to 6 or 8 inches. Add to that any possible tremor or flinch — human error — when the hammer falls, and it's easy to see how much simple luck plays a part when shooting at extreme ranges.

I'm not saying rangefinding and trajectory-compensating scopes can't be useful. If the rifleman takes the time to learn his rifle's capabilities, and similarly learns how deep the chest cavity of the animal he'll be hunting is likely to be — then figures out how to compensate for a depth larger or smaller than the 18-inch setting most such scopes are calibrated at — these devices can prove helpful.

I like to keep things as simple as possible when I'm in the hunting field. I tend to rely on my ability to get within 250 or, at the most, 300 yards, and use a flat-shooting rifle that requires little if any holdover at those distances. Even if I misjudge the range a bit (which is always more of a probability than mere possibility), I'm not likely to miss the vitals of the animal I'm shooting at. I've taken longer shots, but not without giving the whole matter some careful thought first. And I'll never attempt such feats without a rock-solid rest and a good idea of how high to hold the crosshairs. Even then, I keep my fingers crossed when I squeeze the trigger (and if you don't think *that's* tough, try it sometime).

A good pair of binoculars are another necessity when hunting desert sheep and antelope. A quality 7x35 pair of field glasses can be a big help in searching for distant game, and a 9x35 or 10x40 model is even better. A spotting scope is also a must if you're looking for a real trophy.

Rifle and Ammo Choices

Nearly any rifle and cartridge combination suitable for hunting deer works well on antelope and desert sheep. A few notable exceptions: slow-moving numbers such as the .44 magnum

and .45-70 are poor choices, and saddlegun rounds such as the .30-30 and .35 Remington also sport rainbow trajectories that eliminate them from serious consideration.

Either the .243 Winchester or 6mm Remington make fine pronghorn rounds as long as you limit your shooting to reasonable rifle range. In my opinion, any distance out to 300 or 325 yards is "reasonable" when gunning for these desert critters. Some riflemen stretch things a bit farther than that, but if they do they should use a more potent cartridge. The 6mm's deliver less than 1,000 foot-pounds of energy at 400 yards, and that's getting marginal even for antelope. It's decidedly on the weak side for dropping a big, desert ram.

As with deer, the heavier bullet weights (100 to 110 grains) should be used. The light 80-grain projectiles are designed for varmint use, and don't hold together well enough on larger animals. Too, the lighter the bullet, the faster it sheds both energy and velocity.

The .250 Savage and .257 Roberts both make good antelope and sheep loads, but they're at their best at ranges under 200 yards. Of the quarter bores, the .25-06 is by far the best for longer-range work. With a 117- or 120-grain projectile, the .25-06 is usable out to 400 yards. But at that extended distance, you'd have to use a 22-inch holdover with a 200-yard zero.

Either the .264 Winchester or 6.5mm Remington magnums make fine desert rounds, but these are no longer in popular use.

One of the best all-around choices for hunting antelope or desert sheep is the .270 Winchester. The 130-grain load is the bullet weight of choice. This combination is fine medicine even past the 400-yard mark, and has proven itself many times afield.

Any of the commercial 7mm cartridges are useful here, particularly when loaded with 140- or 150-grain bullets. This includes the 7x57mm Mauser, Remington's new 7mm-08, the 7mm Express Remington and the potent 7mm Remington Magnum.

As far as the .30 calibers are concerned, the .308 Winchester or the .30-06 are fine long-range selections. For sheep and pronghorn, the 150- and 165-grain projectiles are perhaps best suited. The spitzer-shape or boattail slugs provide the best efficiency at extended distances. Both the 150-grain .308 load and factory 165-grain .30-06 fodder show 9 inches of drop (below point of aim) at 300 yards when sighted to print 2½ inches high at 100. At 200 yards, both bullets are dead on.

The .300 magnums all provide more power than really is necessary for antelope, although some desert-sheep hunters like this round for the knockdown it provides at extreme range. The 150-grain .300 Winchester factory load shoots flatter than just about any medium-game combination you can find. With a 2.6-inch 100-yard zero, it's right at the point of aim at not 200, but 250 yards, and just 3½ inches low at 300. With Federal's 200-grain premium load, the .300 Winchester still has nearly a full ton of striking force at 500 yards. Potent medicine!

Since it takes an awfully good man to stalk within normal handgun range of these cautious critters, the pistol-packing hunter would do well to consider the flattest-shooting rounds available. The .30 and .357 Herrett wildcats are likely the best choice, and a Thompson/Center Contender or some other long-barrel single shot chambered for one of these should do the job out to 200 yards. A 1½ or 2½X long-eye-relief handgun scope is advised.

It's not impossible to get closer, though, and if you'd like the challenge of closing the range to under 100 yards before attempting a shot, the .357 or .44 magnum revolvers would be adequate. Iron sights will do here.

Any accurate .45 or .50 caliber muzzleloading rifle can be used to hunt pronghorn or sheep, but again you must first stalk as close as possible to the game.

One final note: if and when you bag your desert trophy, lose no time in getting the animal dressed, skinned and hung—and don't leave it hanging long! Meat spoils fast in the dry, desert heat, and if you want to enjoy the fine table fare this game provides you'll have to cool the carcass fast.

Matching the Gun to the Game

RECOMMENDED LOADS FOR PRONGHORN AND DESERT BIGHORN

(Courtesy Remington Arms Co., Inc., Federal Cartridge Corp., and Winchester-Western)

CALIBERS	BULLET		VELOCITY FEET PER SECOND						ENERGY		
	Wt.-Grs.	Style	Muzzle	100 Yds.	200 Yds.	300 Yds.	400 Yds.	500 Yds.	Muzzle	100 Yds.	200 Yds.
243 WIN.	100	Pointed Soft Point	2960	2697	2449	2215	1993	1786	1945	1615	1332
6mm REM.	100	Pointed Soft Point	3130	2857	2600	2357	2127	1911	2175	1812	1501
250 SAVAGE	100	Pointed	2820	2467	2140	1839	1569	1339	1765	1351	1017
257 ROBERTS	117	Pointed Soft Point	2650	2291	1961	1663	1404	1199	1824	1363	999
25-06 REM.	120	Pointed Soft Point	3010	2749	2502	2269	2048	1840	2414	2013	1668
6.5mm REM. MAG.	120	Pointed Soft Point	3210	2905	2621	2353	2102	1867	2745	2248	1830
264 WIN. MAG.	140	Pointed Soft Point	3030	2782	2548	2326	2114	1914	2854	2406	2018
270 WIN.	130	Pointed Soft Point	3110	2823	2554	2300	2061	1837	2791	2300	1883
	130	Pointed	3110	2849	2604	2371	2150	1941	2791	2343	1957
	150	Soft Point	2900	2550	2225	1926	1653	1415	2801	2165	1649
7mm MAUSER	140	Pointed Soft Point	2660	2435	2221	2018	1827	1648	2199	1843	1533
7mm-08 REM.	140	Pointed Soft Point	2860	2625	2402	2189	1988	1798	2542	2142	1793
280 REM.	165	Soft Point	2820	2510	2220	1950	1701	1479	2913	2308	1805
7mm EXPRESS REM.	150	Pointed Soft Point	2970	2699	2444	2203	1975	1763	2937	2426	1989
284 WIN.	150	Pointed Soft Point	2860	2595	2344	2108	1886	1680	2724	2243	1830
7mm REM. MAG.	150	Pointed Soft Point	3110	2830	2568	2320	2085	1866	3221	2667	2196
30-06 SPRINGFIELD	150	Pointed Soft Point	2910	2617	2342	2083	1843	1622	2820	2281	1827
	150	Pointed	2910	2656	2416	2189	1974	1773	2820	2349	1944
	165	Pointed Soft Point	2800	2534	2283	2047	1825	1621	2872	2352	1909
308 WIN.	150	Pointed Soft Point	2820	2533	2263	2009	1774	1560	2648	2137	1705
	165	Boat-tail Soft Point	2700	2520	2330	2160	1990	1830	2670	2310	1990

FOOT-POUNDS			TRAJECTORY† 0.0 Indicates yardage at which rifle was sighted in.														BARREL LENGTH
			SHORT RANGE						LONG RANGE								
			Bullet does not rise more than one inch above line of sight from muzzle to sighting in range.						Bullet does not rise more than three inches above line of sight from muzzle to sighting in range.								
300 Yds.	400 Yds.	500 Yds.	50 Yds.	100 Yds.	150 Yds.	200 Yds.	250 Yds.	300 Yds.	100 Yds	150 Yds.	200 Yds.	250 Yds.	300 Yds.	400 Yds.	500 Yds.	
1089	882	708	0.5	0.9	0.0	− 2.2	− 5.8	−11.0	1.9	1.6	0.0	− 3.1	− 7.8	− 22.6	− 46.3	24"
1233	1004	811	0.4	0.7	0.0	− 1.9	− 5.1	− 9.7	1.7	1.4	0.0	− 2.7	− 6.8	− 20.0	− 40.8	
751	547	398	0.2	0.0	− 1.6	− 4.9	−10.0	−17.4	2.4	2.0	0.0	− 3.9	−10.1	− 30.5	− 65.2	24"
718	512	373	0.3	0.0	− 1.9	− 5.8	−11.9	−20.7	2.9	2.4	0.0	− 4.7	−12.0	− 36.7	− 79.2	24"
1372	1117	902	0.5	0.8	0.0	− 2.1	− 5.5	−10.5	1.9	1.6	0.0	− 2.9	− 7.4	− 21.6	− 44.2	
1475	1177	929	0.4	0.7	0.0	− 1.8	− 4.9	− 9.5	2.7	3.0	2.1	0.0	− 3.5	− 15.5	− 35.3	24"
1682	1389	1139	0.5	0.8	0.0	− 2.0	− 5.4	−10.2	1.8	1.5	0.0	− 2.9	− 7.2	− 20.8	− 42.2	24"
1527	1226	974	0.4	0.8	0.0	− 2.0	− 5.3	−10.0	1.7	1.5	0.0	− 2.8	− 7.1	− 20.8	− 42.7	24"
1622	1334	1087	0.4	0.7	0.0	− 1.9	− 5.1	− 9.7	1.7	1.4	0.0	− 2.7	− 6.8	− 19.9	− 40.5	
1235	910	667	0.6	1.0	0.0	− 2.5	− 6.8	−13.1	2.2	1.9	0.0	− 3.6	− 9.3	− 28.1	− 59.5	
1266	1037	844	0.2	0.0	− 1.7	− 5.0	−10.0	−17.0	2.5	2.0	0.0	− 3.8	− 9.6	− 27.7	− 56.3	24"
1490	1228	1005	0.6	0.9	0.0	− 2.3	−6.11	−11.6	2.1	1.7	0.0	− 3.2	− 8.1	− 23.5	− 47.7	24"
1393	1060	801	0.2	0.0	− 1.5	− 4.6	− 9.5	−16.4	2.3	1.9	0.0	− 3.7	− 9.4	− 28.1	− 58.8	24"
1616	1299	1035	0.5	0.9	0.0	− 2.2	− 5.8	−11.0	1.9	1.6	0.0	− 3.1	− 7.8	− 22.8	− 46.7	24"
1480	1185	940	0.6	1.0	0.0	− 2.4	− 6.3	−12.1	2.1	1.8	0.0	− 3.4	− 8.5	− 24.8	− 51.0	24"
1792	1448	1160	0.4	0.8	0.0	− 1.9	− 5.2	− 9.9	1.7	1.5	0.0	− 2.8	− 7.0	− 20.5	− 42.1	24"
1445	1131	876	0.6	0.9	0.0	− 2.3	− 6.3	−12.0	2.1	1.8	0.0	− 3.3	− 8.5	− 25.0	− 51.8	
1596	1298	1047	0.6	0.9	0.0	− 2.2	− 6.0	−11.4	2.0	1.7	0.0	− 3.2	− 8.0	− 23.3	− 47.5	
1534	1220	963	0.7	1.0	0.0	− 2.5	− 6.7	−12.7	2.3	1.9	0.0	− 3.6	− 9.0	− 26.3	− 54.1	24"
1344	1048	810	0.2	0.0	− 1.5	− 4.5	− 9.3	−15.9	2.3	1.9	0.0	− 3.6	− 9.1	− 26.9	− 55.7	
1557	1269	1028	0.2	0.0	− 1.8	− 5.2	−10.4	−17.7	2.6	2.1	0.0	− 4.0	− 9.9	− 28.9	− 58.8	

These Browning Mountain Rifles are modern replicas of percussion muzzleloaders designed by Jonathan Browning in the 1830s. They're made in calibers .45, .50 and .54 for hunting all types of North American game.

Browning's BAR is the only current autoloading sporting rifle offered in 7mm Remington Magnum and .300 Winchester Magnum. This rifle can be ordered with handsomely engraved receiver.

For rifle hunting of small game such as rabbits and squirrels, scoped rimfire lever-actions and bolt-actions are very popular.

Doe mule deer are often accompanied by several bucks, so the hunter must be on the lookout for the best rack.

Hunter Connie Brooks kneels with a nice pronghorn taken on the Wyoming plains. Her rifle is a single-shot Ruger.

Eager hounds surround this treed cougar. Lion hunts with dogs usually mean short-range shooting, and many veteran hunters prefer to use open-sighted handguns.

This is a bear camp in the North Country. Fall can bring cold weather, and sportsmen must be prepared to rough it.

Rockchuck hunting provides lots of springtime targets for long-range riflemen. Such hunts combine enjoyable sport with valuable practice.

A short, light, fast-handling, accurate carbine such as this Interarms Mark X—in a suitable caliber like 7mm Mauser—is excellent for deer.

On packstring hunt in wilderness country, there's a need to travel light, and that often means choosing one rifle in a caliber that handles anything from mountain goat to grizzly.

This is typical Northern sheep country—and promising habitat f
mountain goats, too. Such open terrain demands long-range accura

Guide is using spotting scope to check whether distant game
is good enough trophy to be worth stalking. Goat and sheep hunts
require frequent use of binoculars as well as spotting scope.

Noted shooting and hunting writer Bob Brister carefully approaches
downed moose. He's ready for second shot if it's needed; it wasn't.

Here are bolt-action deer rifles of several makes and with different barrel lengths. Three are carbines stocked in the Mannlicher style—with wood to the muzzle. These are among the author's favorites.

Deer hunter waits and watches for a buck from a promising morning stand in open woods. An accurate bolt-action is a good choice for this.

Running, bouncing jackrabbits are sporty game for shotgunners and, like cottontails, they often stop —or simply sit still in hope of escaping detection— so they can also be hunted with rifle or handgun. Rabbits are America's favorite small game.

Top-ejecting carbines present scoping problems, but aperture sights are well suited to a .30-30 lever-action and are fast to use on moving game in heavy cover.

Author uses antlers to rattle up a buck. This is a popular Southwestern hunting technique during the rut. He's using a .308 with 150-grain bullets in handloaded cartridges.

Clair Rees is shown during deer hunt, waiting on stand with light, short Sako .308. He strongly favors scoped carbines of this sort.

When a buck crashes out of the brush, the hunter needs a fast-handling rifle. It's wise to practice getting off quick, accurate shots.

Author is shown with a fine mountain caribou bull taken in British Columbia's Skeena Range. Note double-shovel antlers on this excellent trophy. Rifle is scoped .30-06 Colt Sauer.

Author sights-in an 8mm Remington Magnum model 700. This belted magnum is a flat-shooting cartridge suitable for elk and moose. Proper sighting-in is crucial for clean kills of such big game.

Scoped Remington model 700 bolt-action rifle is shown on sighting-in target displaying a tight group that testifies to excellent 200-yard accuracy. In fact, this rifle would be deadly at 300 yards or more.

Firearms for Cougar, Wolf and Coyote 6

Cougars—Rifle or Handgun

My lungs felt close to bursting as I plunged through the February snow, doing my best to keep up with my long-striding guide. We'd been alternately running and walking through the ankle-deep powder for nearly an hour, and the pace was beginning to tell.

The guide's hounds had struck the lion's trail 4 miles back, and their noses now told them the prey wasn't far ahead. This news was communicated by the higher-pitched sound of their baying, and increased volume to convey greater urgency. When the baying turned to short, chopping barks, we'd know the cat was treed.

The chase had already led us up two rocky cliff walls and through a steep, slippery-sided canyon. Because of the rough, southern Utah terrain, we'd left the horses behind. Cougars aren't notably long-winded when chased, but this one had a lot more stamina than I could muster. If he didn't tree soon, I was going to run out of steam.

My guide—who appeared to be breathing normally—carried a .22 magnum revolver holstered at his hip, while I was armed with a 35mm camera. I would have thought twice about selecting a rimfire handgun to dispatch a 150-pound cougar, but since my guide had been doing this sort of thing for years I didn't question his choice. Personally, I'd have preferred at least a .357 magnum revolver, or better yet, a .30-30 rifle.

At least that's what I thought at the beginning of the hunt. Now, with my breath coming in sharp, cloud-condensing gasps, I could begin to see the wisdom of leaving the rifles home. Following a pack of lion hounds gives all but experienced cougar men more exercise than they'd ever counted on. When you're fresh-trailing on foot, running through stands of cedar, climbing up steep canyon walls and making your way over broken rimrock, a rifle is a burden you can clearly do without.

Since your chances of ever seeing a mountain lion that wasn't first treed by dogs are about

Because most cougars are shot at close range, many hunters tote handguns rather than rifles. The author recommends .357 magnum, although many cats are taken with .22 rimfires.

the same as your chance of winning a million at Lotto, long shots are almost never called for. And treed cats are dispatched at close range, making handguns ideal.

When this cat, a big, handsome tom measuring an even 8 feet from nose tip to tail, finally came to bay barely 6 feet off the ground in a low cedar tree, the dogs kept him on his perch until the two-legged hunters finally arrived.

Our plan was to simply photograph the cougar, then collar the hounds and hold them until the cat took the hint and skedaddled. That way, the local houndmen could enjoy another rematch the next time the tom showed up in the neighborhood.

The cat quickly put an end to that idea by streaking down the trunk while I was still focusing my camera. He took off up the canyon with the hounds on his heels, and soon came to bay in a clump of heavy brush. This time, the animal was on the ground where the dogs could reach him. Unfortunately, the cat had backed into a narrow tunnel through which the dogs could only attack one at a time. That gave the lion a big advantage, and the pack leader was getting the full buzz-saw treatment while the other hounds tried frantically to shoulder their way into the fray.

That changed the complexion of things fast, and my guide quickly strode up, poked his gun through the brush to within a foot of the big cat's head, and fired. At that range, the .22 magnum slug was all that was needed to end the fight, and the dogs swarmed the now-inert carcass.

While mounted hunters often use .30-30 or .44 magnum saddle carbines to drop a treed cougar, the average houndman favors a belt gun. It doesn't take much to kill a mountain lion at a range of just a few yards — or feet — and many are taken with .22 rimfires. However, a .38 Special or .357 magnum is a considerably more prudent choice, as a wounded cat may have enough fight left when he drops from his tree to badly mangle a few dogs before he succumbs. It's important to make that first shot count, as there's always a danger of hitting one of the hounds in the following melee.

This is one kind of hunting a cap-and-ball revolver could be legitimately used for. A .44 ball from a black-powder percussion handgun packs plenty of punch for a mountain cat. A modern .41 or .44 magnum wheelgun would be another good choice, as would be a 9mm, .38 Super or .45 ACP auto pistol.

Guns for Wolves

Wolves are usually shot by Canadian or Alaskan hunters seeking larger game. As a result, anything from a .270 Winchester to a .338 or even .375 magnum may be used. These and similar cartridges provide far more power than needed for these animals, which seldom exceed a live weight of 150 pounds. Farther south, the average timber wolf will weigh less than 100 pounds, while the smaller red wolf tips the scales at just 60 pounds or so.

In the far north country, a .243 or 6mm rifle would more than suffice, and a .22-250 could be counted on to do the job. Most shots must be taken at ranges beyond 200 yards, so a flat-

This Idaho coyote was taken with .284 factory load at 380 yards.

shooting caliber is called for. A scoped rifle or handgun is needed unless the animal can be lured close with a varmint call.

At one time, wolves were killed from low-flying airplanes by shotgun-wielding pilots who flew close enough for buckshot to do the job. Since wolves are now rightly protected in many areas, this kind of "control" is no longer popular, and is, in fact, illegal.

Firearms for Coyotes

While wolves are now seldom hunted in the "Lower 48," the reverse is true for the "prairie wolf," or coyote. The adaptable yodel dog is widely distributed throughout the United States and Canada. Wherever he's found in huntable numbers, he's popular prey for riflemen and handgunners alike.

In the western and midwestern states, many farmers and ranchers carry a lightweight .223 carbine in the cab of their pickup truck, just on the off chance of spotting a coyote. Every sheepman keeps a rifle handy, and not a few rabbit hunters keep a scope-sighted centerfire in the car trunk in case *Canis latrans* is sighted.

While the wily coyote but rarely becomes a "target of opportunity," a number of nimrods hunt the animal seriously. Not too many years ago the ubiquitous canine was widely boun-tied, and even today a prime pelt fetches substantial sums when the market is right. Thus coyote hunters can enjoy their sport, and when they're successful the sale of the hides may even pay for the gas and ammunition expended during the hunt.

Because the pelt is valuable, most hunters prefer a cartridge and bullet combination that won't seriously damage the hide. For riflemen, two viable options are available. The first is to use a lightly constructed bullet in a fast-stepping .22 centerfire, loaded hot enough to disin-tegrate immediately after contact. Ideally, the bullet will make a small entry hole, and then break completely up inside. The full energy of the bullet is then expended without exiting the animal. The resulting shock kills the coyote almost instantly, and there's no gaping exit hole in the hide.

Things sometimes happen that way, and when they do the animal is killed cleanly, and the pelt remains virtually undamaged. But if an animal isn't hit properly—if the bullet isn't centered, but instead hits high or low, the explosive nature of the light, high-speed projectile can all but ruin a hide.

Similarly, some riflemen have favored a solid, nonexpanding bullet. Unfortunately, even a solid driven at high velocities can create a gaping exit wound, and there's always the possi-bility of merely wounding an animal.

If a solid bullet is used, it should be larger and heavier than a .22-caliber projectile. A 90-

A long-range rifle is needed for hunting wolves and coyotes, unless you can lure the quarry in close. Be sure to check your rifle's zero before the hunt to assure accurate shots that keep pelt damage minimal.

grain solid from a .25-06, or a 130-grain .270 slug driven at around 2,700 feet per second (muzzle velocity) hits solidly enough to put an animal down *without* mushrooming. A .22-caliber solid may produce wounds that later kill, but fail to anchor a coyote. I should point out that there are exceptions to every rule. Rick Jamison, in his excellent book, *Calling Coyotes*, mentions hitting a desert wolf in the chest with a 172-grain solid from a .300 Winchester Magnum — and then watching it run 200 yards before succumbing.

For hunters interested in preserving pelts, the best coyote medicine is either a .22-250 or a .220 Swift with hollow-point bullets, or a larger "deer caliber" shooting solids. If the condition of the hide is of no importance, just about any flat-shooting centerfire will do the job. The tiny .17 Remington, with its Lilliputian 25-grain slug, is on the light side for coyote, but any of the .22 centerfires can be counted on. The 6mm's (.243 Winchester and 6mm Remington) make outstanding long-range yodel-dog cartridges, but they tend to make large exit holes.

Perhaps the most productive way to hunt these critters is to lure them in close with a varmint call. If you're successful enough, you may do your shooting at 50 yards or a lot less. In this case, a fast-handling shotgun makes good medicine. Chances are, the animal will be on the move by the time you're "on" him, and the scattergun's pattern is ideal medicine for a coyote caught double-clutching into second gear.

A 12 gauge, with full or modified choke, is best, loaded with No. 4 buckshot or copper-plated BBs. No. 1 buck loads may work okay if they pattern well in your shotgun, but the denser shot spreads provided by the smaller pellets give better coverage. At the same time, standard lead shot smaller than 2's lack the penetration necessary for consistent kills on a winter-furred coyote.

Whichever load you choose, be sure to test it in your shotgun before going afield. Tack up a sheet of butcher paper, and see what kind of patterns you get at 30, 40 and 50 yards. Scatterguns can be temperamental, and sometimes moving up or down one shot size works wonders for pattern efficiency.

At shotgun range, handguns can be used with excellent results. I personally favor .357 magnum factory loads throwing 140- or 158-grain bullets, as these shoot flatter and have greater reach than .38 Special combinations. For long shots of 80 yards or more a scoped Thompson/Center Contender or some other single-shot pistol works well. Chambered for the .222 or .223 Remington or the above-mentioned .357 magnum, a long-barrel one-shooter will reach out well past 100 yards to anchor coyotes.

Black-powder rifles can also be used, and either the .36- or .45-caliber models will do a fine job. Because of their lobbing trajectories and relatively coarse iron sights, muzzleloaders are best restricted to ranges shy of 125 yards or so.

While coyotes have been shot and killed with .22 rimfires, these little cartridges lack the oomph to be sporting when yodel dogs are the prey. Most coyotes shot with a low-velocity .22 round (which includes "high velocity" .22 long-rifle fodder and the somewhat warmer .22 WMRF loads) aren't anchored. If they make their escape, they'll likely die a lingering death.

On the other hand, a .22 revolver or auto pistol in a belt holster can be legitimately used to give a mortally wounded coyote the *coup de grace*. A .22 lead solid in the skull does a clean job, and doesn't ruin the pelt.

One final note regarding firearm selection. When attempting to lure a yodel dog in close, you may have varying degrees of success. One animal may be fooled into venturing mere feet away, while the next may spot a hunter move or get his scent while still 150 yards off. The rifle-toting nimrod at least has a chance to bag both, but those with short-range guns can only watch while the more cautious animals turn tail and vanish over the horizon.

Because both close- and long-range shots may be offered, a variable scope is the best sighting equipment for flat-shooting rifles. The scope should be left on its lowest power setting while you're calling, as you need maximum field of view if a coyote pops up mere feet away. For long shots, you may get the chance to crank up to more magnification, but if not, 2X or 3X is sufficient. If a fixed-power scope is chosen, avoid magnification greater than 4X.

Rifles and Handguns for Varmints 7

As a youth, I spent many hours harassing rockchucks with my grandfather's .22. It was a worn Winchester single shot that had to be manually cocked by pulling back the striker knob before each shot, and its iron sights weren't very conducive to long-range marksmanship. As I recall, the front bead totally obscured the body of a chuck at 50 yards.

Those rockchucks and ground squirrels soon learned the effective range of the little rimfire, and would vanish every time I approached within 80 yards. Beyond that distance, I and my grandfather's rifle posed little threat. The diminutive animals lived in an exposed, rocky outcropping on a barren hillside, and no cover was available to let me approach closer unseen.

At 100 to 125 yards, I could always get at least a couple of shots off before the noise, or a ricochet in their midst alarmed them. But at that distance, I hit very few of the little rodents. I wasted many hours and countless rounds of half-cent-a-shot .22 long-rifle fodder trying to score at extended range. I was getting a lot of shooting practice, and the chucks were about convinced it was all harmless fun.

Then a cousin visited my grandfather's ranch one summer while I was there. He proudly showed me a new bolt-action rifle chambered for the .22 Hornet cartridge, and wearing a 4X scope sight. Except for a .30-30 saddle carbine, it was the first centerfire rifle I ever shot. And it was certainly the first scope sight I'd ever used.

Together, we quickly re-educated the complacent chucks. Since my cousin was a year or so older than I and it was his rifle, I didn't get to fire too many of the bottleneck cartridges. But I shot enough of them to fall in love with the rifle.

By the time I could finally afford a .22 centerfire, the Hornet had pretty well passed from vogue. More than a decade had passed, and the then-new .222 Remington was the varmint cartridge of choice unless you wanted a real barn-burner like the .220 Swift. The Swift had been around since 1935, and was the first factory cartridge to actually deliver velocities faster than 4,000 feet a second.

The .222 Remington is still one of the best varmint loads available for ranges up to 250 yards. Accuracy is excellent in a properly tuned rifle, and recoil is all but absent. In spite of this fact, the diminutive .22 Hornet is enjoying a resurgence in popularity among American

Marmot on the lookout is vulnerable to the long-range rifleman.

riflemen. The Hornet has always been popular in Europe, where it has the metric designation of 5.6x35R, but stateside varmint hunters are only now rediscovering its virtues. Out to 175 or 200 yards, the little Hornet makes a fine varminter, and it's much quieter than any other .22 centerfire on the market. This makes it a natural for use in populated areas where the sharper report of a .22-250 would draw complaints. A number of excellent bolt-action and single-shot rifles are now chambered for the .22 Hornet, and its popularity continues to grow.

For hunting bobcats, foxes and other small, carnivorous critters, a good .22 centerfire is probably the best all-around choice. Burrowing chucks and ground squirrels are other likely targets for the rifleman armed with a long-range .22. However, the two types of animals are hunted in different ways, so somewhat different types of armament are called for.

Foxes and other predators are most effectively hunted by fooling them with a varmint call. By sounding like a rabbit in distress, the skillful caller can usually toll his prey to within 100 yards or less — often much less, if the hunter isn't seen or scented. The caller must be camouflaged or hidden from view, and the rifle brought into play at the very last minute.

Too, the varmint caller usually moves to a new site every hour, or even more often, and may walk miles through the desert in the course of a single hunt. He needs a relatively lightweight rifle that won't tire him needlessly, and that can be swung on target fast. He also needs a scope sight of only moderate power, 4X or less. More magnification only narrows the field of view, making close, running shots next to impossible.

Small, burrowing rodents such as marmots, ground squirrels and prairie dogs are usually shot from a distance. Ranges up to 300 yards or more aren't uncommon, and the hunt is more of a test of rifle and marksmanship than of stalking or woodsmanship skills.

This kind of varmint hunting calls for a highly accurate, bull-barrel rifle topped by a quality scope of 10X or greater magnification. A bipod or some other type of rest is used, and a flat-shooting cartridge is a must. If the rifleman is lucky enough to find a grassy slope well-populated by sunning rodents, he may shoot all day from the same stand.

The .222 Remington throws a 50-grain projectile at a starting velocity of 3,140 feet per second (fps). Sighted to print a half-inch high at 50 yards, the bullet falls only 2½ inches at 200. On windless days, it's extremely accurate.

The .222 case doesn't hold a lot of powder, and reloads are relatively inexpensive. Factory ammo groups well in most .222 rifles, and handloading can produce exceptionally tight spreads.

While the .222 Remington is a nice, little cartridge, the .222 Remington Magnum is a bit more potent. Factory loads push a 55-grain slug at an advertised 3,240 fps, giving it from 50 to 75 yards greater effective range than its non-magnum namesake. Accuracy is about the same.

At one time, the .222 Remington Magnum enjoyed high popularity among varmint hunters, but the development of the .223 Remington, the civilian version of the military 5.56mm round, has pretty well stolen the thunder from the triple-deuce magnum. Case capacity differs by about 5 percent between the two rounds, and performance is all but identical. The availability of surplus military ammo and cartridge cases at attractively low prices has assured the popularity of the .223. Many modern rifles are chambered for the round, and the cartridge is a fine choice for varmints.

For long-range varmint work, the .22-250 is the first choice of knowledgeable riflemen. Factory loads hustle a 55-grain pill along at more than 3,700 fps, and handloading can improve on that. Weatherby's .224 Varmintmaster, a proprietary cartridge, is closely comparable.

Sighted to print 2 inches high at 100 yards, the .22-250 Remington shoots flat enough to require just 3½ inches of holdover at the 300-yard mark. This makes it a 300-yards-plus cartridge, and in a highly accurate rifle it can kill at surprising distance. It's the favorite choice of the heavy-barrel varminter bunch.

The .220 Swift, which earned an early reputation for burning out barrels in short order with its 4,000-fps muzzle velocities, is now loaded to much milder pressures. Hornady-Fron-

Camouflage clothing, including gloves and head net, helps when trying to call foxes and other small predators into close range.

tier factory loads register 100 fps slower than .22-250 fodder, and at those speeds the .220 Swift makes a highly useful, dependable varmint round. It no longer wears out rifling after a few hundred firings, and delivers fine accuracy in most rifles.

The .22-250 Remington, .224 Weatherby Varmintmaster and .220 Swift all make top long-range varmint loads. Because of the extra power these cartridges have, they're better suited to taking largish varmints such as bobcats and coyotes than the smaller-capacity, slower-moving .22's.

While the double-deuce centerfires are our premier varmint numbers, long-range accuracy is adversely affected by high winds. In flat, gusty country, many riflemen prefer the .243 Winchester or 6mm Remington for varmint-hunting work. Most of the same bull-barrel varmint rifles chambered for the .22-250 Remington are also available in .243 or 6mm chambering.

With 75- to 90-grain bullets, either of these two rounds buck wind reasonably well, and kill large varmints with more surety than any .22, particularly at extended range. Their main drawbacks are that they recoil with considerably more force, and cost more to reload. Not that the kick of a .243 Winchester is all that fearsome, but when you plan on firing several hundred rounds in a single day, even this much recoil becomes bothersome.

An even more potent choice for long-range work is the .240 Weatherby Magnum. It out-hustles by a couple of hundred fps either of the other 6mm's commercially loaded, but is available only in Weatherby or custom-made firearms.

The largest caliber considered by sportsmen for specialized varmint use is the quarter bore. With light, 87-grain bullets, both the .250 Savage and .257 Roberts make fine long-range varmint cartridges. As loaded by the factory, the .257 Roberts has about a 140-fps edge over the Savage round. Both shoot flat enough for 300-yard work.

The premier .25-caliber varmint cartridge, though, is the .25-06. This is nothing more than the popular .30-06 case necked down to handle .257-inch-diameter bullets. This has the powder capacity to really hustle an 87-grain projectile along. The factory load produces an advertised 3,440 fps from a 24-inch barrel, and some rifles digest hot handloads that yield more than 3,600 fps.

For top long-range performance and high wind-bucking ability, the .25-06 has no peer. The 90- and 100-grain bullets work better than the light 87-grain slug on windy days, while the 117- and 120-grain slugs are better yet. An accurate .25-06 rifle is useful out to 400 yards or even farther, although you need both skill and a fair amount of luck going for you at that distance.

Other, larger-caliber cartridges can also be used for shooting varmints. Popular deer and

Long-range rockchuck shooting calls for .222 Remington or some other .22 centerfire.

big-game rounds like the .270 Winchester and .30-06 Springfield are factory loaded with 100- and 110-grain projectiles, and these rounds are designed for varmint hunting. However, these more potent cartridges feature greater recoil, and they're usually fired from sporter-weight hunting rifles lacking the accuracy of a heavy-barrel varminter.

Remington offers a .22-caliber Accelerator load for the .308 Winchester, .30-30 and .30-06. A .22 projectile is retained in a plastic container, or sabot, until it exits the bore. Then the sabot drops away, and the bullet continues downrange alone. The .22-caliber Accelerator slugs weigh 55 grains, and turn the .30-caliber rifles they're designed for into middling-fair varmint shooters. But again, they lack the accuracy of a legitimate .22 centerfire varmint rifle.

Because of accuracy considerations, nearly all honest-to-goodness varmint rifles on the market today are either bolt-action or falling-block single-shot models. Scope sights are necessary, with most shooters opting for 6X or better magnification. Heavy-barrel varmint rifles are typically topped by a 10X to a 16X glass.

Varmint hunting is highly popular among handgunners, and several specialized pistols on the market are designed for long-range rodent shooting. Remington's bolt-action XP-100 pistol chambered for the hot .221 Remington Fire Ball cartridge is one example. This combination groups under 1 inch at 100 yards and shoots flat enough to be useful at more than twice that distance.

The Thompson/Center Contender is also chambered for the .221 Fire Ball, and for a whole flock of other varmint rounds, besides. These include the .22 Hornet, .222 and .223 Remington, .256 Winchester Magnum and .357 magnum. Other one-shooters in this same general class are the Sterling X-Caliber and the Merrill Sportsman. Wichita Arms offers yet another single shot, a custom-priced bolt gun, that digests rifle-power-class cartridges.

Long-eye-relief scopes are generally mounted on these guns, as iron sights are too coarse for hunting tiny rodents at extended range.

Revolvers and auto pistols can be used to take varmint-size critters lured close by calling,

Chet Brown custom-made 6mm rifle with fiberglass stock weighs just over 5 pounds and makes a fine long-range varmint rifle. For distance shots at small critters, a support of some sort is helpful.

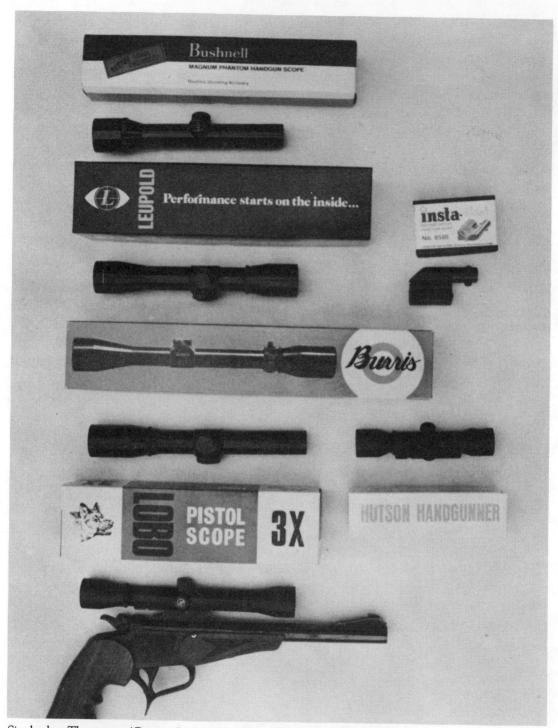

Single-shot Thompson/Center Contender is chambered for a variety of hunting cartridges and accepts several different long-eye-relief scopes. Accurate and powerful, it is a good choice for varmint-hunting handgunners.

The javelina, or peccary, was once considered a varmint but now is protected by hunting seasons and bag limits. (Photo by Leonard Lee Rue III.)

and just about any centerfire cartridge is suitable out to 30 yards or so. Wheelguns are more popular, though, and a .357 magnum revolver with a 6- or 8-inch barrel works well out to 100 yards, particularly when fitted with a 1½X or 2½X pistol scope.

Rimfire rifles and handguns can be used on the smallest varmints, but even magnum .22's lack the oomph for anything but relatively short-range use. If possible, the rifleman should shoot for the head when using a .22 rimfire.

Thirty-six-caliber muzzleloaders make good varmint rifles at moderate range, and shooting one of these black-powder burners can be a lot of fun. The same holds true for percussion revolvers and pistols.

Even shotguns can be used to take small carnivores that respond to calling, but the effective range is limited to 35 or 40 yards.

Hunting varmints is a year-round sport, and there's no bag limit on most species. In some states, a hunting license isn't even required, but be sure of those regulations before venturing afield without one. Varmint hunting allows a sportsman to shoot at a lot of animated targets each year and can help him to develop marksmanship skills before deer and big-game hunting seasons roll around. Almost any rifle or handgun can be used, but success and satisfaction mount when the armament is designed for the sport.

Ground squirrels' burrows are disliked by ranchers, and the pesky little animals have unprotected pest status.

At one time, the javelina, or peccary, was relegated to varmint status in Arizona, southwest Texas and other states in which *Pecari angulatus* is found. That has long since changed, and these unusual little game animals now enjoy the protection they deserve, with regular seasons and limits set.

Wild boar or feral pigs, on the other hand, are still considered bothersome pests in some states. Feral hogs or hybrids can be shot out of hand in many areas, although where imported European boar are hunted game rules usually apply.

The javelina is a fearsome-looking beast, but is too small (a big one may weigh 65 pounds and stand 22 inches high) and far too shy to be dangerous. A 450-pound wild boar with 6-inch tusks, on the other hand, makes a highly respectable hunting opponent. A nimrod going after one on foot runs a real, though not highly likely, risk of injury.

Both javelina and wild boar are hunted with rifles and handguns, and in some states only shotguns may be allowed for taking the latter. If a scattergun is used, 12-gauge guns with rifled slugs are recommended.

Any rifle caliber from the .243 or 6mm upwards is suitable for the peccary, while a .38 Special or .357 magnum handgun will suffice. For the much larger boar and feral hogs, a .308 Winchester, .30-06 or some larger caliber makes a good rifle choice, although some sportsmen prefer fast-firing .444 Marlin or .45-70 lever rifles. These larger calibers make better stoppers at hog-hunting range, which can become heart-thumpingly close. Handgunners should tote .41 or .44 magnums, as a first choice. With either rifles or handguns, open sights should be used, as a scope lacks the needed field of view when the range is measured in feet, rather than multiple yards. For hunting the desert javelina, scoped rifles work fine.

Handgunners find real challenge in varmint hunting. Several pistols are available especially for long-distance hunting.

RECOMMENDED LOADS FOR VARMINTS

(Courtesy Remington Arms Co., Inc., Federal Cartridge Corp., and Winchester-Western)

CALIBERS	BULLET Wt.-Grs.	BULLET Style	VELOCITY FEET PER SECOND Muzzle	100 Yds.	200 Yds.	300 Yds.	400 Yds.	500 Yds.	ENERGY Muzzle	100 Yds.	200 Yds.
17 REM.	25	Hollow Point	4040	3284	2644	2086	1606	1235	906	599	388
22 HORNET	45	Pointed Soft Point	2690	2042	1502	1128	948	840	723	417	225
	45	Hollow Point	2690	2042	1502	1128	948	840	723	417	225
222 REM.	50	Pointed Soft Point	3140	2602	2123	1700	1350	1107	1094	752	500
	50	Hollow Point	3140	2635	2182	1777	1432	1172	1094	771	529
	55	Metal Case	3020	2562	2147	1773	1451	1201	1114	801	563
222 REM. MAG.	55	Pointed Soft Point	3240	2748	2305	1906	1556	1272	1282	922	649
	55	Hollow Point	3240	2773	2352	1969	1627	1341	1282	939	675
223 REM.	55	Pointed Soft Point	3240	2747	2304	1905	1554	1270	1282	921	648
	55	Hollow Point	3240	2773	2352	1969	1627	1341	1282	939	675
	55	Metal Case	3240	2759	2326	1933	1587	1301	1282	929	660
22-250 REM.	55	Pointed Soft Point	3730	3180	2695	2257	1863	1519	1699	1235	887
	55	Hollow Point	3730	3253	2826	2436	2079	1755	1699	1292	975
243 WIN.	80	Pointed Soft Point	3350	2955	2593	2259	1951	1670	1993	1551	1194
	80	Hollow Point	3350	2955	2593	2259	1951	1670	1993	1551	1194
6mm REM.	80	Pointed Soft Point	3470	3064	2694	2352	2036	1747	2139	1667	1289
	80	Hollow Point	3470	3064	2694	2352	2036	1747	2139	1667	1289
	100	Pointed Soft Point	3130	2857	2600	2357	2127	1911	2175	1812	1501
250 SAVAGE	87	Pointed Soft Point	3030	2673	2342	2036	1755	1504	1773	1380	1059
	60	Hollow Point	2760	2097	1542	1149	957	846	1015	586	317
256 WIN. MAG.	87	Pointed Soft Point	3170	2802	2462	2147	1857	1594	1941	1516	1171
257 ROBERTS	100	Pointed	2900	2541	2210	1904	1627	1387	1867	1433	1084
25-06 REM.	87	Hollow Point	3440	2995	2591	2222	1884	1583	2286	1733	1297
	100	Pointed Soft Point	3230	2893	2580	2287	2014	1762	2316	1858	1478
270 WIN.	100	Pointed Soft Point	3480	3067	2690	2343	2023	1730	2689	2088	1606
284 WIN.	125	Pointed Soft Point	3140	2829	2538	2265	2010	1772	2736	2221	1788
30-30 WIN. ACCELERATOR	55	Soft Point	3400	2693	2085	1570	1187	986	1412	886	521
30-06 SPRINGFIELD ACCELERATOR	55	Pointed Soft Point	4080	3485	2965	2502	2083	1709	2033	1483	1074
30-06 SPRINGFIELD	110	Pointed Soft Point	3380	2843	2365	1936	1561	1261	2790	1974	1366
	125	Pointed Soft Point	3140	2780	2447	2138	1853	1595	2736	2145	1662
308 WIN. ACCELERATOR	55	Pointed Soft Point	3770	3215	2726	2286	1888	1541	1735	1262	907
308 WIN.	110	Pointed Soft Point	3180	2666	2206	1795	1444	1178	2470	1736	1188
	125	Pointed Soft Point	3050	2697	2370	2067	1788	1537	2582	2019	1559

FOOT-POUNDS 300 Yds.	400 Yds.	500 Yds.	TRAJECTORY† 0.0 Indicates yardage at which rifle was sighted in. SHORT RANGE Bullet does not rise more than one inch above line of sight from muzzle to sighting in range. 50 Yds.	100 Yds.	150 Yds.	200 Yds.	250 Yds.	300 Yds.	LONG RANGE Bullet does not rise more than three inches above line of sight from muzzle to sighting in range. 100 Yds	150 Yds.	200 Yds.	250 Yds.	300 Yds.	400 Yds.	500 Yds.	BARREL LENGTH
242	143	85	0.1	0.5	0.0	− 1.5	− 4.2	− 8.5	2.1	2.5	1.9	0.0	− 3.4	− 17.0	44.3	24"
127	90	70	0.3	0.0	− 2.4	− 7.7	−16.9	−31.3	1.6	0.0	− 4.5	−12.8	−26.4	− 75.6	−163.4	24"
127	90	70	0.3	0.0	− 2.4	− 7.7	−16.9	−31.3	1.6	0.0	− 4.5	−12.8	−26.4	− 75.6	−163.4	
321	202	136	0.5	0.9	0.0	− 2.5	− 6.9	−13.7	2.2	1.9	0.0	− 3.8	−10.0	− 32.3	− 73.8	
351	228	152	0.5	0.9	0.0	− 2.4	− 6.6	−13.1	2.1	1.8	0.0	− 3.6	− 9.5	− 30.2	− 68.1	24"
384	257	176	0.6	1.0	0.0	− 2.5	− 7.0	−13.7	2.2	1.9	0.0	− 3.8	− 9.9	− 31.0	− 68.7	
444	296	198	0.4	0.8	0.0	− 2.2	− 6.0	−11.8	1.9	1.6	0.0	− 3.3	− 8.5	− 26.7	− 59.5	24"
473	323	220	0.4	0.8	0.0	− 2.1	− 5.8	−11.4	1.8	1.6	0.0	− 3.2	− 8.2	− 25.5	− 56.0	24"
443	295	197	0.4	0.8	0.0	− 2.2	− 6.0	−11.8	1.9	1.6	0.0	− 3.3	− 8.5	− 26.7	− 59.6	
473	323	220	0.4	0.8	0.0	− 2.1	− 5.8	−11.4	1.8	1.6	0.0	− 3.2	− 8.2	− 25.5	− 56.0	24"
456	307	207	0.4	0.8	0.0	− 2.1	− 5.9	−11.6	1.9	1.6	0.0	− 3.2	− 8.4	− 26.2	− 57.9	
622	424	282	0.2	0.5	0.0	− 1.5	− 4.3	− 8.4	2.2	2.6	1.9	0.0	− 3.3	− 15.4	− 37.7	
725	528	376	0.2	0.5	0.0	− 1.4	− 4.0	− 7.7	2.1	2.4	1.7	0.0	− 3.0	− 13.6	− 32.4	24"
906	676	495	0.3	0.7	0.0	− 1.8	− 4.9	− 9.4	2.6	2.9	2.1	0.0	− 3.6	− 16.2	− 37.9	
906	676	495	0.3	0.7	0.0	− 1.8	− 4.9	− 9.4	2.6	2.9	2.1	0.0	− 3.6	− 16.2	− 37.9	24"
982	736	542	0.3	0.6	0.0	− 1.6	− 4.5	− 8.7	2.4	2.7	1.9	0.0	− 3.3	− 14.9	− 35.0	
982	736	542	0.3	0.6	0.0	− 1.6	− 4.5	− 8.7	2.4	2.7	1.9	0.0	− 3.3	− 14.9	− 35.0	24"
1233	1004	811	0.4	0.7	0.0	− 1.9	− 5.1	− 9.7	1.7	1.4	0.0	− 2.7	− 6.8	− 20.0	− 40.8	
801	595	437	0.5	0.9	0.0	− 2.3	− 6.1	−11.8	2.0	1.7	0.0	− 3.3	− 8.4	− 25.2	− 53.4	24"
176	122	95	0.3	0.0	− 2.3	− 7.3	−15.9	−29.6	1.5	0.0	− 4.2	−12.1	−25.0	− 72.1	−157.2	24"
890	666	491	0.4	0.8	0.0	− 2.0	− 5.5	−10.6	1.8	1.5	0.0	− 3.0	− 7.5	− 22.7	− 48.0	24"
805	588	427	0.6	1.0	0.0	− 2.5	− 6.9	−13.2	2.3	1.9	0.0	− 3.7	− 9.4	− 28.6	− 60.9	24"
954	686	484	0.3	0.6	0.0	− 1.7	− 1.8	9.3	2.5	2.9	2.1	− 0.0	− 3.6	− 16.4	− 39.1	
1161	901	689	0.4	0.7	0.0	− 1.9	− 5.0	− 9.7	1.6	1.4	0.0	− 2.7	− 6.9	− 20.5	− 42.7	24"
1219	909	664	0.3	0.6	0.0	− 1.6	− 4.5	− 8.7	2.4	2.7	1.9	0.0	− 3.3	− 15.0	− 35.2	
1424	1121	871	0.4	0.8	0.0	− 2.0	− 5.3	−10.1	1.7	1.5	0.0	− 2.8	− 7.2	− 21.1	− 43.7	24"
301	172	119	0.4	0.8	0.0	− 2.4	− 6.7	−13.8	2.0	1.8	0.0	− 3.8	−10.2	− 35.0	− 84.4	24"
764	530	356	0.4	1.0	0.9	0.0	− 1.9	− 5.0	1.8	2.1	1.5	0.0	− 2.7	− 12.5	− 30.5	24"
915	595	388	0.4	0.7	0.0	− 2.0	− 5.6	−11.1	1.7	1.5	0.0	− 3.1	− 8.0	− 25.5	− 57.4	24"
1269	953	706	0.4	0.8	0.0	− 2.1	− 5.6	−10.7	1.8	1.5	0.0	− 3.0	− 7.7	− 23.0	− 48.5	24"
638	435	290	0.2	0.5	0.0	− 1.5	− 4.2	− 8.2	2.2	2.5	1.8	0.0	− 3.2	− 15.0	− 36.7	24"
787	509	339	0.5	0.9	0.0	− 2.3	− 6.5	−12.8	2.0	1.8	0.0	− 3.5	− 9.3	− 29.5	− 66.7	
1186	887	656	0.5	0.8	0.0	− 2.2	− 6.0	−11.5	2.0	1.7	0.0	− 3.2	− 8.2	− 24.6	− 51.9	

Guns for Rabbits and Other Small Game 8

Of all the nimrods in the country, there's no question that rabbit hunters are by far the most numerous. Every deer hunter I've ever met cut his shooting teeth on rabbits, and most of us have never outgrown the sport. These small, tantalizing targets may get neglected during big-game season, but that neglect is only temporary. Once the bigbore rifles are put away, it's time to hunt rabbits again!

As a matter of fact, many sportsmen never graduate to larger game. They become addicted to hunting rabbits early on, and soon find themselves having so much fun that they simply don't bother with the larger critters.

When I talk about "rabbit hunting," I'm not being taxonomically accurate. A western nimrod on his way to a "rabbit hunt" is likely gunning for the ubiquitous jackrabbit (*Lepus*), which isn't a rabbit at all but a hare. These oversize, long-eared speedsters range from 4 to 10 pounds and may be more than 2 feet long.

Similarly, the snowshoe rabbit so enticing to winter sportsmen is actually a varying hare. These animals are brown in the summer, mottled in late autumn, and all white by the time snow coats the ground.

Only the cottontail is a true rabbit. *Sylvilagus* comes in a half-dozen different varieties, and in a few areas in the United States the European rabbit is found.

Rabbit Rifles and Handguns

But regardless of the type of rabbit or hare being hunted, the term "rabbit hunting" is universally applied. One of the most popular forms of rabbit hunting is done with a .22 rimfire rifle. This requires good marksmanship, as a rabbit requires a solid hit in the head or thorax to bring it down cleanly.

When rabbit hunting with a rifle or handgun that digests .22 short, long or long-rifle ammunition interchangeably, use only .22 long-rifle fodder. The .22 long and short cartridges

Kimber .22 rimfire model 82 is a classic bolt rifle of top quality. It's deadly on squirrels and jackrabbits.

both throw light 29-grain bullets (as compared to the 40-grain solids and 36-grain hollow points featured in long-rifle loads), and these fail to generate enough energy to kill reliably.

A .22 long-rifle, high-velocity load throwing a 40-grain solid exits a rifle bore at some 1,250 fps and has 140 foot-pounds of striking force. At 100 yards (pretty much the top effective range of any non-magnum .22 rimfire), the speed is down to 1,015 fps, and the energy has fallen off to 92 foot-pounds. In contrast, a .22 long, high-speed slug churns up only 99 foot-pounds of energy at the muzzle, and but 60 foot-pounds at 100 yards. The .22 short load (pushing the same 29-grain projectile as the .22 long) yields 77 and 52 foot-pounds, respectively, at those ranges.

When high-speed, .22 long-rifle loads are used, both solid lead and hollow-point projectiles have their proponents. Those who use hollow points claim they kill better when the animal is hit in the body area, while those who favor solids say they're more accurate and have more force when they arrive on target.

I've used both with about equal success over the years, and I'll confess I haven't been able to detect much difference between solid and hollow-point .22 long-rifle slugs as far as killing power is concerned. I do my best to shoot for the head, and if the bullet connects it generally anchors the animal, whether it's a hollow point or solid. If the bullet goes astray and strikes the animal's body, a follow-up shot is almost always required.

Again, popular wisdom dictates that only "high-velocity" .22 rimfires be used for hunting rabbits and other small game. That seems to make sense, as the "standard velocity" target and plinking loads start their slugs off around 100 fps slower and hit with 23 foot-pounds less force at point-blank range. Out where rabbits are killed, the story is a bit different. At the 100-yard mark, the standard-velocity load gives up only 7 foot-pounds of striking energy to the high-speed load. And since the standard-velocity fodder tends to be a bit more accurate, I'd call it an almost even tradeoff. Make no mistake, when I go rabbit hunting, I almost always fill my pockets with high-speed ammunition. But I've also used the standard-velocity stuff with good effect.

A relatively recent development in .22 long-rifle fodder is the "hyper velocity" load that throws a light 31- to 36-grain bullet at 1,400–1,500 fps. Remington's Viper .22 and CCI's Stinger ammo are good examples. These churn up higher energy figures at the muzzle, but because their lighter projectiles lose energy faster than the 40-grain bullets, they aren't as potent as long-rifle loads at longer range. At 100 yards, the 33-grain hollow-point Remington Yellow Jacket load (still another of the "hyper velocity" cartridges) delivers 85 foot-pounds of punch.

The faster-stepping long-rifle loads shoot a bit flatter than the more pedestrian fodder, but the difference isn't enough to get excited about. For instance, the mid-range trajectory of the .22 long-rifle Viper load at 100 yards drops 3.1 inches. The .22 long-rifle, high-velocity load throwing a 40-grain lead slug drops 3.6 inches at that distance, while the slower standard-velocity loads show a drop of 4 inches even. That's a difference of less than 1 inch at 100 yards, which for all practical purposes is insignificant.

Remember, these statistics are all for .22 rimfire *rifles*—the same ammo performs much more poorly from a handgun's much shorter tube. Too, some of the propellant force is leaked between cylinder and barrel of revolvers, and this tends to reduce power even more.

How significant is the difference between rifle and handgun with .22 rimfire ammunition? A .22 long-rifle, high-speed load delivers 100 foot-pounds of energy at the muzzle of a 6-inch handgun barrel. That's about the striking force a .22 rifle delivers at 90 yards. For hunting purposes, the practical effective range of a pistol or revolver firing .22 long-rifle ammo is about 40 yards. The rifle is useful to nearly 100 yards. Since the rimfire rifle is easier to shoot accurately in the first place, it has a much greater edge than the ballistic figures indicate.

An even better choice than the .22 long-rifle round is the .22 WMRF, or .22 rimfire magnum. This ammo is considerably hotter than .22 long-rifle fodder, and is *not* interchangeable. Some rimfire revolvers digest both kinds of ammunition, but only when interchangeable cylinders are used. Chamber dimensions are totally different for the two rounds.

From a rifle barrel, the .22 WMRF throws a 40-grain jacketed hollow-point or full metal case bullet at a starting velocity of more than 1,900 fps. That gives it a muzzle energy of 324 foot-pounds. At 100 yards, the .22 magnum delivers 156 foot-pounds of force, which is more than a high-speed .22 long-rifle round produces at the muzzle. The .22 magnum has a mid-range trajectory of just 1.7 inches, making it an effective 130-yard hunting round.

For jackrabbits, which are seldom prepared for the table, the .22 magnum is a much better choice than any lesser rimfire. It anchors large hares with much more authority than a .22 long-rifle load, and even a wounded jack is less likely to escape. A .22 magnum also has a 30 to 40 percent greater range than a long-rifle load, and in a good rifle it can be very accurate.

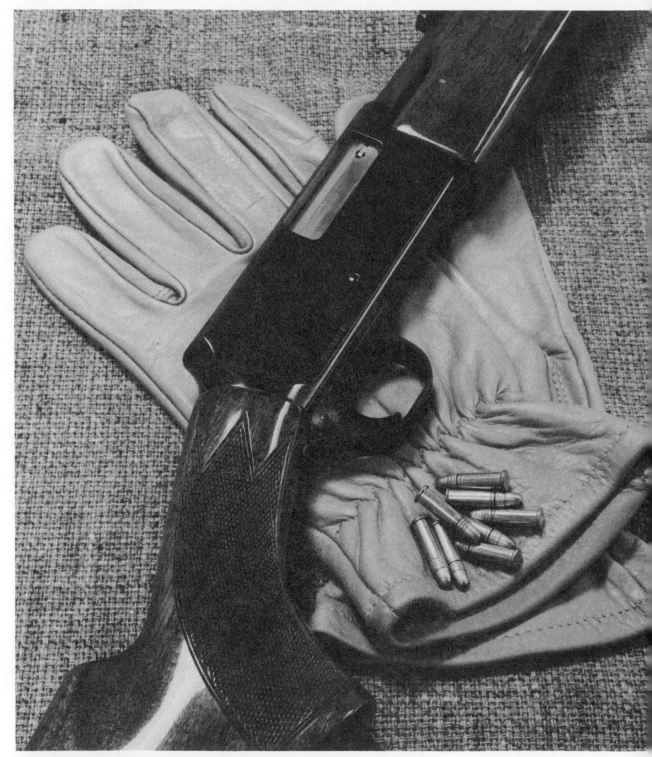

Browning autoloader is a fast-firing, accurate .22 for small-game enthusiasts.

Guns for Rabbits and Other Small Game

The one factor that makes .22 magnum fodder less attractive than standard long-rifle loads is cost, from 2½ to 3 times as much. Too, the rimfire magnum is more destructive of edible small game like cottontails and squirrels. When hunting for the pot, a carefully placed .22 long-rifle slug wastes less meat.

While the high-speed, .22 long-rifle load is the rifle and handgun cartridge of choice for cottontails and squirrels shot for culinary purposes, jackrabbits are often hunted with high-velocity centerfire rounds. Few nimrods of my acquaintance feel the jack is fit table fare, and most hunt them solely for marksmanship practice and sport.

Hunting non-edible game doesn't sit well with many people, but the prolific jackrabbit must sometimes be controlled. When at the peak of its 7- or 8-year reproductive cycle, these hungry hares can lay waste to surprising areas of farmland. In Idaho, these pests periodically become so plentiful that they pose a serious economic threat to farmers and ranchers in the area. Recently, the number of jacks in southern Idaho has reached plague proportions, and mass drives have been held in which thousands of the animals are herded into an enclosure and clubbed to death. Hunting seems a more humane way of dealing with the problem—ending life almost instantly with a high-speed bullet is certainly quicker and less traumatic than driving and clubbing.

Unfortunately, enough hunters aren't available to do the job; the rabbits (sorry—hares) multiply faster than they can be shot! Coyotes and bobcats are controlled by poisoning as well as hunting, so they aren't much help. The jackrabbits will simply continue to increase inexorably until disease or hunger thins their ranks. Few states fear periodic jackrabbit explosions as Idaho does, but when conditions are right these crop-destructive pests can multiply with surprising speed anywhere they're found.

Since jackrabbits are seldom hunted for the pot, there's no reason to limit your rifle or handgun choices to the rimfire variety (short of economics, which certainly favors the .22 long-rifle firearms). As a result, many riflemen hunt jacks with their pet deer or big-game rifles. This provides excellent off-season practice, and the sportsman who learns to score consistently on bounding jackrabbits at 200 yards has little trouble downing larger game.

How large a centerfire can you use to hunt jackrabbits? I know several hunters who've killed many, many more rabbits than deer with their .270 and .30-06 firearms, and a few sturdy souls make it a point to tote .458 Winchester Magnums through the sagebrush deserts at least once or twice each year! In my home state of Utah, one large sporting goods chain tells me a surprising quantity of .375 H&H and .458 magnum "elephant stopper" loads are sold annually. Since I've seen very few pachyderms wandering the state, I'd be willing to bet the bulk of that ammo was fired at bounding, long-eared hares.

Obviously, a few hardy folk tend to go overgunned when only jackrabbits are on the program. I'd hardly call a .458 Winchester—or even a .270—ideal armament for doing in an 8-pound animal, regardless of its ferocity. But a few centerfires do make fine rabbit rounds. These include the full range of centerfire .22's, from the quiet-spoken .22 Hornet to the long-range .22-250 Remington. My own preference is for the .22 Hornet, the .222 or the .223 Remington chambering in a light, easy-to-carry rifle. The heavy, bull-barrel varmint models are

Randy Brooks shoots at running jack with Harrington & Richardson .22 WMRF autoloader, while John Rees waits with Ruger 10/22.

simply too bulky and unwieldy for the job. Jackrabbit hunting is always an on-the-move sport, and there's seldom time to set up shop with a bipod rest and high-powered scope. Many rabbits hunted with centerfire rifles are vaporized on the run, and on slow days the nimrod may walk a mile or more for every target fired at. A 10-pound rifle is definitely out of place.

As far as sights are concerned, a good 2½X or 4X scope does fine, as does any of the popular 2–7X or 3–9X variables. Iron sights are too coarse to let you center distant jacks consistently. The front sight bead obscures the entire body beyond 50 yards or so, which puts you out of the money on most targets offered. Jackrabbits hear you coming as much as 400 yards off, and may start moving that far ahead of your position. Those rabbits are probably safe, but the tardy hares that wait until you are 150 or 200 yards away should be in serious trouble.

While many hares won't wait around for you to come within range, you can always count on a few to simply sit motionless, relying on their natural camouflage until you pass. *Then* they'll dart off behind you, zigzagging as they go.

If you can spot these crafty critters, those are the ones you can take with a head shot from your .22 rimfire. These are also likely targets for a handgun, be it of rimfire or centerfire design. A .22 WMRF handgun is good medicine, but an accurate .38 Special or .357 magnum revolver is even better. A jack startled by a 125-grain .357 slug isn't likely to survive the surprise. Auto pistols also work well, and any .380 ACP, 9mm Parabellum or .45 ACP load makes short work of any rabbit.

While centerfire rifles and handguns are often used to hunt jackrabbits and other non-edible game, cottontails, squirrels and other animals destined for the cooking pot are best harvested with a carefully placed 40-grain solid lead slug from a .22 rimfire. Bushytails are generally shot at much closer range than are cottontails, and either an iron-sighted or scoped .22 rifle makes an ideal choice for this work.

Muzzleloaders for Small Game

Black-powder burners also get in on the fun, and a .36- or .45-caliber muzzleloader makes an efficient squirrel killer. Traditionalists looking for a way to harvest the makings of a squirrel pie without damaging much meat should try the age-old method known as "barking."

"Barking" a squirrel doesn't refer to any kind of sound made by the hunter. Sharpshooters of a century or so ago killed the critters by aiming *underneath* them to hit the limb or branch

Ruger Single-Six convertible, which has cylinders for shooting either standard .22 Long Rifle loads or .22 WMRF fodder, is an excellent small-game handgun.

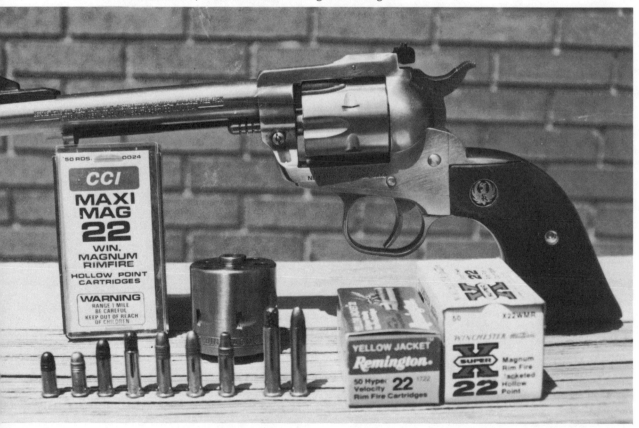

they were standing on. Properly done, this chips a chunk of bark *and* the squirrel off the branch, and the animal falls dead without a mark on its body. The squirrel is killed by shock rather than by a direct wound. It takes a carefully placed ball to accomplish the task, but it can be done.

Anyone who can consistently bounce tin cans high in the air with a rifle or handgun should be up to barking a squirrel. The principle is the same, with the shot placed exactly at the juncture of can and ground (or squirrel and tree limb). This is best done with a muzzle-loading rifle of .36 caliber or larger, or with a modern centerfire. A .22 long-rifle load doesn't generate enough shocking power to do the trick reliably.

The .22 magnum rimfire may be the best all-around jackrabbit load on the market. Teamed with Harrington & Richardson's deluxe autoloader, it shoots just fine.

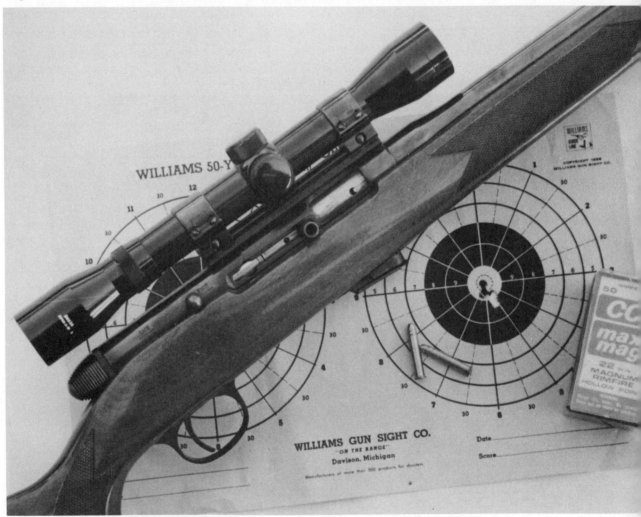

In snowshoe rabbit country, most shots are at close range with the semi-invisible target moving fast. A scattergun is the right choice here.

Shotguns for Small Game

Rabbits, hares and squirrels can all be hunted successfully with a shotgun, although the game changes considerably with this kind of armament. With a rifle or handgun, the marksman must take careful aim when the animal is at rest. Shooting at running game is tricky, and a hastily placed shot is liable to wound, rather than kill cleanly, particularly when a .22 rimfire is used.

Shotgunners, on the other hand, generally shoot only at a moving target. It's not really considered sporting to shoot an animal "on the sit" with a scattergun, but a rabbit that's busily going through the gears is a different story entirely. And a squirrel that's flitting from branch to branch or scurrying around a tree trunk requires a fair degree of shooting skill.

Just about any shotgun gauge is suitable for harvesting rabbits or squirrels, although the diminutive .410 (which isn't a "gauge" at all, but a caliber designation) is the least effective bore size a hunter can use. Twenty- and 12-gauge guns are by far the most popular.

Matching the Gun to the Game

A 28-gauge Remington pump proved to be the right armament on this snowshoe rabbit hunt.

Again, nearly any choke constriction is usable, but guns throwing open cylinder or improved cylinder patterns are best for running game this side of 35 yards. A tightly constricted full-choke pattern either misses cleanly at short range (20 to 30 yards) or kills decisively. At close range, *any* shotgun pattern can be overly destructive. Squirrel hunters may prefer a modified-choke or even a full-choke gun for shooting into tall trees, although a true full choke would be my last choice for such work.

Either high-velocity "express" loads or light field loads will do. No. 5, 6 and 7½ shot sizes work best for rabbits and squirrels, and anything from ⅞ to 1¼ ounces gets the job done. You don't want 3-inch magnum 12 loads throwing 1⅞ ounces of shot to hunt squirrels or rabbits with.

Choosing between rifle and shotgun is a personal matter for small-game hunters. Invariably when you're toting a rifle, rabbits seem to literally swarm at your feet, then dart away offering the kind of close, moving shot that scattergunners love and riflemen despise. And when you've brought the shotgun, the long-eared targets show themselves only at a distance—well out of range of your pellet pattern. Well-heeled European nimrods solve this problem by toting a drilling, or a rifle-shotgun, combination afield. These guns are expensive, but the American rabbit and squirrel hunter can have the same kind of versatility by acquiring a Savage model 24 over-under rifle-shotgun combination. These are available with either .22 rimfire or .22 (or larger) centerfire barrels positioned over a 20-gauge smoothbore tube. Several importers offer similar guns, but the ones I've seen are priced much higher than our domestic Savage offering. The one drawback these two-in-one guns have is the inability to provide fast follow-up shots.

Hunting rabbits and squirrels will always remain popular, as these tasty little critters are found almost everywhere and they're prolific enough to withstand fair to heavy hunting pressure. Seasons are long, and bag limits are often generous. And where jackrabbits are concerned, hunting is usually available on a year-round basis.

RECOMMENDED SHOTSHELL LOADS FOR SMALL GAME

(Courtesy Winchester-Western)

Game Loads

Gauge	Length of Shell Inches	Power Dram Equivalent	Ounce Shot	Standard Shot Sizes
12	2¾	3¾	1¼	5, 6, 7½
16	2¾	3¼	1⅛	6, 7½
16	2¾ Mag.	3¼	1¼	6
20	2¾	2¾	1	5, 6, 7½
20	2¾ Mag.	2¾	1⅛	6, 7½
20	3 Mag.	3	1¼	6, 7½
28	2¾	2¼	¾	6, 7½
410	3	Max.	$^{11}/_{16}$	6, 7½

Upland Field Loads

Gauge	Length of Shell Inches	Power Dram Equivalent	Ounce Shot	Standard Shot Sizes
12	2¾	3¼	1⅛	6, 7½
12	2¾	3¼	1¼	6, 7½
16	2¾	2¾	1⅛	5, 6, 7½
20	2¾	2½	1	5, 6, 7½

Trap Loads

Gauge	Length of Shell Inches	Power Dram Equivalent	Ounce Shot	Standard Shot Sizes
12	2¾	2¾	1⅛	7½
12	2¾	3	1⅛	7½

International Trap Loads

Gauge	Length of Shell Inches	Power Dram Equivalent	Ounce Shot	Standard Shot Sizes
*12	2¾	3¼	1⅛	7½, 8
12	2¾	3¼	1⅛	7½, 8

*nickel plated shot

Guns for Rabbits and Other Small Game

Target Loads (Paper)

Gauge	Length of Shell Inches	Power Dram Equivalent	Ounce Shot	Standard Shot Sizes
12	2¾	2¾	1⅛	7½
12	2¾	3	1⅛	7½

Target Loads

Gauge	Length of Shell Inches	Power Dram Equivalent	Ounce Shot	Standard Shot Sizes
12	2¾	3¼	1¼	7½

RECOMMENDED RIMFIRE LOADS FOR SMALL GAME

(Courtesy Winchester-Western)

Rimfire Rifle Cartridges

Cartridge	Bullet Wt. Grs.	Type	Velocity (ft/s) Muzzle	100 yds.	Energy (ft. lbs.) Muzzle	100 yds.	Nominal Mid-Range Traj. (in.) 100 yds.
22 Long Rifle	40	L*	1255	1016	140	92	3.6
22 Long Rifle H.P.	37	L*	1280	1013	135	84	3.5
22 WMRF	40	JHP	1910	1326	324	156	1.7
22 WMRF	40	FMC	1910	1326	324	156	1.7
22 Long Rifle	40	Lead*	1150	975	117	84	4.0

Rimfire Pistol and Revolver Cartridges

Cartridge	Bullet Wt. Grs.	Type	Barrel Length	Muzzle Velocity (ft/s)	Muzzle Energy (ft. lbs.)
22 Long Rifle	40	L*	6"	1060	100
22 Long Rifle	40	Lead*	6"	950	80
22 Long Rifle Match	40	Lead*	6¾"	1060	100
22WMRF	40	JHP	6½"	1480	195
22 WMRF	40	FMC	6½"	1480	195

Specifications subject to change without notice.

FMC-Full Metal Case   *Wax Coated   L-Lubaloy   JHP-Jacketed Hollow Point

Specifications are nominal. Test barrels are used to determine ballistics figures. Individual firearms may differ from test barrel statistics.

RECOMMENDED HANDGUN LOADS FOR SMALL GAME

(Courtesy Winchester-Western)

Caliber	Bullet Wt. Grs.	Bullet Type	Velocity-fps Muzzle	Velocity-fps 50 Yds.	Velocity-fps 100 Yds.	Energy ft-lbs Muzzle	Energy ft-lbs 50 Yds.	Energy ft-lbs 100 Yds.	Mid Range Trajectory Inches 50 Yds.	Mid Range Trajectory Inches 100 Yds.	BARREL LENGTH
.22 Rem. Jet	40	SP	2100	1790	1510	390	285	200	0.3	1.4	8⅜
.221 Rem. Fireball	50	PSP	2650	2380	2130	780	630	505	0.2	0.8	10½
256 Winchester Magnum	60	HP	2350	2030	1760	735	550	415	0.3	1.1	8½
30 Luger (7.65mm)	93	FMC	1220	1110	1040	305	255	225	0.9	3.5	4½
32 Automatic	71	FMC	905	855	810	129	115	97	1.4	5.8	4
32 Automatic	60	STHP	970	895	835	125	107	93	1.3	5.4	4
32 Smith & Wesson (inside lubricated)	85	Lead	680	645	610	90	81	73	2.5	10.5	3
32 Smith & Wesson Long (inside lubricated)	98	Lead	705	670	635	115	98	88	2.3	10.5	4
32 Short Colt (greased)	80	Lead	745	665	590	100	79	62	2.2	9.9	4
32 Long Colt (inside lubricated)	82	Lead	755	715	675	100	93	83	2.0	8.7	4
357 Magnum Jacketed Hollow Point	110	JHP	1295	1094	975	410	292	232	0.8	3.5	4V
357 Magnum Jacketed Hollow Point	125	JHP	1450	1240	1090	583	427	330	0.6	2.8	4V
357 Magnum Hollow Point	145	STHP	1290	1155	1060	535	428	361	0.8	3.5	4V
357 Magnum (inside lubricated)	158	Lead	1235	1104	1015	535	428	361	0.8	3.5	4V
357 Magnum Jacketed Hollow Point	158	JHP	1235	1104	1015	535	428	361	0.8	3.5	4V
357 Magnum Jacketed Soft Point	158	JSP	1235	1104	1015	535	428	361	0.8	3.5	4V
9mm Luger (Parabellum)	95	JSP	1355	1140	1008	387	274	214	0.7	3.3	4
9mm Luger (Parabellum)	100	JHP	1320	1114	991	387	275	218	0.7	3.4	4
9mm Luger (Parabellum)	115	FMC	1155	1047	971	341	280	241	0.9	3.9	4
9mm Luger (Parabellum)	115	STHP	1225	1095	1007	383	306	259	0.8	3.6	4
9mm Winchester Magnum	115	FMC	1475	1264	1109	556	408	314	0.6	2.7	5
38 Smith & Wesson (inside lubricated)	145	Lead	685	650	620	150	135	125	2.4	10.0	4
38 Special (inside lubricated)	158	Lead	755	723	693	200	183	168	2.0	8.3	4V
38 Special Semi-Wad Cutter	158	Lead SWC	755	721	698	200	182	167	2.0	8.4	4V
38 Special Super Police (inside lubricated)	200	Lead	635	614	594	179	168	157	2.8	11.5	4V
38 Special Jacketed Hollow Point +P	110	JHP	1020	945	887	254	218	192	1.1	4.8	4V
38 Special Jacketed Hollow Point +P	125	JHP	945	898	858	248	224	204	1.3	5.4	4V
38 Special Hollow Point +P	95	STHP	1100	1002	932	255	212	183	1.0	4.3	4V
38 Special (inside lubricated) +P	150	Lead	910	870	835	276	252	232	1.4	5.7	4V
38 Special (inside lubricated) +P	158	Lead-HP	915	878	844	294	270	250	1.4	5.6	4V
38 Special Semi-Wad Cutter (inside lubricated) +P	158	Lead-SWC	915	878	844	294	270	250	1.4	5.6	4V
38 Special Match and Match Mid-Range Clean Cutting (inside lubricated)	148	Lead-WC	710	634	566	166	132	105	2.4	10.8	4V
38 Special Match (inside lubricated)	158	Lead	755	723	693	200	183	168	2.0	8.3	4V
38 Short Colt (greased)	130	Lead	730	685	645	150	130	115	2.2	9.4	6
38 Long Colt (inside lubricated)	150	Lead	730	700	670	175	165	150	2.1	8.8	6

Guns for Rabbits and Other Small Game

Caliber	Bullet Wt. Grs.	Bullet Type	Velocity-fps Muzzle	Velocity-fps 50 Yds.	Velocity-fps 100 Yds.	Energy ft-lbs Muzzle	Energy ft-lbs 50 Yds.	Energy ft-lbs 100 Yds.	Mid Range Trajectory Inches 50 Yds.	Mid Range Trajectory Inches 100 Yds.	BARREL LENGTH
38 Automatic Hollow Point +P	125	STHP	1240	1130	1050	427	354	306	0.8	3.4	5
*38 Automatic +P	125	JHP	1245	1105	1010	430	340	285	0.8	3.6	5
*38 Automatic +P	130	FMC	1280	1140	1050	475	375	320	0.8	3.4	5
38 Automatic (For all 38 Colt Automatic Pistols)	130	FMC	1040	980	925	310	275	245	1.0	4.7	4½
380 Automatic	95	FMC	955	865	785	190	160	130	1.4	5.9	3¾
380 Automatic	85	STHP	1000	921	860	189	160	140	1.2	5.1	3¾
41 Remington Magnum (inside lubricated)	210	Lead	965	898	842	434	376	331	1.3	5.4	4V
41 Remington Magnum Jacketed Soft Point	210	JSP	1300	1162	1062	788	630	526	0.7	3.2	4V
44 Smith & Wesson Special (inside lubricated)	246	Lead	755	725	695	310	285	265	2.0	8.3	6½
44 Remington Magnum (Gas Check) (inside lubricated)	240	Lead	1350	1186	1069	971	749	608	0.7	3.1	4V
45 Colt Hollow Point	225	STHP	920	877	839	423	384	352	1.4	5.6	5½
45 Colt (inside lubricated)	255	Lead	860	820	780	420	380	345	1.5	6.1	5½
45 Automatic	185	STHP	1000	938	888	411	362	324	1.2	4.9	5
45 Automatic	230	FMC	810	776	745	335	308	284	1.7	7.2	5
45 Automatic Match Clean Cutting	185	FMC-WC	770	707	650	244	205	174	2.0	8.7	5
45 Winchester Magnum	230	FMC	1400	1232	1107	1001	775	636	0.6	2.8	5

Specifications subject to change without notice

Met. Pierc.-Metal Piercing   FMC-Full Metal Case   JHP-Jacketed Hollow Point   JSP-Jacketed Soft Point   Met. Pt.-Metal Point
XP-Expanding Point   HP-Hollow Point   WC-Wad Cutter   SWC-Semi-Wad Cutter   STHP-Silvertip Hollow Point
Specifications are nominal. Test barrels are used to determine ballistics figures. Individual firearms may differ from these test barrel statistics.

+P Ammunition with (+P) on the case head stamp is loaded to higher pressure. Use only firearms designated for this cartridge and so recommended by the gun manufacturer.

V-Data is based on velocity obtained from 4" vented barrels for revolver cartridges (38 Special, 357 Magnum, 41 Rem Mag, and 44 Rem Mag.).

Data not marked V obtained from unvented (solid) test barrels of the length specified.

*For use only in 38 Colt Super and Colt Commander Automatic Pistols.

RECOMMENDED CENTERFIRE LOADS FOR SMALL GAME

(Courtesy Remington Arms Co., Inc., Federal Cartridge Corp., and Winchester-Western)

CALIBERS	BULLET		VELOCITY FEET PER SECOND						ENERGY		
	Wt.-Grs.	Style	Muzzle	100 Yds.	200 Yds.	300 Yds.	400 Yds.	500 Yds.	Muzzle	100 Yds.	200 Yds.
17 REM.	25	Hollow Point	4040	3284	2644	2086	1606	1235	906	599	388
22 HORNET	45	Pointed Soft Point	2690	2042	1502	1128	948	840	723	417	225
	45	Hollow Point	2690	2042	1502	1128	948	840	723	417	225
222 REM.	50	Pointed Soft Point	3140	2602	2123	1700	1350	1107	1094	752	500
	50	Metal Case	3140	2602	2123	1700	1350	1107	1094	752	500
	50	Hollow Point	3140	2635	2182	1777	1432	1172	1094	771	529
222 REM. MAG.	55	Pointed Soft Point	3240	2748	2305	1906	1556	1272	1282	922	649
	55	Hollow Point	3240	2773	2352	1969	1627	1341	1282	939	675
223 REM.	55	Pointed Soft Point	3240	2747	2304	1905	1554	1270	1282	921	648
	55	Hollow Point	3240	2773	2352	1969	1627	1341	1282	939	675
22-250 REM.	55	Pointed Soft Point	3730	3180	2695	2257	1863	1519	1699	1235	887
	55	Hollow Point	3730	3253	2826	2436	2079	1755	1699	1292	975
243 WIN.	80	Pointed Soft Point	3350	2955	2593	2259	1951	1670	1993	1551	1194
	80	Hollow Point	3350	2955	2593	2259	1951	1670	1993	1551	1194
6mm REM.	80	Pointed Soft Point	3470	3064	2694	2352	2036	1747	2139	1667	1289
	80	Hollow Point	3470	3064	2694	2352	2036	1747	2139	1667	1289
25-20 WIN.	86	Soft Point	1460	1194	1030	931	858	797	407	272	203
256 WIN. MAG.	60	Hollow Point	2760	2097	1542	1149	957	846	1015	586	317
257 ROBERTS	87	Pointed Soft Point	3170	2802	2462	2147	1857	1594	1941	1516	1171
25-06 REM.	87	Hollow Point	3440	2995	2591	2222	1884	1583	2286	1733	1297
30-30 WIN. ACCELERATOR	55	Soft Point	3400	2693	2085	1570	1187	986	1412	886	521
30-06 SPRINGFIELD ACCELERATOR	55	Pointed Soft Point	4080	3485	2965	2502	2083	1709	2033	1483	1074
308 WIN. ACCELERATOR	55	Pointed Soft Point	3770	3215	2726	2286	1888	1541	1735	1262	907
32-20 WIN.	100	Lead	1210	1021	913	834	769	712	325	231	185
	100	Soft Point	1210	1021	913	834	769	712	325	231	185

| FOOT-POUNDS | | | TRAJECTORY† 0.0 Indicates yardage at which rifle was sighted in. | | | | | | | | | | | | | BARREL LENGTH |
| | | | SHORT RANGE Bullet does not rise more than one inch above line of sight from muzzle to sighting in range. | | | | | | LONG RANGE Bullet does not rise more than three inches above line of sight from muzzle to sighting in range. | | | | | | | |
300 Yds.	400 Yds.	500 Yds.	50 Yds.	100 Yds.	150 Yds.	200 Yds.	250 Yds.	300 Yds.	100 Yds	150 Yds.	200 Yds.	250 Yds.	300 Yds.	400 Yds.	500 Yds.	
242	143	85	0.1	0.5	0.0	− 1.5	− 4.2	− 8.5	2.1	2.5	1.9	0.0	− 3.4	− 17.0	− 44.3	24"
127	90	70	0.3	0.0	− 2.4	− 7.7	−16.9	−31.3	1.6	0.0	− 4.5	−12.8	−26.4	− 75.6	−163.4	24"
127	90	70	0.3	0.0	− 2.4	− 7.7	−16.9	−31.3	1.6	0.0	− 4.5	−12.8	−26.4	− 75.6	−163.4	
321	202	136	0.5	0.9	0.0	− 2.5	− 6.9	−13.7	2.2	1.9	0.0	− 3.8	−10.0	− 32.3	− 73.8	
321	202	136	0.5	0.9	0.0	− 2.5	− 6.9	−13.7	2.2	1.9	0.0	− 3.8	−10.0	− 32.3	− 73.8	24"
351	228	152	0.5	0.9	0.0	− 2.4	− 6.6	−13.1	2.1	1.8	0.0	− 3.6	− 9.5	− 30.2	− 68.1	
444	296	198	0.4	0.8	0.0	− 2.2	− 6.0	−11.8	1.9	1.6	0.0	− 3.3	− 8.5	− 26.7	− 59.5	24"
473	323	220	0.4	0.8	0.0	− 2.1	− 5.8	−11.4	1.8	1.6	0.0	− 3.2	− 8.2	− 25.5	− 56.0	
443	295	197	0.4	0.8	0.0	− 2.2	− 6.0	−11.8	1.9	1.6	0.0	− 3.3	− 8.5	− 26.7	− 59.6	
473	323	220	0.4	0.8	0.0	− 2.1	− 5.8	−11.4	1.8	1.6	0.0	− 3.2	− 8.2	− 25.5	− 56.0	24"
622	424	282	0.2	0.5	0.0	− 1.5	− 4.3	− 8.4	2.2	2.6	1.9	0.0	− 3.3	− 15.4	− 37.7	24"
725	528	376	0.2	0.5	0.0	− 1.4	− 4.0	− 7.7	2.1	2.4	1.7	0.0	− 3.0	− 13.6	− 32.4	
906	676	495	0.3	0.7	0.0	− 1.8	− 4.9	− 9.4	2.6	2.9	2.1	0.0	− 3.6	− 16.2	− 37.9	
906	676	495	0.3	0.7	0.0	− 1.8	− 4.9	− 9.4	2.6	2.9	2.1	0.0	− 3.6	− 16.2	− 37.9	24"
982	736	542	0.3	0.6	0.0	− 1.6	− 4.5	− 8.7	2.4	2.7	1.9	0.0	− 3.3	− 14.9	− 35.0	
982	736	542	0.3	0.6	0.0	− 1.6	− 4.5	− 8.7	2.4	2.7	1.9	0.0	− 3.3	− 14.9	− 35.0	24"
165	141	121	0.0	−4.1	−14.4	−31.8	−57.3	−92.0	0.0	−8.2	−23.5	−47.0	−79.6	−175.9	−319.4	24"
176	122	95	0.3	0.0	− 2.3	− 7.3	−15.9	−29.6	1.5	0.0	− 4.2	−12.1	−25.0	− 72.1	−157.2	24"
890	666	491	0.4	0.8	0.0	− 2.0	− 5.5	−10.6	1.8	1.5	0.0	− 3.0	− 7.5	− 22.7	− 48.0	24"
954	686	484	0.3	0.6	0.0	− 1.7	− 4.8	− 9.3	2.5	2.9	2.1	0.0	− 3.6	− 16.4	− 39.1	
301	172	119	0.4	0.8	0.0	− 2.4	− 6.7	−13.8	2.0	1.8	0.0	− 3.8	−10.2	− 35.0	− 84.4	24"
764	530	356	0.4	1.0	0.9	0.0	− 1.9	− 5.0	1.8	2.1	1.5	0.0	− 2.7	− 12.5	− 30.5	24"
638	435	290	0.2	0.5	0.0	− 1.5	− 4.2	− 8.2	2.2	2.5	1.8	0.0	− 3.2	− 15.0	− 36.7	24"
154	131	113	0.0	−6.3	−20.9	−44.9	−79.3	−125.1	0.0	−11.5	−32.3	−63.8	−106.3	−230.3	−413.3	24"
154	131	113	0.0	−6.3	−20.9	−44.9	−79.3	−125.1	0.0	−11.5	−32.3	−63.8	−106.3	−230.3	−413.3	

Shotguns and Loads for Upland Game 9

The first repeating shotgun I ever owned was a 12-bore Ithaca pump. I bought it equipped with a 30-inch full-choke barrel and fed it nothing but 1¼-ounce express loads of No. 6 shot.

With that combination, I hunted everything from rabbits to greenheads, but with decidedly mixed results. The gun did fine in the duck blind, and I killed many mallards and pintails on those bluebird days when everything flew high. But I didn't do so well on upland game. Flushing pheasants were often missed clean, and when one did fall it was usually too mangled for decent table fare. A downed quail was an even rarer bird, but for some reason, I had pretty good luck hunting doves, which are even smaller.

In my part of the country during the 1950's, if you bought a shotgun off the rack it almost always wore a tight, full choke. Western nimrods wanted a gun that would "reach out and gettem," and hardware and sporting goods stores that sold scatterguns stocked full-choke models almost exclusively. There were a few skeet shooters around, but these target gunners usually bought their guns special order. The guy who walked in the day before pheasant season to buy a new pump or autoloader wanted a tight-choke 12, and if you could drop a dime down the muzzle he'd look at another gun, thank you.

Like most weekend hunters of the time, I knew little of choke theory or performance. The only time I came even close to patterning that gun was when I blasted the door of an old, junked Plymouth someone had abandoned in the desert. I doubt if I was 20 yards away when I centered the door, and I remember being awed at the destructiveness of the shot pattern at that close range. For the first time, I began to realize why most of the Chinese cacklebirds I shot were so badly chewed up. I vowed then and there to let my targets get a little farther from the gun.

Even so, I never considered using a more open choke until I went hunting with a friend who was somewhat eccentric in his taste of firearms. While everyone else I knew shot a full-choke 12 trombone gun or autoloader, he affected a 20-gauge double. What's more, the barrels were just 26 inches long, and were choked improved cylinder and modified. It wasn't a fancy import, but a Stevens 311; all the same, it was pretty exotic as far as I was concerned.

145

Short barrels make for fast gun handling on upland game without sacrificing pattern, velocity or efficiency.

We were hunting pheasants in corn country, and the birds were holding tight in the tall stubble. My buddy was really wiping my eye with his short-coupled double. While I was waiting my birds out to let them get a fair distance from the gun before shooting, he was on those ringnecks almost as soon as they cleared the ground. He had his limit in short order, while I had but a lone bird hanging from my belt.

At that point, he offered to trade me guns for a few minutes, and I took him up on it. I was frankly curious about how it felt to tote and shoot the little 20. If I'd had any misgivings about the effectiveness of the lighter gauge, they'd pretty well vanished during the previous hour.

Right from the first I was tickled with the light weight and fast-handling capabilities the little gun displayed. It was easy to carry and much lighter at the muzzle than my long-barrel pump. After killing the next three birds that got up with as many shots, I was hooked. A month later I bought a twin-tube 20 of my own, and it wore the same combination of improved cylinder and modified chokes.

That was a pivotal purchase in my gunning career. It opened a previously closed mind with relation to gauge, choke and barrel length, and I soon began experimenting with other guns and gauges. I even began to pattern each gun by shooting at a sheet of butcher paper, then evaluating the pellet distribution. Was the shot all bunched-up toward the middle, or was it evenly distributed over the paper? Were there quail-size holes a bird could escape through? Did the barrel shoot close to the point of aim, or did the pattern print low and off to the side?

Those experiments led me to try other loads and shot sizes. I soon learned that each gun had its preferences. One shotgun seemed to give more uniform performance with low-base 7½'s throwing only 1⅛ ounces of shot, while another liked high-velocity 5's. It didn't take me long to learn that a grouse or pheasant could be made very dead by an even ounce of shot from a gun that threw a decent pattern.

I also discovered that an open-choke skeet or improved cylinder barrel was deadly at close range, and would kill game a lot farther out than I thought it would. When I began using more-open chokes on upland game, my success ratio soared.

Chokes and Shot Patterns

Without going into choke theory or the effect barrel length has on range and shot velocity (that's all covered in Chapter 16), the general rule for choke selection is "short range—open choke, long range—tight choke." For flying game or rabbits that flush at your feet, a skeet or straight cylinder choke makes a fine choice. These are at their best at a maximum of 25 or maybe 30 yards, which means longer shots should be ruled out. Skeet-choke guns work very well when you're hunting over a well-trained dog that holds a bird until you're very close. I've hunted in Idaho beet fields with such dense cover that the ringnecks hiding there felt safe until you almost kicked them in the tailfeathers. For this kind of gunning, a cylinder or skeet tube is ideal. You can get on the birds right away without having to wait them out, and the pattern is large enough to be forgiving if you fail to center your target perfectly.

The improved cylinder choke, which throws slightly tighter patterns, is good out to 35 yards. This is the least degree of choke constriction generally offered in field model "hunting guns," and is an excellent choice for most upland scattergun work. This is the first choice of many quail hunters, and the best ringneck shots I've known habitually hunted with improved cylinder (or wider) choke shotguns. Come to think of it, that may be one reason they were such deadly shots.

At one time, the modified choke was considered the best choice for all-around gunning work. In theory, this is still true, but in point of fact today's modern shot-cup protected pellet loads pattern much tighter than scattergun ammo did a couple of decades ago. As a result, many modified-choke shotguns are actually throwing full-choke patterns. By the same token, not a few improved cylinder tubes are giving true "modified" performance.

A modified choke is supposed to put from 45 to 55 percent of the pellets it throws inside a 30-inch circle at a range of 40 yards. If it prints a 55 to 65 percent pattern, it's giving "improved modified" performance, while anything tighter (denser) than 65 percent falls in the full-choke realm.

A gun that actually delivers modified-choke performance is good medicine at ranges from 25 to 45 yards. At closer range, the pattern is too dense to give best results, and if the target is more than 45 yards from the gun the pattern is theoretically too thin to kill reliably.

Of course, you can make any shotgun throw a denser pattern by simply using small shot; there are just 87 pellets to the ounce in a load of No. 2 shot, and approximately 585 individual lead spheres in an ounce of 9's. So if you need a denser pattern for long-range shooting, all you need to do is use smaller pellets—right?

Wrong! While increasing pattern density is desirable for long-distance gunning, the small shot sizes that allow you to do this without drastically increasing the weight of the shot load thrown lose velocity and energy too fast to do you much good at extreme range. This is particularly true with larger game and birds. At 25 or even 30 yards, a load of 8's will kill a grouse or pheasant, but at 45 or 50 yards the same shot charge isn't likely to down a bird this size unless a lucky pellet penetrates its head.

A general rule for selecting shot size is "large game, long range—large shot; small game, short range—small shot."

Getting back to chokes, guns with tight improved-modified or full-choke constriction should only be used where long shots are the rule, not the exception. Late-season ringnecks can be awfully fleet of foot, and have learned to flush only at extreme range. By the same token, jackrabbits hunted in open desert country often take a long headstart. A full-choke gun (or a modified-choke barrel that delivers tight "full-choke" patterns) can be a handy thing to have in these situations. But for most typical upland gunning conditions, a full-choke barrel is too tight. At close ranges, the densely packed pattern has a tendency to either miss or mangle.

Western grouse often flush at long range, calling for modified- and full-choke guns throwing 5's or 6's.

Gauges and Loads

As far as bore size is concerned, the larger 12-gauge barrels inevitably give better pattern density than do smaller 16-, 20-, 28- and .410-bore guns. A 12-gauge shotshell simply holds more shot than a 20-gauge hull, all other things equal. Granted, a 3-inch 20-gauge magnum throws

A slide-action repeater is favored by many upland gunners.

as much shot as a 2¾-inch non-magnum 12-gauge high-velocity load, and the two can be considered approximate equals. However, when 3-inch magnums are used in both gauges, the 1⅞ ounces of lead contained in the 12-gauge hull easily "out-magnums" the 1¼-ounce load carried by the 3-inch 20-gauge fodder.

Because 12-gauge loads throw more shot than any others except the big 10-gauge magnum hulls, the 12 is considered the best all-around gauge for all kinds of scattergunning. If the mighty 10-gauge loads, and the massive maulers chambered for them, were lighter, handier and packed less recoil, the 10 would likely be the most popular gauge.

Thus, a properly choked 12-gauge gun is the upland hunter's most effective choice for a wide variety of upland game. It'll do everything a smaller bore will do, and more. For shotgunning, the 12 is never a mistake.

However, 16-gauge guns have their fans, as do the smaller 20, 28 and .410 bores. Most of these guns are lighter and handier than the larger 12's, and they make up in speed and handling ability what they lack in effectiveness.

Lightweight 20-bore doubles are favored by many grouse and quail hunters. Ithaca makes a slide-action 20 that weighs even less than most double guns, and other easy-toting 20-bore guns are available to please the laziest nimrod.

While the small-gauge guns are fast and handy enough to be popular with many sportsmen, another rule should be remembered: the smaller the gauge, the better shot you need to be. An ounce of shot kills the biggest pheasant as long as the range is reasonable, and both 12- and 20-gauge guns deliver this quantity, and more. But when you drop to the ¾-ounce pellet load thrown by the little 28, you're definitely handicapping yourself. Consequently, the 28 should be reserved for experts only when hunting upland game. The tiny .410 (which isn't a true "gauge," but a measure of the bore size in inches) throws only ½ or ¹¹⁄₁₆ ounces of shot, and is far less effective than the 28.

At one time, 1-ounce magnum loads were available for the 28, and Federal made a fine ⅞-ounce 28-gauge hunting load. Apparently too few of these mini-bore powerhouse loads were sold to justify their continued production, and they've since been dropped. More's the pity.

The Best Combinations

What constitutes the best choke, gauge and load combination for upland game? The choice depends on the bird being hunted and the terrain. Sage grouse hunted on the endless sagebrush deserts of the western United States are big birds that typically fly several hundred yards once flushed, and then remain in the landing area until the gunners arrive to have another go at them. The first time a flock is flushed, shots may be offered at very close range, and the action can be furious. Very often a hunter walks into the center of a flock of a dozen to two dozen birds, totally unaware of them until the sky is full of 4- to 8-pound feathered bodies. When the first bird flushes, the rest follow in short order. This can startle an unwary nimrod long enough to let most of the birds get well under way.

As a result, many experienced "sage chicken" hunters like 12-gauge modified- or full-choke guns fed 1¼-ounce loads of 5's or 6's. These tightly choked guns also come in handy late in the day when the birds tend to flush wildly at extreme range.

But for a gunner with fast reflexes, an improved cylinder 12 or 20 bore can be deadly. The first, mass flush can offer several close-range targets, and if you have a light, short-coupled shotgun that throws a wide pattern you can harvest your two- or three-bird daily limit in short order. A 1- or 1⅛-ounce load of 6's or even 7½'s does for this close-in work, but later in the day you should switch to shot one size larger. Some sage hen hunters even use 4's, but 5's and 6's are the all-around favorites. A modified choke is probably the most practical compromise when hunting these desert-dwelling birds.

Pinnated grouse and sharptails are smaller birds, weighing 2 pounds or so. Again, these are found on relatively flat, open land, and the same gauges and chokes used to hunt sage grouse are popular. But shy away from the larger shot sizes—7½'s work fine early in the season, while 6's are the best all-around choice.

Chukar partridge are also found in open country, usually at high elevation. Unfortunately, the "open country" these birds inhabit is seldom flat. Because the chukar-hunting sportsman spends his day literally running up and down mountains (or at least, steep slopes), lightweight scatterguns are definitely favored. Shots can be offered at close range or at discouragingly long distance. The modified choke makes a pretty good compromise, although an improved cylinder/modified-choke double seems the ideal choice. Either a 12- or 20-gauge gun throwing anywhere from 1 to 1¼ ounces of 7½ shot is the preferred medicine.

The widely prized ruffed grouse makes a flitting, hard-to-hit target often found where the cover is thick overhead. An open-choke gun throwing 7½'s or 8's makes a fine choice here. On the other hand, blue grouse and other related forest grouse are typically much less wary. Called the "fool hen" in many parts of the country, both blue and spruce grouse often allow a hunter to approach within a dozen feet—and oftentimes even then refuse to flush unless prodded into the air.

You can't always count on this behavior, though, as these birds smarten up when under any kind of hunting pressure. Once these grouse become man-wary, they may fly from their perches before the hunter is in decent range. Still, an improved cylinder 12- or 20-gauge gun is best, with a modified-choke tube as second choice. I like low-base loads of 6's or 7's for these birds. Where they're not heavily hunted, it's possible to kill them with head shots using a full-choke .410. That's not very sporting, though, and most hunters pass by sitting shots unless they're looking for a change of camp diet.

For hunting pheasants, I choose a load of 6's almost every time, although 7½'s work fine for close-range shooting. Later on in the season when the birds tend to run on ahead or flush wild, 5's make good sense. For early season hunting or over a good dog, light loads from an

Over-under shotguns, with their two different chokes, make fine choices for most upland hunting.

Ithaca ultra-lightweight 20 gauge is a fine dove gun. At 5 pounds or less (depending on wood density), this is the lightest 20-gauge pump on the market.

open choke are the right medicine. A fast-handling 20-gauge improved cylinder/modified-choke double makes a fine choice, and an ounce of shot is plenty. Later on when the roosters are wilder, a modified-choke 12 throwing 1¼ ounces of shot is better. If the birds are really wild and in top running form, a full-choke magnum may not be too much gun.

Doves and pigeons are much smaller birds, and can be very hard to hit. It doesn't take many pellets or large shot to kill them, but you need to put a lot of No. 7½ or 8 shot in the air to have much chance of filling your bag. For water-hole shooting, a cylinder or improved-modified choke works well, but I do most of my dove and pigeon gunning with a modified tube. Lightweight 20 bores are tempting, particularly when hunting dry, dusty desert country on foot. But 12-gauge gunners score with better consistency.

The eastern woodcock, or timberdoodle, is typically hunted in dense cover, and a short-coupled 20 bore throwing a ⅞- or 1-ounce field load of No. 8 or 9 shot works best. Some wood-cock buffs also favor 28-gauge guns. A double-barrel gun in either gauge is ideal, partly because these arms are light, short and handy, and partly because they offer two very fast shots with an instant choice of choke constriction. An improved cylinder/modified-choke model is best, although skeet-choke guns work well, too.

Quail are found in densely wooded, brush-choked areas and in vast, western deserts alike. The desert-dwelling birds (of whatever subspecies) tend to flush at a distance or even tuck their heads down and flee on foot. They require modified- or full-choke guns throwing 1⅛ or 1¼ ounces of 7½'s or 8's.

Their more pastoral cousins are hunted with open-choke guns where the cover warrants and with modified tubes in more open country. A lightweight 20 gauge is a top choice for this work when paired with an ounce of 8's or 9's. In really tight cover, a straight cylinder or skeet choke is recommended.

Since the 16 gauge has long been considered a fine compromise between the 20 and 12, it can be substituted for either. However, the 16 has fallen on hard times and is not nearly as popular as it once was. That fact doesn't reduce its effectiveness, but 16-gauge guns and loads are hard to find in all but a few parts of the country. The advent of the magnum 20, with its 1¼ ounces of shot, has pretty much killed off the "sweet 16."

Turkey Guns 10

I saw my first wild turkeys while honeymooning. No, I didn't take my new bride bird hunting to celebrate our nuptials. We were driving through the Kaibab forest to the Grand Canyon lodge (which, it turned out, had just closed for the season—but that's another story), when I was startled by a band of four large birds that suddenly dashed from the forest and onto the road. I had to brake hard to avoid the little flock, and my equally startled wife asked, "What *are* they?"

"Wild turkeys," I answered, grabbing for the camera I had in the glove compartment. Because I'd read so many accounts of how wily and hard to hunt these birds were, I could hardly believe that four of the dark-colored fowl were now milling about on the far side of the asphalt, just a few yards from the car. If the turkey was all that shy and cunning, these birds were clearly having an off day. They were behaving as stupidly as any pen-reared gobbler, and anyone who's ever visited a turkey ranch knows how moronic *those* birds act!

Surprisingly, the birds hung about until I could locate and extricate my camera, then leap from the car and dash within photo range. The camera had a standard 50mm lens—no telephoto—yet I was able to get close enough to take two or three excellent portraits and one group photo that looked like it'd been posed in an advertising studio before the turkeys finally legged it to the safety of the woods.

That day, my estimation of the wild turkey as a hard-to-hunt game bird took a nose dive. I didn't gain a full appreciation for *Meleagris gallopavo*'s true talents until many years later, when I participated in my first spring gobbler hunt.

Without going into the trials and tribulations I suffered on that first turkey hunt—or my ignominious defeat at the hands (claws?) of an ignoble tom that bamboozled me not once, but twice during the course of the weekend—let me just say that my estimation of the bird's wariness and intelligence took several mighty leaps upward. Maybe those first turkeys I encountered were simply vain enough to stand around posing when anyone produced a camera.

If anything, my esteem for these magnificent trophy birds has continued to grow. For trophy birds they are, in the truest sense. Anyone who outwits a wily tom in the bird's own territory deserves a few minutes of quiet pride, or even an hour or two of unselfconscious boasting at the end of the day, when there's an audience of unsuccessful nimrods to entertain.

To hunt wild turkeys successfully, you must learn the big birds' behavior patterns. You must know when a tom is thinking about sex, breakfast or a place to nap, and have a pretty good idea of where he'll head for each activity.

Entire books have been written about turkey hunting tactics, so I'll not attempt to make a turkey hunter of you here. But I will tell you the kind of armament most gobbler-seeking nimrods tote afield.

Handguns

First, let me acknowledge that turkeys can be taken with a handgun. Just about any decent centerfire cartridge will do the job, although I'd favor a flat-shooting round like the .357 magnum over others. A .38 Special would also be a good choice, and it tends to destroy less tender flesh. That's assuming a revolver is used.

A .45 ACP or .38 Super auto pistol would also put a turkey down, if properly placed. Loads like the .380 and .32 ACP are on the light side; moreover, the guns chambered for these numbers are usually designed more for concealment than top accuracy. And the one thing you must have in a turkey pistol is accuracy. Only the top-grade target pistols can be relied on to place their shots accurately enough for this exacting sport.

If a good, scope-sighted single-shot pistol such as the Thompson/Center Contender or Sterling X-Caliber gets the nod, the .22 Hornet, .221 Fire Ball, .222 Remington, and .223 or .256 Winchester would all be excellent cartridges for turkey hunting. If I were going to use a handgun to hunt turkeys, this would be the way I'd go. You're not apt to get more than one shot at a turkey anyway unless you're toting a shotgun, and these one-shooter handguns offer top precision. Speaking from personal experience, it's going to be a few years yet before I have enough confidence in my turkey hunting abilities to tote a handgun, rather than a rifle or shotgun, into the woods. These birds come tough enough without imposing additional handicaps on myself.

Handgunners are successful on turkey hunts every year, and my hat's off to them. Maybe in a couple of more years...

Rifles

The cartridges I've listed for handgun use (at least where the Contender is concerned) are nearly identical to the choices most riflemen make when headed for the turkey woods. Some sharpshooters rely on the .22 WMRF (rimfire magnum), but most sportsmen who favor rifles over shotguns opt for one of the .22 centerfires: the .22 Hornet, .222 Remington, .222 Remington Magnum or .223 Remington. Faster-stepping numbers like the .220 Swift and .22-250 are generally avoided, as they cause excessive damage and destroy fair amounts of turkey meat.

The wary wild turkey is a true trophy bird. (Photo by Leonard Lee Rue III.)

Some riflemen also use reduced loads in such cartridges as the .250 Savage, .257 Roberts and even the .270 Winchester and .30-06. Cast-lead bullets are sometimes employed.

Any turkey rifle should be scoped, although the magnification needn't be excessive. A 2½X or 4X glass is a good choice, and 6X is almost more than enough. Turkeys aren't shot at long range, even with a rifle, and a scope with too much magnification only makes it more difficult to find the bird in the reticle.

Rifle and scope combinations should be sighted in to print dead on point of aim at 50 yards, and the hunter should then shoot some groups at both shorter and longer ranges to

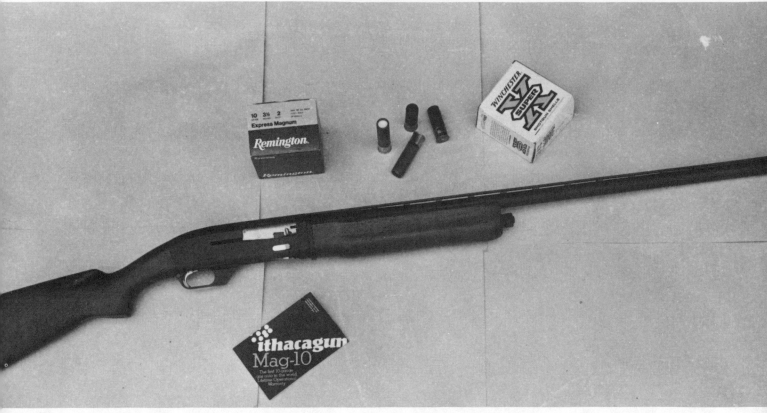

Ithaca's Mag-10 10-gauge autoloader is a potent gobbler getter, although it's 11½-pound weight is formidable.

see how far above and below the crosshairs the bullet prints at those distances. The reason this kind of care is needed to insure pinpoint accuracy is because an experienced hunter doesn't shoot at the entire bird. Instead, he concentrates on the small area where the neck joins the body. An accurately placed bullet here kills quickly, yet damages little edible meat.

You hear of some old-timers who "shoot for the head" (or even "aim for the eye"). That's all well and good, but I'm here to tell you a turkey's head is an awfully small mark. To make matters worse, it's the first thing that moves whenever the bird decides to take another step. Just watch a barnyard turkey, or even a chicken, move. When any significant motion occurs, the head first juts forward (and up or down) jerkily. Then the feet move, and finally the body follows.

Shooting for a turkey's head is a very sporting tactic. When you connect, the bird dies instantly. And if you miss, chances are the bird escapes scot free and unharmed. Me, I'll aim for the juncture of body and neck. Every time.

Rifles are usually used when a hunter expects to see his tom at some distance, and that means anything over 35 or 40 yards. Most shotgunners like to shoot their turkeys in close, as these hardy birds take a fair amount of killing to keep them down. At the same time, shots at extreme range should be avoided. Most consider 100 yards to be a long shot, even with an accurate rifle you're sure of.

The expanding bullets used in most .22 centerfire loads can be destructive, but if you shoot for the lower part of the neck you won't waste much meat.

Shotguns

Most turkey hunters use shotguns to bag their prey. Any gun of 20 gauge or larger will kill turkeys, but magnum loads of largish shot should be used exclusively when the bird is on the wing. As I've said before, a big tom is a tough, hardy bird and can pack a lot of lead.

But again, many sportsmen do their best to shoot while the bird is still on the ground. This is *not* considered unsporting; it's a real challenge to lure a wary tom within decent range.

If the bird can be lured close enough for a deliberate head shot, 4's or 6's make a good choice. Again, you don't necessarily shoot for the head, but rather for the head-neck area. If you're lucky—and your pattern performs as it should—you should nearly decapitate the bird if a heavy load of 6's is used and the range is right.

Because large, experienced toms aren't often fooled into too-close range, many gunners favor 4's for the first shot and follow that first load with BB's or 2's in the magazine. If the bird is missed, or manages to get skyborne, the heavier shot can be counted on to put him down.

Tightly choked guns are favored, and while some nimrods do tote 16's and 20's into the turkey woods, most experienced hunters prefer 12-gauge guns. Magnum loads are also favored, as the more shot a gunner can throw at one of these large birds, the better.

For this reason, the 10-gauge magnum has earned a lot of turkey-hunting fans. Perhaps the favorite 10 bore is Ithaca's autoloading Mag-10, which digests the largest magnum loads without nearly the fuss other 10-gauge guns put up. Many have called the Mag-10 the "turkey hunting gun supreme," although its 11½-pound weight makes it less than a delight to lug very far.

Still another type of gun popular among some turkey hunters is the double-barrel combination gun featuring a .22 rimfire magnum or .222 Remington rifle barrel atop a 12- or 20-gauge shotgun tube. Savage offers rifle and scattergun combinations, as does the Finnish firm of Valmet. These are available with various combinations, although the various Savage guns are available with a 20-gauge shotgun tube only. The Savage model 24-V, with either a .22 Hornet or .222 Remington rifle barrel and a 3-inch magnum 20-gauge tube, is perhaps the best domestic combination turkey gun available.

The more expensive Valmet model 412KE features a more potent 12-gauge shotgun barrel, in combination with a .222, .223, .243, .308 or .30-06 rifle tube. Either of the .22 centerfires makes this a premier turkey gun. Other imported combination guns are available, but they're relatively expensive items.

Savage Model 24-V, with its .22 centerfire rifle barrel atop a 20-gauge shotgun tube, makes a fine turkey gun for those who want to take long and short shots.

Camouflage for Turkey Hunting

Regardless of the turkey gun you choose, you'll likely want to apply some form of camouflage before you head for the woods. Turkeys can recognize colors (unlike deer and some other animals, who are more or less color blind), and have notoriously sharp eyesight. Accordingly, any turkey hunter desirous of success must do something to hide both himself and his armament.

Some dedicated nimrods go so far as to paint their pet turkey guns dead-flat green, or in a camouflage pattern. The oil-based paints they use are permanent (water-based pigments wash off in the rain), and unless the guns are extensively refinished later, they remain mud-ugly from that point on. But they're beautiful to the turkey hunters who own them.

A less drastic course is to use removable camouflage tape. This is the same stuff bow-hunters use, and it comes off without damage to the gun's finish if you don't leave the tape on too long. If the tape is allowed to cure, it becomes tough to remove and may take a bit of finish along with it. But if the tape is removed at the end of the hunt, you should have no problems.

Camouflage waxes or stick-paint can also be used, and these wipe right off. The same stuff is used on the hunter's face, neck and hands. Camouflage "gun socks" are available, too.

Of course, once you've gone to all that trouble to camouflage your gun, *you* deserve the same kind of treatment. It's all part of the game, and if you chance into a turkey hunter who *looks* like a hunter strolling through the woods, chances are he won't be toting a trophy tom. If he looks like a bush, a tree or a rotting stump, he's likely to be successful.

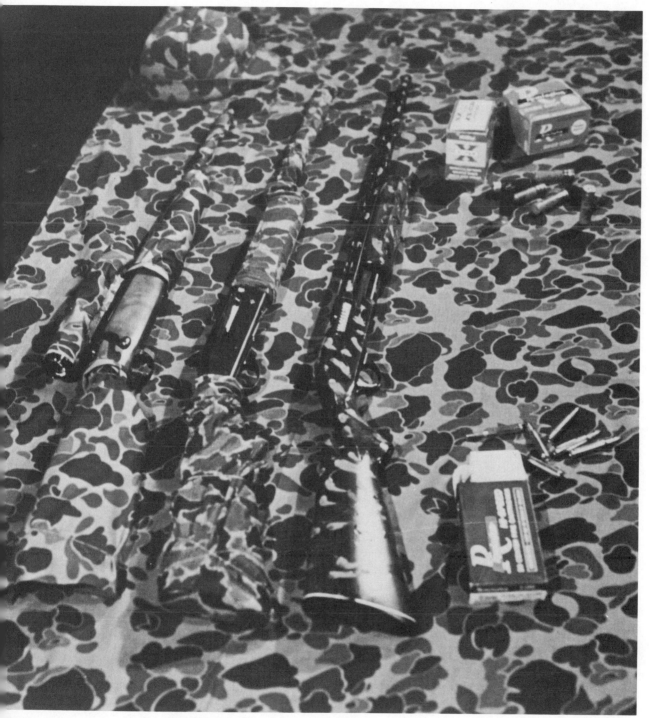

Turkey guns can be camouflaged with patterned covers or paint (don't use permanent pigments).

Gauges and Loads for Hunting Ducks **11**

For several decades the 12-gauge, full-choke pump or autoloader was widely regarded as the only sensible choice for hunting ducks. These waterfowling guns wore elongated 30- or 32-inch barrels, and were invariably fed heavy 1¼-ounce (or heavier) express loads of 4's or 5's.

Not everyone doted on long barrels and tight chokes, but that was surely the most popular choice in the duck blind. Even today, this same combination is a heavy favorite among waterfowlers. And there are times and places when a Long Tom 12 throwing a dense, tight pattern is called for. Ocean-going ducks attracted to rafted decoys are often shot at long range, and a full-choke magnum 12 is exactly what the smart gunner wants for these situations.

A full-choke tube might also be justified on those cloudless "bluebird" days when the few shots that may be offered come out past the 40-yard mark. Pass shooters need long-range guns and loads, too. I once shot pintails from a pass-shooting blind along the Snake River. This unusual blind was located high on the side of a gorge overlooking the river, and you shot *down* at the ducks as they passed upriver beneath you. That day provided an unforgettable lesson in the amount of lead necessary to stop a fast-flying duck at long range. You could easily see where the shot pattern splashed into the water—almost always a surprising distance behind the intended target. The ducks were flying only 8 or 10 feet above the waves, and you couldn't have asked for a more graphic, or accurate, picture of lead requirement. Anyone without a full-choke magnum and a good, strong-hearted retriever would only waste his time hunting from that blind.

But the average duck gunner so armed is handicapping himself. Most ducks are shot over decoys from a blind. If the decoys are properly rigged and there's an experienced caller in the blind, incoming birds will be shot at a known distance after their wings are set. That distance is more likely to be this side of the 35-yard mark than farther out, and many mallards perish less than 20 yards from the muzzle.

This means heavy charges of large shot aren't really necessary, and a tight, full choke is the last thing you need for this kind of waterfowling. On days when the ducks were decoying well, I've had excellent luck with both skeet-choke and improved-cylinder–choke guns. I've

Modified-choke 12-gauge pump is a good all-around waterfowl gun and also handles many upland hunting chores.

even killed a number of fat greenheads and more than a few teal with a little 28-gauge skeet gun under such conditions. Not that the 28 deserves serious consideration as a duck gun—it doesn't, particularly with the ¾-ounce factory loads that are the heaviest available today. But any halfway decent shot is reasonably well armed with a 20 gauge, particularly if it's fed 1⅛-ounce magnum loads. Even an ounce of shot kills ducks out to 30 or 35 yards.

While a surprising number of ducks are shot close to the gun, a skeet- or improved-cylinder choke is hardly ideal for the long shots that are invariably offered during a day of waterfowling. Even when the birds do try to land in the decoys, you need a tighter pattern than an improved-cylinder choke provides if you're trying for a double. Once that first round is fired, incoming puddle ducks exhibit a remarkable aptitude for executing that classic maneuver known as "getting the hell out of there." They can gain 10 yards of altitude almost immediately when they flare, and it takes only a few frantic wingbeats to carry them safely out of range. The gunner who wants a second chance needs to be fast on the trigger and throw a shot pattern with a fair amount of reach.

Shooting Decoyed Ducks

Perhaps the ideal firearm for shooting decoyed ducks is a twin-tube 12 or 20 gauge, choked improved cylinder and modified. Since most 20-gauge side-by-side and stackbarrel guns made today come with 3-inch chambers and handle 1¼-ounce magnum loads, they give up little to the standard 12 in terms of range or pattern density. Most 12-gauge guns, however, produce slightly better patterns, with the pellets more evenly distributed, than do 20-gauge scatterguns throwing the same amount of shot. This is because the 12's larger bore size allows for a shorter shot column, so fewer pellets come in direct contact with the bore. This, in turn, creates fewer flat-sided shot pellets, and leaves more perfectly spherical shot to fly straight and true.

The 20 isn't equal to the 12 in yet another important area—steel shot. In many parts of the country, waterfowlers must use steel (actually, soft-iron) shot exclusively, although regulations are anything but uniform across the United States and have a way of changing, sometimes radically, from year to year. As a result, a duck hunter in one locality may be forced to fire steel shot exclusively, while a gunner in a neighboring marsh is free to use either steel or lead pellets at his discretion. A waterfowling ban against traditional lead shot may be statewide, enforced on a strictly local, marsh-by-marsh basis, or nonexistent—all depending on the area and the legislative mood at the time.

One fact remains clear: steel shot seems to be here to stay, and it's something waterfowlers are going to have to live with. If you must use steel-shot loads for hunting ducks, a 12 gauge is the only logical choice because the only 20-gauge steel-shot load currently available consists of an even ounce of 4's stuffed into a 3-inch magnum case. Twelve-gauge loads are available in 1⅛-, 1¼- and 1⅜-ounce weights, in BB size or No's. 1, 2 and 4.

The fact that a 3-inch 20-gauge magnum load carries only an ounce of steel shot doesn't mean you're sacrificing much in pattern density over the 1⅛- and 1¼-ounce 20-gauge mag-

An over-under 20 gauge was used to collect these winter mallards.

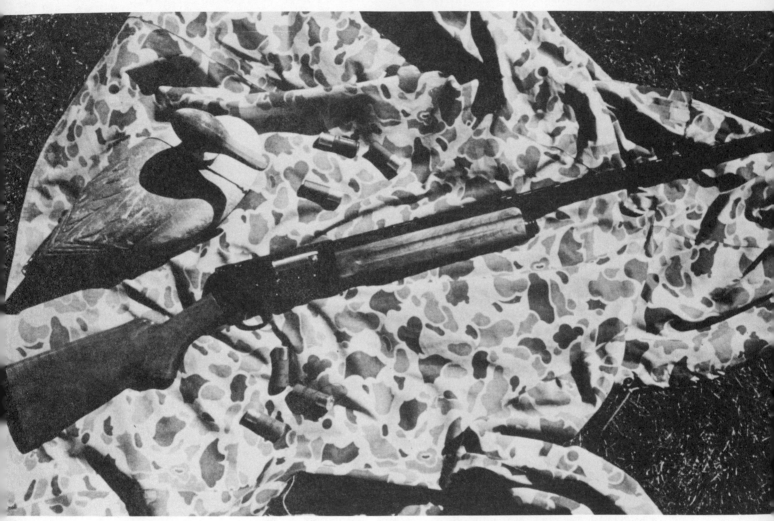

Classic Auto-5 Browning was the first successful autoloading shotgun, and it is still in production.

num lead-pellet loads. Since steel shot is lighter than lead, it contains more pellets per ounce. For instance, an ounce of lead 4's gives you 135 pellets, while the same weight of steel 4's has 192. But this same ratio holds true with 12-gauge loads, which means the gunner with a 20 gauge labors under a real handicap when steel pellets are used.

All things considered, the 12 gauge remains the number one choice of duck hunters, and rightly so. The magnum 20 will give a non-magnum 12 a run for the money when steel shot

isn't required, but even then the 12 offers greater versatility. All you need do to increase the effective range and killing power of a 12 is to slip a 2¾-inch magnum into the chamber. The baby magnum 12 throws 1½ ounces of (lead) shot, fully 20 percent more than the 3-inch magnum 20 carries. And if your 12 has 3-inch chambers, you have a full 1⅞ ounces at your disposal.

Ten-gauge guns throw even more shot, but they're a lot heavier and bulkier. These big-bore behemoths are reserved for goose and turkey hunters and are most popular with the pass-shooting set. A few duck hunters I know used 10's at one time, but most of these have since switched back to 12's. An 11½-pound 10-gauge autoloader quickly becomes tiresome when you're slogging through the marsh burdened with decoys, Thermos bottles and folding stools. It's more gun than you really need for bagging ducks.

Which Type of Shotgun?

As far as gun type is concerned, an over-under or side-by-side double gives you the advantage of two different degrees of choke to choose from. The ideal combination for hunting over decoys (*good* decoys set not too far out on the water) would be an improved cylinder/modified-choke stackbarrel 12. A side-by-side double would work as well, but the single sighting plane of the over-under barrel arrangement makes long-range marksmanship easier. For hunting mallards, pintail and teal, I load the more open barrel with a 1¼-ounce express load of 6's. The modified tube gets a 1¼-ounce or 1½-ounce baby magnum load of 4's or 5's to reach out and drop escaping ducks.

There's been some concern about using steel shot in double-barrel guns, and the concern is legitimate where older guns are concerned. Some fine, European doubles have been damaged by steel shot, and even some autoloader and pumpgun tubes have reportedly been "ringed" by the hard, metal pellets. This damage is only superficial, as the barrels aren't seriously weakened. But the cosmetic appearance is certainly harmed by any rings or bulges that may appear.

In modern doubles featuring harder steel and chromed bores, there's little likelihood of such damage. I've fired steel loads through a Ruger over and under, and it digested them just fine. Any American shotgun manufactured after the early 1970's should handle steel shot without problems. On older guns with softer barrels and relatively abrupt choke configurations, the possibility of cosmetic damage does exist, particularly with full-choke guns. Most manufacturers have made the choke configurations in their guns more gradual in recent years, eliminating one potential trouble source when steel shot is used.

While a twin-tube gun offers two different degrees of choke, single-barrel magazine guns have their advantages, too. Even when plugged to conform to federal migratory birdshooting regulations, pumps and autoloaders offer a trio of shots before reloading is necessary. Sometimes it takes that third load to bring down that second mallard before it dodges out of range. Too, a magazine gun is often easier to reload in the cramped confines of a duck blind. The barrels of an over-under shotgun strike a long arc when the action is broken, but you

Ducks coming in! Slide-action gun with 3 shots available gives hunter an edge.

can thumb shells into an under-the-barrel tubular magazine while holding the gun in the "ready" position.

Autoloaders have a particular advantage over the other shotgun types available. Either a modern gas-operated or classic recoil-operated self-loader generates less apparent recoil than a fixed-breech pump or double. Actually, your shoulder receives the same amount of force, but it's spread over a longer duration as the action cycles. This is felt as more of a push than a sharp jolt, and the sensation is much less punishing.

Since duck guns are often fed heavy express or magnum loads, the autoloader makes a lot of sense. The gunner goes home a lot less battered at the end of the day, and he's less likely to develop a bird-saving flinch. Today's auto shotguns are highly reliable and make fine choices for waterfowling.

Trombone guns are also highly favored. They offer absolute reliability under terrible weather conditions, and a practiced operator can get aimed repeat shots away as rapidly as any autoloader owner can trigger them off. Purists will be quick to point out that you don't really "aim" a shotgun, but point it ahead of the moving target and keep it swinging until well after the shot load is on its way. The point I'm trying to make is that a good pumpgun man can knock as many ducks out of the sky in the same amount of time as an autoloading fan can. Another point in their favor is that pumpguns are relatively inexpensive, almost always costing less than a good stackbarrel or self-loader.

With either of the magazine guns mentioned, only one degree of choke is available unless you tote extra, interchangeable barrels along to the marsh or attach a variable choke device. If I had to rely on a single choke setting for all my duck gunning, I'd unhesitatingly choose "modified." A good modified choke throwing honest 45 to 55 percent patterns (and not the 65 to 70 percent concentrations some ammo may produce) works well for reasonably close targets, as well as for ducks who manage to put some distance between themselves and the hunter before the gun goes off. It makes a fine compromise choice where one is needed.

Loads, Shot Size and Barrel Length

Choice of load and shot size depends on the size of the game and the conditions. I've often used 1⅛-ounce field loads of 7½'s to take teal and even larger puddle ducks, as long as I knew the range wouldn't be excessive. Nothing smaller is recommended.

For most duck gunners, 5's and 6's are the all-around standard, while 4's are generally favored for long-distance shooting. If the range is going to be on the extended side, magnum loads are recommended to give you the necessary pattern density with this largish shot.

That's actually all a magnum load does for the shooter—it puts more shot in the air to keep the pattern deadly at longer ranges. The shot doesn't fly any harder or farther, there's just more of it to work with.

By the same token, Long Tom 30-, 32- and even 36-inch tubes don't materially improve velocity or range. I once took a 36-inch 12-gauge barrel and periodically amputated 2-inch

Both gas-operated and recoil-operated autoloaders help reduce the effect of recoil, making them top choices when magnum loads are used.

chunks until the tube was only half that length. I fired several different factory loads through this barrel at each step and measured the velocities produced with a chronograph. When the test was completed, the results showed less variation between the full yard-long tube and the stubby 18-inch barrel than I have experienced between consecutive factory rounds from the same box of ammo.

Long barrels do give a gun a muzzle-heavy feel, and some waterfowlers like this. They claim it helps smooth the swing and improve their scores on passing ducks and geese. Many also feel a long sighting tube helps in tracking a passing, high-flying target.

Short-barrel fans like the fast-handling characteristics such guns provide. A side-by-side double or stackbarrel firearm with 26- or even 28-inch tubes is particularly lively in the hands, since there's no reciprocating action to extend the gun's overall length.

Barrel length is really a matter of personal choice. If you have a deliberate, point-out-and-swing shooting style, a long barrel may be best for you. Instinctive snap-shooters almost invariably prefer their guns on the stubby side.

Regardless of which gauge, choke constriction and barrel length you choose, don't count on making any 50-plus-yard kills with steel shot. I've already pointed out that steel shot pellets are lighter than their lead twins, which means you get more to the ounce. It also means that the steel spheres lose velocity faster, and that reduces long-range performance.

To partly compensate for this fact, most ammo makers recommend the use of a size larger steel shot than you'd normally employ when lead shot is being thrown. Thus a typically long-range lead-shot magnum 12 load would consist of 1½ ounces of 4's. Its steel equivalent would be 1¼ ounces of No. 2 shot.

If conventional lead 2's are preferred, go to 1's when steel shot becomes necessary. (There are no "No. 1" size lead pellets, incidentally—that's a designation reserved for steel shot only.)

Guns for Geese, Swans and Cranes 12

Geese

It was a sunless, cloud-banked morning. Fresh snow had fallen during the night, turning each desert sagebrush into a miniature Christmas tree. In spite of the low overcast, hoarfrost studded my gun's barrel and my fingers and toes were numb with aching cold.

I was observing my annual pilgrimage to Utah's Uba reservoir to once again sample the unique goose gunning the area offers. The reservoir is located in desert country, but some vast dryland farms are nearby. The combination of food and daytime sanctuary seems irresistible to the large flocks of geese who pause to feed and rest at Uba during their migration south.

The geese typically fly out of the reservoir well before dawn to breakfast on beckoning corn and wheat. They return soon after first light, flying straight to the center of the impoundment, where they set down for a day of rest and contemplation. The swimming birds never venture within a quarter-mile of shore, and they're perfectly safe from two-legged and four-legged predators alike.

The only time they're vulnerable is when they're flying in from their morning meal. If weather conditions are right — foggy, snowy or well overcast — the big Canadas fly in right on the deck, sometimes barely 20 feet above the rolling sage. Their flight path usually takes them over a low hill that's about 150 yards long. If you can position yourself in the right spot on that hill, you're a cinch to get some shooting.

Once the geese begin coming in, birds are in the air for 20 to 30 minutes before the last stragglers set down. Rather than flying in one large flock, the geese appear in small flights of 12 to 18 birds, four or five minutes apart. These groups seldom cross the ridge in the same spot, so smart hunters simply stay put rather than leap-frogging to new positions every time a flight passes by out of range.

This is pass shooting at its finest. When the geese cooperate by flying low, long-range magnums aren't really needed. Sometimes the big, regal birds seem to fly right down your shotgun's muzzle, and you have the feeling you could swing the gun by the barrel and bat

Marlin Super Goose (*left*) and Ithaca Mag-10 are two American-made goose guns throwing the maximum amount of shot skyward towards high-flying honkers.

Magnum-toting goose hunter prepares a pit blind.

them out of the sky. Appearances are deceptive, though, and the wide-open terrain plays tricks on eager gunners. You can see the geese coming from a long way off, and by the time the garrulous birds have flapped and gabbled their way to within 100 yards of a hunter's hiding place the poor guy is in such a state that he's sure they're right on top of him. Many a red-faced nimrod has opened his barrage while the approaching geese were still well out of range. The birds do try your patience, and it takes an experienced hand to still the trigger finger until the honkers are almost directly overhead.

Of course, a gunner on any pass-shooting line must be prepared to reach out and kill birds at extreme range. If you're lucky, you have some close-in shots—but never count on it. Particularly with big Canada geese, you need a gun with plenty of long-distance punch.

I'd been at Uba many times before and knew that the geese sometimes didn't follow the script. If the weather is a touch too good, the birds may fly at oxygen-mask levels until reaching the center of the lake, then spiral down to a perfectly safe landing. Even on a snowy, wind-swept day the black-eyed honkers may maintain 40 or 50 yards of altitude as they pass overhead.

This time, I was ready for them. I was armed with a full-choke Ithaca Mag-10, loaded with big 3½-inch magnums throwing a full 2 ounces of No. 2 shot. The pellets were buffered with a granulated plastic filler to minimize shot damage and maximize performance.

The big Ithaca autoloader is the ultimate in pass-shooting guns for several reasons. In the first place, any 10-gauge scattergun has an advantage over its smaller-bore competition simply because it's capable of putting more shot in the air. That's particularly important where large-shot pellets are used, as pattern density is needed to kill birds reliably, regardless of shot size. The more shot you can get airborne, the greater the effective range.

Unfortunately, most 10-gauge guns produce fearsome recoil, and only a few hardy souls can hit anything with them. The average weekend waterfowler finds himself yanking on the trigger in an eyes-shut grimace after the first few shots. Shooting maximum loads in a magnum 10 isn't an experience that grows on a person. Recoil is even aggravated in some imported doubles featuring excessive stock drop and too-sharp combs. Only a four-star masochist would enjoy shooting one of these bone-crushing behemoths.

But the Ithaca Mag-10 is a real exception. Its gas-fired action soaks up recoil like a wet sponge, and anyone who doesn't mind the moderate recoil produced by a 12-gauge pump shooting high-base 1¼-ounce loads will find the Ithaca self-loader very much to his (or her) liking. I've fired a number of 10-gauge magnums in my time, and the Mag-10 is the only one I'd consider using on a regular basis. That statement isn't intended as an advertisement for Ithaca, but until some other manufacturer decides to produce a 10-gauge autoloader, the Mag-10 is the only real choice available to bigbore buffs who don't appreciate punishment.

My selection of No. 2 shot was something of a compromise. For close-range work, I prefer the better coverage 4's provide, and find that the .13-inch-diameter pellets offer adequate penetration. But for extreme-distance gunning, BB-size shot gets the nod. Out around the 50-yard mark, it takes a big pellet to have enough momentum to punch through a goose's feathered armor and bring him down. The pattern density with BB's gives less than 40 percent of the coverage provided by 4's—but each leaden sphere packs a lot more punch.

Camouflaged goose hunter's hands are all that show in this carefully prepared hide.

By going with 2's, I was effectively hedging my bets. These pellets, sized midway between BB's and 4's, work great on geese at any range. They're not quite as effective on large-bodied birds as BB's are at extended range, and they don't offer the pattern density 4's provide. But when you're not sure how the honkers are going to behave, 2's are your best possible bet.

Since steel shot isn't required at Uba dam, I was pretty sure I could reach out to 55 or even 60 yards, if need be. That's a long shot with any scattergun, and one I wouldn't even attempt with less than a magnum-loaded 10. But long-range shooting is what the 10 gauge is designed for, and the big Federal factory loads had proven their worth at extended distances several times in the past. Unfortunately, hitting a fast-moving target (and a Canada goose is fast,

Goose hunter takes a practice swing with Browning A-5 magnum autoloader before geese arrive. Long barrel helps steady swing but does not make shot fly any harder.

even though he may look like he's loafing along) half a football-field-length from the muzzle is a tough proposition. Even a top wingshot needs more than a little luck going for him past the 40-yard mark.

Hopefully, the birds would pass close enough to obviate the need for *too* much luck. Geese are easy to miss even 30 yards out, but these misses can be attributed simply to poor marksmanship, rattled nerves, the sun in your eyes or whatever decent excuse you can manufacture. Luck can't be counted as a factor when the range is right, unless you want to call those bulletproof honkers that somehow escape your barrage "lucky sons-of-birds."

While a 10-gauge magnum is comforting to have on hand when the geese fly high, you can almost equal its performance with a magnum 12 shooting 3-inch loads. Almost—but not quite. While a 3½-inch magnum 10 loaded to max by the ammo factory pushes an even 2 ounces of lead out the barrel, 3-inch 12-gauge magnums are available loaded with 1⅞ ounces of shot. That means a stretched-12 mag offers nearly 94 percent of the big 10's capacity.

Considering that magnum 12 ammo costs but ⅗ as much as the big 10 loads, the 12 gauge looks awfully good on a dollars-against-performance comparison. Too, a wide variety of 12-gauge magnums are on the market, and most of these are a sight less costly than the only 10-gauge gun I'd ever seriously consider.

Incidentally, anyone considering the purchase of a 12-gauge magnum would do well to think hard about buying an autoloading model in preference to other action types. The same principle that leads me to like the Mag-10 gas gun applies—any auto shotgun is softer on the shoulder than a fixed-breech gun of like size and weight, shooting the same ammunition. And when the ammunition in question is going to be 3-inch magnums, autoloaders look increasingly attractive.

I've used a number of 12-gauge pumps chambered for 3-inch hulls, and liked them—but *not* when they were fed 3-inch magnum loads. One of the nice things about a trombone gun so chambered is that it digests *all* 12-gauge loads interchangeably and without adjustment. The long-chamber magnum autos work fine as long as either 3-inch or 2¾-inch "baby" magnums are fed to it. But try to shoot standard target, field or even 1¼-ounce express loads, and the gun simply fails to feed the next shot into the chamber. In a modern self-loader, the gas that cycles the action is carefully metered through a pair of ports in the barrel, and the gun is designed to function well through a certain range of pressures. Magnum models typically siphon less combustion gas into their operating cylinders, which serves to reduce magnum pressures. When a less robust non-magnum load is fired, there's just not enough pressure available to squeak through the smaller ports and get the job done.

With a slide-action shotgun, the bolt is cycled manually and without regard for pressures within the bore. Thus, a 3-inch-chamber pump functions fine with any and all 12-gauge loads.

Geese—out of range now, but decoys may lure them closer.

Large decoy spread like this should lure geese within good gunning range. Still, heavy magnum 12- or 10-gauge loads are recommended, and so is full choke.

Cornfield goose hunter camouflages barrel with husk-colored masking tape.

Guns for Geese, Swans and Cranes

Winter goose hunter wears snow camouflage and has taped gun barrel to help hide it.

That's a splendid feature to have available when you intend to use the same gun for a wide variety of hunting chores. The average one-shotgun hunter spends a lot more time in the upland game fields or the duck blind than he does hunting geese, and chances are the stray honker or two he drops every year were harvested while sitting over mallard decoys. It's comforting to keep a few 3-inch magnums stuffed with 2's or 4's on hand when hunting ducks. You never know when a lonesome goose may drift past, and those 6's in your pump may not drop a big Canada with authority.

While I've never hunted geese with such diminutive shot, I know a couple of nimrods who do. They're usually successful, too, and that's including the guy who stuffs 1¼-ounce loads of 7½'s in his modified-choke 12. These men specialize in calling the big birds right in on top of them, and then shoot for the outstretched head!

I should point out that these scattergun artists carefully avoid body-shooting their birds, and never pull the trigger unless the target is well within range. Needless to say, their carefully constructed decoy spreads are flawless, and their calling is superb. The geese that fall to them are more victims of artistic mimicry than of gunning skills.

Most experts agree that 4's are the smallest lead pellets that should be used for gunning geese. As I've already pointed out, 4's are best when the targets are likely to appear within reasonable range, say 25 to 35 yards. Beyond that distance, larger shot is needed to penetrate the feather-and-fat armor a big gander wears. Some favor 2's for the denser patterns they provide, while many pass-shooting pros swear by BB-size pellets.

Where steel (soft-iron) shot is required, move up to the next larger size, 2's for close work, BB's or 1's for the long-distance stuff. And don't stretch the range too far when shooting these harder, lighter projectiles.

As far as choke is concerned, either full choke or modified choke will do. Today's cup-protected shot often gives tighter-than-advertised performance, and many modified-choke magnums deliver honest "full" patterns.

Actually, anytime you try to down any flying game at ranges much farther than 40 or 45 yards, the odds begin stacking against you. Not only must you allow proper lead and follow through after the trigger is pulled, but you also need to shoot high to allow for drop at that range. This isn't something a gunner consciously does, so the shot pattern doesn't fall significantly at any truly lethal range. But it remains a factor in the killing equation.

Wind drift, on the other hand, can be significant, particularly at long range. Tests have shown that a load of lead 4's moves approximately 10 inches at 40 yards when buffeted by a 15-mile-per-hour crosswind. At 60 yards, that same crosswind drifts the pattern nearly 2 feet to one side. Smaller shot sizes and steel pellets are affected even more. The same tests showed that 2's and BB-size shot suffer less wind drift, which is yet another reason to stick with relatively large shot for long-range gunning.

Of course, a shot pattern or string is also affected by headwinds and tailwinds, and this is even more likely to cause a miss. This may be a good time to explain that the shot doesn't travel to its target in a tight, little cloud, but is actually strung out over several feet. At 40 yards, the shot string may be from 8 feet to more than 12 feet in length, depending on shot hardness, size and whether or not a buffer of plastic chips or some other medium is used. This means only part of the pattern is likely to hit a fast-moving bird at long range, particularly if the bird hasn't been properly centered by the gunner, but merely "edged."

How does a headwind or tailwind cause misses? Consider a high, oncoming goose laboriously flapping his way upwind. Although his ground speed may appear to be very slow, his air speed is something else again.

What's more, if you shoot with a 20-mile-per-hour wind at your back, that wind could carry the shot string a significant distance behind the bird, even if your lead was otherwise correct. Add these two factors together, and you can see why those frantically flapping geese that seem suspended almost motionless overhead are so easy to miss. Appearances are often deceiving.

Swans

While geese may weigh between 4 and 12 pounds, depending on whether you're hunting snow geese, Canada geese or some other variety, whistling swans are much larger. These stately birds are legal game in several western states, and an adult is likely to tip the scales at 16 pounds or so. The wingspan is an impressive 7 feet.

Swans typically offer long-range targets, so a full- or modified-choke 12- or 10-gauge gun is called for. Magnum loads of BB's or 2's are best for these oversize waterfowl. I've hunted them several times, and can attest that they're tough, hardy birds that require a solid hit with large shot to bring down.

As with all goose-size or larger waterfowl, you should avoid looking at the entire bird as a target, but instead concentrate on the forward third, the head-chest area, of the body. Too many swans and geese have escaped after having their hindquarters peppered by tardy shot. Shooting any gamebird in the fanny is ill advised, but while a duck or pheasant may drop to a load of 4's in the posterior, a goose or swan accorded the same treatment won't miss a beat. If shot up badly enough, the bird may die later or become too stiff and slow to escape predators. These majestic birds deserve a better fate.

Sandhill Cranes

Sandhill cranes weigh from 6 to 16 pounds, depending on variety. The heavier birds (greater sandhill) are protected by law, but the lesser sandhill crane is hunted in several west-central states. The legal lesser bird sports a 5-foot wingspan, and seldom tops 8 pounds or so.

The same armament used in hunting geese is called for here. Full- or modified-choke 12 or 10 gauges work best, and magnum loads help stretch your effective range.

Whistling swans are legal game in some western states. It takes large shot in magnum loads to kill these hardy birds, which weigh about 16 pounds.

The greater sandhill crane is protected by law but the lesser sandhill, rarely topping 8 pounds, is hunted in several west-central states. (Photo by Charles G. Summers, Jr., Leonard Rue Enterprises.)

It's possible to use 16- and 20-gauge guns to kill goose-size waterfowl, but the hunter so armed is greatly handicapping himself. This is particularly true in areas where steel shot is mandatory. The largest steel-shot size currently available in factory 20-gauge loads is No. 4, and that's not the ideal choice for these large birds.

When hunting over decoys, the range is likely to be well this side of 40 yards, and a 16- or 20-gauge gun with heavy express or magnum loads kills geese effectively in such situations. You can't always count on a goose's ready cooperation, though, so it's best to be prepared for less than ideal conditions. That means using bigbore shotguns, large shot and maximum or near-maximum loads. A full-choke barrel isn't always needed—as a matter of fact, large shot such as 2's and BB's often pattern better through a modified tube—but you should be prepared to reach out a ways when geese, swans or cranes are your quarry.

Which Rifle Type For You? 13

A hunter today has no fewer than six basic rifle types to choose from: single shots, autoloaders, bolt-actions, pumps, double rifles or rifle-shotgun combination guns and lever-actions. I lump the double-barrel rifles and combination guns (sometimes called "drillings") into the same general category because they're closely related. Too, both are more popular in Europe than they are in this country, and the average North American nimrod all but ignores multi-barrel rifles.

Which rifle type should you select? When it comes right down to it, this is usually decided by simple, personal taste. Tradition also enters in, and if both Dad and Granddad toted lever rifles in the deer woods, there's a fair chance this preference will be subconsciously passed from father to son. Similarly, if you were taught to shoot with a bolt-action firearm, that's the type you're likely to choose when you go shopping for a big-game rifle.

There's no reason you shouldn't cater to personal taste when building your own rifle battery; when you're laying your own money on the counter there's no reason to please anyone but yourself. Every action type has its proponents. Lever-rifle fans point to the nice balance and the rapid repeat-shot capability their favorites feature, while slide-action addicts are usually familiar with pumpgun handling from their shotgunning days afield. Single-shot owners frankly like the way their sleek rifles look and are more than a little proud of using just a single round to put their game away.

My own personal preference is for stubby, wood-to-the-muzzle-stocked bolt carbines. I can give you any number of excellent (and even semi-scientific) arguments for this predilection, but the honest truth is I simply like the *appearance* of these little rifles. That they're super handy for toting on horseback and in dense cover alike, or that a carbine is the fastest-handling long gun extant, is only window dressing. Short carbines stocked in the classic Mannlicher style attract me in much the same way petite, dark-eyed brunettes do, and I have about the same justification to offer for either choice. Suffice it to say I married a girl of that description, and my gun cabinet has one or two full-stock carbines tucked away inside. No apologies for either will be offered here.

Wood-to-the-muzzle carbines are the author's favorite but may not be what you'd choose. Personal preference plays a large part in selecting a rifle.

Scoped, bolt-action sporter is probably the best all-around choice for taking a wide variety of game in all regions of North America.

The point I'm trying to make is that you should exercise your own taste and preference, and if a self-loader or lever gun suits your style, don't let some self-proclaimed "expert" (myself included) talk you out of it. The fact is, almost every rimfire and centerfire rifle on the American market today is capable of doing a fine job afield. Poor designs simply don't survive long in this highly competitive market.

Some rifles, on the other hand, have been so successful that the design remains basically the same year after year. Certain models—the Savage 99, the Winchester 94, Marlin's 336, the fabled Mauser 98—date back to the last century, yet continue to sell very well. Such designs become known as "classics," and their success is assured in the face of much newer, and sometimes better, designs.

American riflemen are a tradition-minded lot, and most don't take readily to drastic change. Thus, most gunmakers take a conservative approach to adopting new innovations, so the evolution of sporting rifles has been slow and deliberate. This is strongly reflected in the stock materials used in large-scale commercial rifle production. Walnut has long been the wood of choice and is the traditional favorite. Chronic shortages of stock-grade walnut have forced many makers to substitute walnut-stained hardwood on their less costly rifle models, and these have been reasonably well accepted.

However, serious benchrest shooters and a handful of practical-minded hunters have discovered several materials that offer important advantages over wood for stock construction. Bench rifle competitors make common use of fiberglass, aluminum and other modern materials. These offer closer bedding and better stability than wood, and make their rifles shoot better. Nimrods interested in lightweight, yet highly accurate centerfires have also turned to fiberglass and even more exotic materials. Unlike wood, which can absorb moisture, swell and warp as climatic conditions change, fiberglass remains stable and unaffected by changes in temperature or moisture. Because fiberglass can be molded to almost any shape or form, good stock-to-metal fit is fairly easy to attain. A rifle with a fiberglass stock usually weighs significantly less than its wood-stocked twin.

Today, there's sufficient demand for synthetic stocks to keep a handful of custom stockmakers and gunsmiths busy building superlight, highly accurate hunting rifles. Traditionalists, on the other hand, want nothing to do with the homely, dull-finished products.

While you should choose the style and type of rifle that fits your taste, each basic type has its own set of advantages and disadvantages. It pays to be aware of what these are before you make your decision.

Combination Guns

I mentioned that a few sportsmen use double rifles or combination rifle-shotgun firearms. Savage makes an inexpensive rimfire rifle/20-gauge shotgun in a breaktop action that's far and away the most popular gun of its type in use in this country. It gives the small-game and bird hunter the choice of a close-range shotgun pattern or a rifle barrel that kills game out to

Combination rifles (or drillings) featuring both rifle and shotgun tubes are popular in Europe but not in the United States.

Ruger No. 1 single shot (*top*) and Sako bolt rifle (*bottom*) are both well-made, accurate arms available in chamberings for most popular cartridges.

100 yards or so. It's a plinking and small-game gun that's proven very useful, and it's sold in a number of versions.

One problem with the Savage combination is the difficulty in scoping it. An inexpensive scope works fine when shooting the .22 rifle barrel, but shotgun recoil may damage budget-priced optics. A more costly scope can be used, but a magnifying sight is only a hindrance when the smoothbore tube is used.

The centerfire double rifles and drillings now available are both expensive and too heavy to appeal to the average American sportsman. What's more, it's difficult to calibrate two separate barrels to shoot anywhere near the same point of aim, even when a scope is used. They're anything but ideal for precision, long-range marksmanship. Enough said.

Single-Shot Rifles

While most stateside sportsmen consider double rifles impractical, the single-shot centerfire is alive and well in this country. Ruger's strong one-shooters are well-known and sought-after firearms. They're available in a full range of calibers for both large and small game, and they're capable of fine accuracy. Because there's no reciprocating bolt to deal with, the action itself is very short, and this in turn makes the Ruger No. 1 and No. 3 rifles significantly shorter than other rifle types using the same barrel length. Thus, you can have a full-length 26-inch barrel to give you maximum velocities without having a firearm any more unwieldy than a conventional bolt-action rifle with a 22-inch tube.

Single-shot high-powered rifles are capable of fine accuracy; but with no quick follow-up shot possible, the rifleman has to be good—or disappointed.

Savage model 170 .30-30 pump is a quick-shooting, close-range woods rifle. Don't count on it to buck brush, though.

Other pluses include the sometimes not-so-subtle one-upmanship you derive from toting a one-shooter while your companions carry magazine guns afield. In effect, the guy who uses a single-shot hunting rifle is saying, "I can do it with just one shot."

The minuses? Rifles with two-piece stocks can be fussy about bedding tension, but the Ruger mounting system is a good one that requires little pampering. Of course, there's the obvious disadvantage of having no fast backup shot available if the first one fails to go true. Finally, I have experienced one annoyance with my own Ruger No. 1's. While hunting, I habitually carry my rifle slung over my right shoulder. In this muzzle-up position, the rifle has a tendency to hook my jacket pocket with the stubby underlever that operates the action.

As a result, I often find myself carrying the rifle with the action gaping open. Of course the chambered round is lost in the process, leaving the firearm unloaded. I like the Ruger single shots in spite of this tendency. Maybe I'll have to find a pocketless hunting coat.

Other single-shot rifles are on the market, ranging from the budget-priced Harrington & Richardson breaktops to modern replicas of the old Sharps and trap-door Springfields. These latter offerings are chambered for the aging .45-70 and similar rounds. The H&R model 158 hammer rifle can be had with interchangeable rifle and shotgun barrels, incidentally.

Pump Rifles

Only two slide-action centerfire rifles are currently available, the Savage model 170, which is chambered for the .30-30 Winchester and the .35 Remington, and Remington's model Six (and its variations). The Remington pump is chambered for a good selection of modern, high-intensity hunting rounds, ranging from the .243 Winchester up to the .30-06. It gives good hunting accuracy out to 200 yards or so when properly scoped, and provides very rapid fire-power in trained hands.

The pump rifle's weaknesses are that the rotating bolt of the Remington and the action used by Savage provide little camming power to remove recalcitrant cases from their chambers. This means you should avoid hot handloads and take care to see that the chambers are kept clean. The fore end also rattles a bit if you're not careful as you tiptoe through the woods. Long-range accuracy is also lacking.

Rimfire trombone guns are a pleasure to operate. Fast-shucking and plenty accurate enough for .22 range plinking and other chores, the Remington, Rossi and Browning slide actions make fun, practical firearms.

Semi-Automatic Rifles

While self-loading centerfire rifles abound, many of those in current use retain a distinctive paramilitary use most sportsmen prefer to avoid. The Ruger Mini-14 skates along the edge of this, but I think stays safely inside the confines of good taste. This is a .223 Remington carbine more than vaguely reminiscent of the M-1 Garand, and it's a highly popular firearm for short- to medium-range varminting. You see a lot of these little rifles riding in pickup truck gun racks, and ammo makers would probably like to strike Bill Ruger a medal for designing and producing these fast-shooting firearms. Pluses: it's cute, light and handy, and shoots pretty well if the range isn't too long. Typical 100-yard groups run 2¼ to 2½ inches or so.

Minuses: it isn't really accurate enough for shooting small varmints at 200 yards, and it has a habit of chewing through your ammo supply in a hurry if you can't resist the urge to trigger off multiple shots. Too, it throws empty cases clear of the gun, meaning handloaders have to hunt for them.

A number of other more military-looking auto rifles are around, but they're of little use to the average nimrod. The .30 M1 carbine is an example. Like the Ruger Mini-14, it's cute and light, but the .30 carbine ammo is all but worthless for sporting use. Semi-automatic assault rifles deserve no mention here.

Heckler & Koch makes a .308 Winchester self-loader, and both Remington and Browning offer well-developed gas guns chambered for a variety of useful hunting loads. The Browning auto is the only firearm of its type chambered for the potent 7mm Remington Magnum and .300 Winchester Magnum.

These all offer good hunting accuracy at most reasonable ranges, and they make fast shooting possible. In addition, the autoloading actions soak up some recoil, making these centerfires most pleasant to shoot, even with the magnum loads mentioned.

Disadvantages include the fact that these rifles can be fussy regarding the ammo they di-

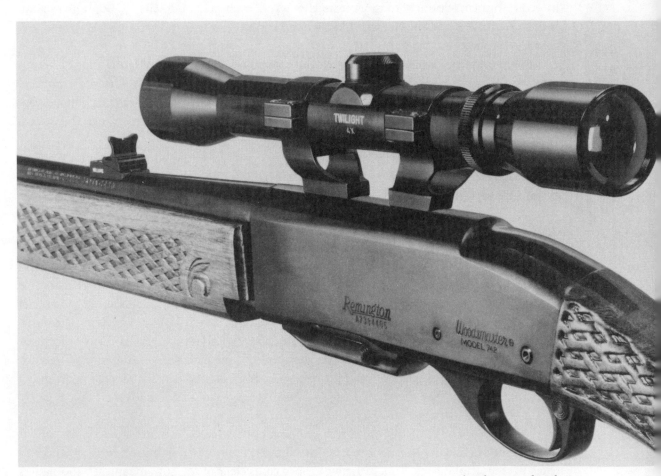

Fast-shooting combination for both close and distant game is the Remington autoloader paired with a 4X Williams scope in low sight-through mount.

Winchester's stubby Trapper model 94 carbine is extremely light and fast-handling. It's chambered for .30-30 Winchester only.

gest. Factory loads rarely cause functioning problems, but hot handloads can be a different story. Because tolerances can be critical, many handloaders use special small-base dies when brewing fodder for an autoloading rifle. And if a case sticks in the chamber, it's sometimes a problem to get it extracted. Until you've succeeded, the rifle stays inoperative.

Pumps or autoloaders work well enough in most states and under most hunting conditions. But for the kind of severe weather Alaska, Canada and the Yukon Territories can serve up at least six months of the year, they may not deliver the desired reliability.

Ruger's .44 magnum autoloader is a fine rifle in the woods and brush. It's short, light and handy, and does a great job within the limitations of its short-range cartridge. That company also makes a look-alike rimfire, the 10/22, which is undoubtedly the most popular .22 auto rifle on the market today.

Speaking of .22's, many autoloading rimfire models are available, and all make fine plinking and small-game rifles. Since .22 rimfire shells aren't reloadable, there's no urge to chase empties. These fast-firing plinkers provide relatively decent accuracy for rimfire shooting, and most models display excellent reliability.

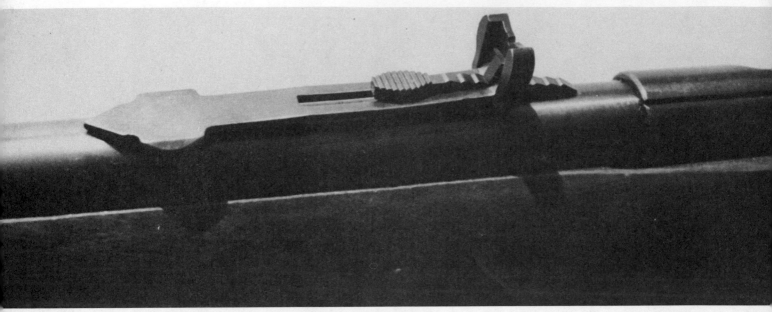

Open sights are fine for short-range lever carbines.

Lever-Action Rifles

Lever rifles are an American favorite. More deer have fallen to .30-30 underlever rifles and carbines than any other firearm and cartridge combination. Lightweight saddle guns in this chambering continue to sell well despite the availability of much better, considerably more modern loads.

The reason the .30-30 lives on in such robust health can be attributed to one thing only—the tremendous continuing popularity of the Winchester and Marlin lever carbines that are made to digest it. These little rifles have a devoted following all out of proportion to their actual utility at this late stage in the twentieth century. There's something almost romantic about the exposed-hammer saddle guns, an image that hasn't been hurt by the countless western movies that have been revived to flicker on home TV screens.

The .30-30 carbine does have a place on today's hunting scene, as these compact little rifles are fast and handy to use. They balance nicely in the hand, and are a delight to carry. The .30-30 is a fair deer round as long as its 150-yard range isn't exceeded, and the lever rifles chambered for it are at their best with open iron sights. While the Marlin lever guns allow top-mounting of a scope, the Winchester carbines do not, but this is academic for close-range woods use.

Marlin makes lever rifles to digest more robust rounds like the bigbore .444 Marlin and the .45-70. These are useful on game larger than deer, but again the range limitations of these cartridges make them relatively short-range propositions. Similar rifles chamber .44 magnum

These revolvers are (from top) single-action Colt, single-action Ruger, double-action Ruger, and double-action Dan Wesson. All are well designed for hunting and are available in appropriate calibers.

Many handgun hunters prefer shoulder holsters, which ride high and out of the way but are easily reached even when heavy clothing is worn. Such holsters are made for every type of sidearm, iron-sighted or scoped. Be sure to choose one that's durable and will keep your gun securely in place.

Compact rangefinder can be useful in many kinds of hunting and can also help a sportsman become more accurate at judging distance, but practice is needed to get consistent readings.

With a braced, two-handed hold, this Ruger .44 Magnum single-action is adequate for deer out to 100 yards, and a long-eye-relief scope could lengthen that range.

This dove hunter shoots a 12-gauge autoloader.
With modified or improved-cylinder choke,
the same gun is fine for a wide variety of upland game.

With plain extractors (rather than ejectors), this
double-barrel shotgun permits empty hulls to be removed
by hand and pocketed for use in reloading.

Waterhole shooting provides steady sport for dove hunters.
Gunner is tracking incoming dove with Superposed Browning.

This Idaho upland hunter uses a Remington autoloader
equipped with a variable choke device that renders
gun versatile enough for everything from chukars to ducks.

Whistling swans are legal game in some Western states. They're also difficult game. Large shot and magnum loads are recommended to bring down these hardy birds.

Late-season hunting is best for snowshoe hares —which make fine eating. Cooperative effort may be needed to get such large hares into the game pocket of your hunting vest.

With a big spread of stick-up decoys, these hunters should lure geese within gun range. Nevertheless, 10- or 12-gauge magnums are recommended, and so is full or modified choke.

Western grouse shooting often means long shots since birds may flush far out. Author likes an over-under with modified and full choke and No. 5 or 6 loads.

For duck shooting over decoy
a 12-gauge gun with modifie
choke is fine. This hunter has connected

Carrying his 12-gauge Ithaca pump gun,
author scurries to fetch mallard
drake. He prefers using a retriever.

Hunting over decoys doesn't
always require a man-made blind.
Cattails like these or bulrushes serve nicely.

Labrador retriever brings pheasant to hand for
Lois Zumbo, wife of well-known outdoor writer
Jim Zumbo. Her shotgun is a 12-gauge
over-under with improved and modified chokes.

Coyotes are generally regarded as rifleman's
quarry, but skillful calling can lure
them into shotgun range. This one was taken
with a 12-gauge load of buckshot.

This handsome cock pheasant was bagged with
12-gauge over-under firing No. 6 handloads.

and .357 magnum handgun rounds. The .44 is suitable for woods use on deer, while the .357 magnum is better left to smaller game.

The disadvantages of these lever rifles are primarily due to the cartridges they're chambered for. They're fine out to 150 yards or so, but beyond that distance they're outclassed by other firearm and load combinations.

Browning's modern BLR and the Savage model 99 are a pair of lever offerings much bet-

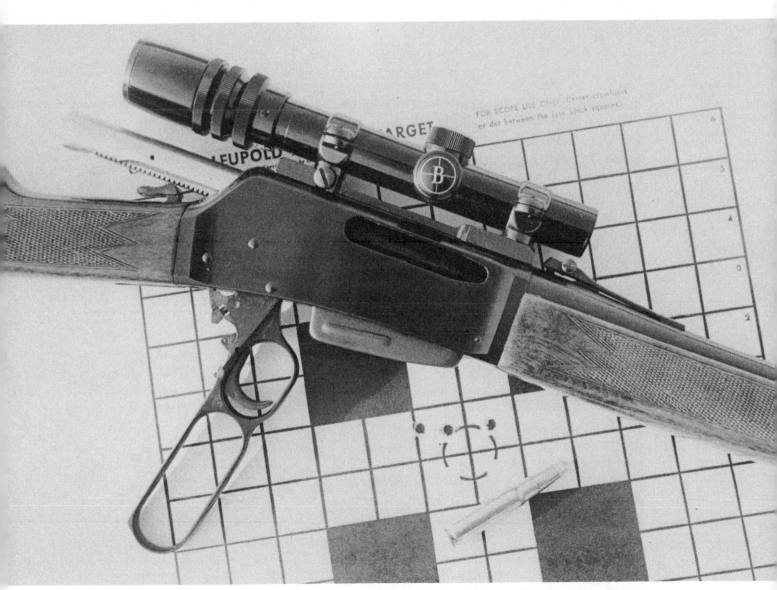

While some lever rifles chamber relatively short-range loads, this Browning BLR handles .358 Winchester, a good mid-range moose, elk and bear load.

ter suited to big-game use. A variety of loads is available, including the popular .308 Winchester. That makes these rifles a good choice for elk and other large deer, and they're usually accurate enough to make 250-plus-yard shots feasible. The Browning lever rifle is even chambered for the .358 Winchester, which is potent medicine for moose-size critters.

These lever rifles deserve being paired with high-quality scopes, as they have a lot more reach than the lever carbines mentioned earlier. They make fine all-around rifles for hunting all but dangerous game such as the Alaskan grizzly. Come to think of it, I know a lot of knowledgeable nimrods who wouldn't hesitate to tackle *any* bear with a .358 Winchester loaded with heavy bullets.

Lever- and slide-action rifles like these offer fast follow-up shots.

On the negative side, these lever rifles lack the camming power to yank a frozen cartridge case clear of the chamber or to force home a partly sized reload. They're not as accurate as a good bolt-action model for long-distance shooting, and under very extreme weather conditions they are a bit less reliable. By "very extreme" I'm referring to winter hunts in Alaska and the surrounding environs, where wet weather and plunging temperatures give any gun a severe test. Sportsmen sticking to the "lower 48" needn't overly concern themselves with this consideration.

Marlin, Winchester (now U.S. Repeating Arms), Browning and other companies offer fine rimfire lever rifles, and these make top choices for .22 sport. If your deer or big-game rifle is a lever action, it makes good sense to pair it with a similar rimfire.

There's nothing wrong with any of the action types mentioned above. I want to stress this, along with the point that you should use the kind of rifle that pleases you best. I've used all the types described, and continue to do so.

Bolt-Action Rifles

Most truly serious nimrods today prefer bolt-action centerfires to all other rifle types. In some cases, the bolt rifle is the only type available simply because of its cartridge requirements. Excepting the very strong Ruger No. 1 single shot, only bolt rifles digest such charge-stopping loads as the .357 Holland & Holland and .458 Winchester magnums. The same thing holds true for high-intensity, long-range rounds like the 8mm Remington Magnum and .338 Winchester Magnum. I've noted that you can buy a Browning autoloader chambered for the 7mm Remington Magnum and the .300 Winchester, but by far the bulk of the models offered to digest this fodder are bolt rifles.

Handloaders love the bolt rifle, too. This kind of action offers the ultimate in camming power, and if you have a bolt rifle featuring a large, Mauser-like extractor claw that won't pull through the cartridge case head, extraction is virtually guaranteed. No rifle type is more reliable, and under extreme weather conditions, a good Mauser or Mauser-inspired bolt design functions dependably where other actions fail.

For hunting truly dangerous game where reliability can be a life-or-death matter, you simply can't beat a Mauser action. The Mauser bolt-face sports that massive, clawlike extractor I've already mentioned, while ejection is assured by a mechanical stop. Many more-modern designs feature considerably smaller extractor assemblies and spring-loaded plunger ejectors. This arrangement is fine for 99 percent of all hunting situations, and bolt rifles so equipped remain among the most reliable available anywhere. No flies on them at all.

But don't look down your nose at the aging Mauser. The classic and much sought-after pre-64 Winchester bolt rifles are almost pure Mauser in design, and the excellent Ruger M77 features the huge Mauser extractor claw. Sako takes another tack with its bolt rifles, abandoning the oversized extractor in favor of more modestly sized equipment, but retaining the lug-cut mechanical ejector that always works so positively. Both Harrington & Richardson and Interarms offer genuine Mauser-action hunting rifles, and many of the costly custom sporters being built to order today feature surplus or new commercial Mauser actions.

In addition to providing excellent camming power and reliable operation, the bolt rifle offers the best overall accuracy. For long-range shooting at tiny targets, the bolt rifle reigns supreme. Some heavy-barrel varminters are capable of printing surprisingly small groups and consistently hit small rodents out to 250 or even 300 yards. By the same token, mountain rifles for hunting goats, sheep and other distant game are usually bolt-fed models.

Disadvantages? Bolt rifles are somewhat slower to operate than the other repeaters mentioned, making fast follow-up shots on running game more difficult. Still, a good bolt man familiar with his rifle can pump out bullets with surprising speed under the right kind of incentive.

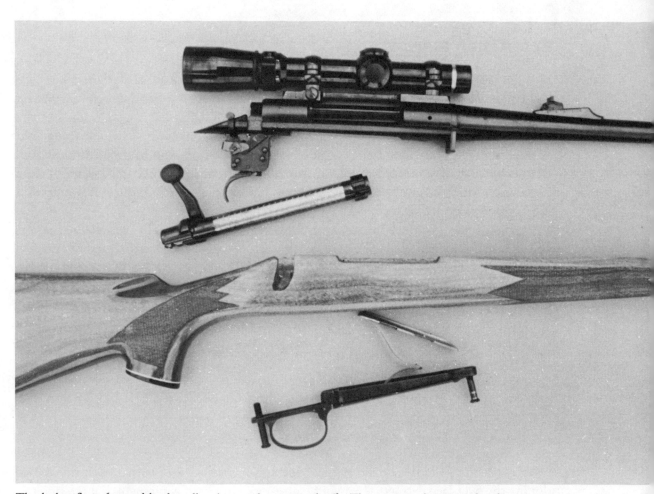

The bolt rifle is favored by handloaders and accuracy buffs. This action also provides the greatest camming power for extracting recalcitrant empties.

Bolt-action rifles come in several different varieties and in a wide choice of chamberings.

You don't need to spend a fortune to get a highly accurate bolt rifle, either. The Remington model 788 is a highly affordable firearm, yet it's one of the most accurate out-of-the-box sporters I've ever fired. And that opinion is based on several samples I've had the opportunity to test over the years. A number of other top bargains are around.

Many of the finest .22 rimfire rifles currently on the market are bolt-action designs. The Kimber .22 is one such offering that comes to mind, and both Harrington & Richardson and Remington have quality bolt .22's in their lineup. These make fine companion guns to a quality bolt-action centerfire. Numerous budget-priced models are available, too.

If you're looking for a serious target rifle of either rimfire or centerfire persuasion, chances are you'll pick a bolt design. Anschutz and Remington lead this field where rimfires are concerned, although a number of competitive makes are well worth considering.

Custom bolt carbine (*left*) and Marlin lever rifle are approximately the same length. The bolt is chambered for .358 Norma magnum, while the Marlin shoots .45-70 ammo.

Barrel Length

Once you've decided on caliber, load and action type, there's still the matter of barrel length to consider. If you shop the catalogs a bit, you can often find two or even three different barrel lengths available for the cartridge you have in mind. Anything at or under 20 inches in length qualifies as a carbine, while most sporter-size rifles have 22- or 24-inch tubes. Some magnums come with 26-inch barrels.

Regardless of the barrel length you prefer, you'll be making some kind of tradeoff. A 24-inch tube delivers close to maximum velocities, but can be unhandy in close quarters. Another plus is that a longer barrel is less noisy.

An 18- or 20-inch carbine tube makes for a very fast-handling little rifle, but at the cost of lost velocity and punch. As a rough rule of thumb, you can figure from 20 to maybe 30 feet per second of velocity lost for every inch of barrel you sacrifice. In other words, a round that exits a 24-inch tube at 3,000 feet per second drops to 2,900 fps when fired from a 20-inch carbine barrel. This varies with caliber, cartridge and load, but the principle remains the same.

Which rifle type is best for you? I've given you the facts. You take your choice. Remember, it's *your* rifle, and it need please no one else!

Calibers for Multiple Use 14

While we'd all like to own several different rifles, economic considerations sometimes dictate getting along with a bare minimum of shooting equipment. For that matter nearly all hunting batteries are begun with the purchase of a single firearm, and added to later as circumstances permit.

That means a single rifle is often called upon to handle a wide variety of shooting chores. If there is such a thing as an "all-around" hunting rifle, this is what the one-gun sportsman must have.

I know, I did all my serious hunting for years with a single centerfire. As a matter of fact, while I used several different such rifles when I began hunting deer and other medium-size game, I only owned one at a time for a long period. My first deer rifle was a bolt-action .308 Winchester, which I later traded for a 6mm Remington. A .270 came next, followed by a .30-06. All these chamberings did the job they had to do very well.

It is possible to use a single rifle for all your hunting chores. Granted, your choice is likely to be a compromise if you intend to hunt everything from ground hogs to grizzlies with the same firearm, but it can be done. Fortunately, few of us intend to get quite this much utility from just one rifle.

The average American nimrod needn't seriously consider the grizzly-slaying characteristics of his one-gun hunting cartridge. Unless he lives in Alaska, or happens to be a Canadian citizen living in the western part of the country, grizzly hunts are simply too costly for the budget-minded sportsman to consider. If you can afford the expense of a guided grizzly hunt, you can certainly afford to buy a magnum rifle for the occasion.

By the same token, many riflemen needn't take elk or moose into consideration when buying their all-around armament. If you live in Illinois or Georgia, you're going to have to spend a fair chunk of cash to get an elk hunt under way. Including a new rifle in the budget shouldn't stretch the total all that much.

The point is, the more you can narrow down the type and size of game you'll actually be hunting, the better your selection of an "all-around" rifle is likely to be. The limiting factor

Two good bolt-action choices for doing double duty as varmint and deer rifles: *left*, .25-06 Remington; *above*, .243 Winchester.

on cartridge selection is always the size and life-tenacity of the largest critter on the menu. And the guy who feels he has to have a .338 Winchester Magnum on the off chance of one day venturing north for Alaskan brown bear isn't going to enjoy shooting ground squirrels very much with the same rifle.

Most North American nimrods in the "Lower 48" fall into the varmint- and deer-hunter category. While these riflemen eagerly anticipate and plan for the fall deer season several months in advance, most of the shooting they do each year is at much smaller targets like chucks and prairie dogs. Hundreds of rounds may be expended at these tiny rodents, as well as at foxes, coyotes or jackrabbits during the 11½-month-long "off season." Only one or two shots are likely to be fired at deer.

Small Calibers

The confirmed chuck hunter may be tempted to try using his pet .223 or .22-250 varmint rifle to take his yearly venison supply. This would be a serious mistake. In the first place, .22-caliber rifles of any persuasion are illegal for hunting deer in many states. The .22 centerfires mentioned will kill deer, but the consensus is that they don't do a good enough job of it. A good marksman who knows how to place his shots and has sufficient stalking skills to get close to his quarry before pulling the trigger can kill deer with any .22—and that includes the diminutive .22 long-rifle rimfire cartridge. But that doesn't make these rounds a good choice for this purpose.

The lightest cartridge class that should be seriously considered for hunting deer is the 6mm centerfires. That includes both the .243 Winchester and its 6mm Remington competitor. With 100-grain (or heavier) bullets, either of these rounds do a fine job in the deer woods. I've taken some very large mule deer with a 6mm, and was very happy with its performance. These cartridges make fine pronghorn loads, too, and with lighter 70- or 80-grain projectiles serve very well for varminting.

A good, accurate .243 or 6mm bolt rifle shoots well enough to nail varmints at considerable distances. What's more, the 6mm bullets are heavier than .22-caliber projectiles and are less affected by wind drift. Although recoil is heavier than with a .22 centerfire heavy-barrel varmint rifle, it's pleasantly light when compared to other calibers used for hunting deer. This is yet another reason so many once-a-year deer hunters like these rounds—they simply don't punish the shooter. Women and teenage boys aren't the only fans; a lot of burly he-men dote on these 6mm's, as they find they can shoot them a lot better than they can most other, larger-caliber loads.

For the varmint hunter who goes afield once or twice a year for medium-size game no larger than deer or antelope, the 6mm Remington and .243 Winchester are the best choices. Incidentally, this is one application where the 3–9X variable scopes make excellent sense. Cranked down to 3X or 4X, this sight is fine for hunting deer. When small varmints are the quarry, twist the adjustment knob to its 9X setting. A tapered or stepped-down crosshair is the ideal reticle for this dual duty.

The quarter-bore calibers likewise make fine deer and varmint loads. The .250 Savage, .257 Roberts and .25-06 Remington, along with the proprietary .257 Weatherby Magnum fill this category. Factory loads are available in 87- and 100-grain bullet weights for the .250 Savage, and from 87- to 117- and even 120-grain weights for the other .25's mentioned. The heav-

Scoped 6mm Remington works equally well on long-range chucks and pronghorns.

ier bullets are even more effective on deer-size game than the 100-grain 6mm factory loads available (although handloaders can find 120-grain slugs for the 6mm's), and some hunters have used the heavier quarter bores on elk with success. I don't personally feel the .25's are up to hunting elk and other critters larger than mule deer, but not everyone agrees with that assessment.

The .25's have long been considered excellent for long-range varmint shooting, although they generate a bit more recoil than the lesser varmint loads. While the first few rounds through a .25-06 cause little discomfort, shooting 50 or more shots in the course of a summer afternoon can soon have you flinching.

The .25-06 is the heaviest hunting cartridge varminting purists will consider. A number of bull-barrel varmint rifles are chambered for this load, which has an excellent reputation

These .270 bolt rifles are tops for long-range mountain hunting and also work well in the desert and deer woods.

for accuracy. At the same time, the .25-06 makes a superb deer killer, and is a fine choice for mountain goat and sheep.

The above-named calibers are all first-class selections for the hunter who goes after varmint and small game more often than deer-size critters. That's the category most nimrods fall into, so it's little wonder the .243 Winchester, 6mm Remington and the .25-06 are so popular. The old .257 Roberts is enjoying a current revival, too.

Medium Calibers

For hunting larger game, it's necessary to move up to the 7mm, .30-06 class. This includes the excellent .270 Winchester, which has been used to take all manner of North American and European game. It is one of the top choices for western nimrods who sometimes hunt mule deer, elk and other critters at extended range.

With 130-grain bullets of the proper construction, the .270 does a first-class job on all western big game. This is the classic bullet weight for this cartridge, and it's an exceptional long-range performer. Heavier projectiles are available for woods use on moose and the like, but since these don't shoot as flat, most sportsmen stick with 130-grain (or the new 140-grain) loads.

When loaded with lighter 100-grain bullets, the .270 works well for shooting varmints. The cartridge has a reputation for top accuracy, and in the right rifle it will shoot right alongside many of the smaller varmint calibers. However, recoil is greater, and shooting too many rounds in a single day can cause discomfort.

The 7mm Mauser, 7mm-08 Remington and the 7mm Express Remington, which are in the same general class as the .270, will do just about anything this fine cartridge will. Because larger-diameter, heavier bullets are used, some prefer the 7mm to the .270 for large game. But for all intents and purposes, anything I've said about the latter applies to the former. The 7mm Express Remington (formerly known as the .280 Remington) is one of the finest North American hunting cartridges on the market. It's a bit more potent than the other non-magnum 7mm's and has slightly greater range. It and the .270 Winchester come pretty close to tying for the "most useful" centerfire hunting cartridge title, at least in "second place" position. In my opinion, the .30-06 remains our most versatile commercial centerfire. But the race between these three is very close, indeed.

One reason the .30-06 has long been known as our most versatile hunting cartridge is the wide range of projectiles available for it. Factory loads are offered in weights of 110, 125, 150, 165, 168, 180, 200 and 220 grains, while handloaders have an even greater variety of projectiles to choose from. These loads make the '06 suitable for all kinds of game, from the smallest to all but the very largest. I can't honestly think of an animal that hasn't been killed by .30-06–toting riflemen, although the caliber is far too light for some of the most dangerous species. I know the '06 has accounted for any number of grizzlies, including the oversize brown bears of the Alaska peninsula. While I wouldn't choose a .30-06 for serious *arctos* hunting, I did use one once to back up a fine marksman armed with a magnum rifle when he took on a grizzly. My help wasn't needed, but no intelligent nimrod willingly tackles a big, northern grizzly solo. I and my .30-06 were along merely for moral support.

When Remington introduced its .30-06 Accelerator load a few years back, it succeeded in making this cartridge even more versatile. This round uses a plastic sabot to enclose a 55-grain .22-caliber projectile and hustle it through the '06's .30-caliber bore. When the sabot exits, it drops away, leaving the little .22 traveling along at 4,000 fps or so.

Thus the .30-06 becomes a variety of .22 centerfire. Accuracy isn't up to heavy-barrel varminting standards, but is often surprisingly good. Out to 200 yards this ammo usually shoots well enough to give you a pretty fair chance of nailing a chuck. Beyond that distance, a lot of luck enters the equation.

Perhaps the chief advantage the Accelerator ammo offers is relative lack of recoil. Even the 110-grain .30-06 factory loads generate a certain amount of kick. Recoil from the Accelerator rounds is negligible by comparison. A disadvantage is that components aren't readily available for reloaders. The expended cartridge cases can be reloaded with conventional .30-caliber bullets, but the Accelerator sabots aren't offered over the counter. This makes shooting them a costly proposition.

Accelerator loads are also offered in .308 Winchester and .30-30 cases. The stubby .308 will handle almost any game you'd care to tackle with a .30-06, although this doesn't include oversize, ill-tempered bruins. Otherwise, all the comments made about the .30-06 apply. I'm a big fan of the .308, primarily because it can be operated through a shorter action than the .30-06 requires. Thus the .308 chambering is available in both Savage and Browning lever rifles (while the '06 isn't) and in several ultralight, compact bolt-action models. I am a real fan of featherweight hunting arms and usually don't mind sacrificing the 100-fps edge in velocity that the .30-06 has over the .308.

The .30-30, on the other hand, has only limited usefulness in the hunting field. It's a short-range deer load, pure and simple, and no amount of doctoring turns it into anything like an all-around cartridge. And that includes adding a .22-caliber Accelerator load to the repertoire.

To summarize, a .270 Winchester, 7mm Mauser, 7mm-08 Remington, 7mm Express Remington, .308 Winchester or .30-06 all make excellent choices for the sportsman intent on hunting everything up to and including moose, caribou and elk. These rounds are potent enough for tackling the largest black bear (and some of these critters attain very respectable size) and shoot flat enough for long-distance mountain work.

Furthermore, these are all readily adaptable to varmint hunting. With the right loads, they can be used for any game hunted south of the Canadian border, and for just about anything a Canadian or Alaskan hunt can provide. Again, a good variable scope makes an in-

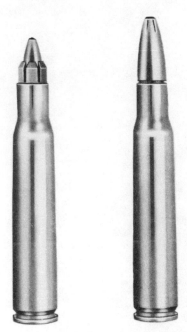

Remington's Accelerator encases a 55-grain .22 bullet in a plastic sabot and loads the combination into a .30-06 case. With this ammo, a larger-bore hunting rifle becomes a .22 varminter of sorts.

telligent choice if varmints may be included in the bill of fare. The 3–9X variables are the number-one choice of American sportsmen, but I prefer a 2–7X or 2.5–8X variable. These slightly less powerful optics come in smaller, lighter packages and provide all the magnification I'll ever need in the game field.

Large Calibers

While the varmint and big-game rifle combination makes a lot of sense to many riflemen, some nimrods care little for hunting rodents and other vermin. Their interest is centered around critters ranging in size from deer and antelope upward. Many of these sportsmen are serious big-game buffs. By that, I mean they regularly hunt (or at least, hope to hunt) elk, moose and even Alaskan grizzly. They're looking for a rifle that will let them hunt the upper end of the North American game spectrum.

While most nimrods fortunate enough to fit this category can afford to own several firearms, the facts are they may be limited by space or duffel weight considerations to packing a single rifle along for an extended hunt. Thus the "all-around" hunting rifle problem can easily apply to them.

Top, Remington Accelerator bullet leaving muzzle at 4,080 feet per second. *Bottom*, sabot and bullet 24 inches from muzzle.

Calibers for Multiple Use

A number of experienced hunters dote on relatively small-bore rounds such as the 7mm Remington Magnum or .300 Winchester. These belted mid-size cartridges develop relatively tame recoil by magnum rifle standards and shoot with very flat trajectories. Excellent long-range killers, they make top-notch sheep and goat rounds. They also do the job on grizzlies, although they're lighter than the big bear loads I personally like.

If I seem to be weighting these selections too heavily toward their grizzly-killing abilities, it's simply because this is the only North American game widely hunted today that can be considered truly dangerous. An Alaskan brownie can be a marrow-chilling beast to contemplate up close, and if he's taken a dislike to you he (or she—never discount a mama bear's wrath if the cubs are too near) is not above taking immediate steps to indelibly convey this attitude.

Experienced hunters shoot for the bear's front shoulders. If either or both shoulders are put out of commission, the shock may kill the bear in short order. If it fails to, the animal will at least stay put until a finisher can be applied. The beast is simply too heavy in the front quarters to remain very mobile without both forward legs in reasonable working order. The rear legs are less critical, and if you're unwise (or unlucky) enough to break a grizzly's *back* leg, you're not likely to have a lot of extra time to get another shot away. Those big, front legs are enormously strong, and a grizzly can move along on them very well. And very fast.

Oh yes. Try not to be directly downslope from a grizzly (or black bear) when you shoot it. They have a disconcerting tendency to tumble and roll downhill, and their path often coincides with the hunter's position. The results can be unfortunate, and maybe even fatal.

To get back to the point, serious grizzly loads need to be pretty potent to crunch a massive shoulder or two. And that eliminates the lesser calibers from real consideration. I wouldn't hesitate to shoot a grizzly from 150 yards or so with a 7mm or a .300 magnum. These rounds will kill the largest bear, but maybe not as quickly as you'd like. With a little distance between you, there's always time for a second or third shot, so there's little danger of an accident.

But for a bear that unexpectedly appears at close range, you need something that won't merely kill the animal, but do it *right now!* You need a *stopper.* And for my money, the smaller magnums just don't qualify.

The 8mm Remington and .338 Winchester magnums do. These generate nearly 2 full tons of energy at the muzzle, and shoot tough, heavily constructed bullets.

These two belted magnums are also highly popular among elk and moose hunters, and they shoot flat and hard for long-range kills. The drawback is that they do kick harder than the lesser cartridges we've discussed. For the serious big-game hunter who will very likely tackle a grizzly or two in the not-too-distant future, these two maggies may be the finest possible choices available. They're big, they bellow, and they tend to buck a bit, but they're not so monstrously powerful to have but narrowly limited usefulness.

Not a few western hunters dote on either a .338 Winchester or 8mm Remington belted magnum, and most of these men will never lay eyes on a grizzly. They use their rifles on mule deer and elk, and couldn't be happier with the way they perform.

When using the 7mm to .338 magnum class of "all-around" hunting rifles, I'd choose a good 1–4X or 1.5–4.5X variable sight. Cranked down to the lowest power setting, such scopes

227

Many centerfire cartridges can be made to serve double duty by careful handloading. This .300 Winchester Magnum is primarily an elk and moose rifle, but it can be used on smaller game.

provide a comfortingly generous field of view for close-in work on critters with fangs and claws, or for running shots at any game. And at 4X, they furnish all the magnification a deer or elk hunter could ever ask for. That setting will even do for hunting sheep and goats (another area in which these rounds excel). A 2–7X variable would also work well, although the field of view is narrowed a bit.

A case can be made for the .358 Norma Magnum and .375 Holland & Holland as "all-around" medium- to large-game hunting cartridges, but that's stretching the point. The .358 Norma is currently available only in custom-made rifles in this country, while the .375 Holland & Holland Magnum is simply too potent for anything but our largest bruins. It's a great all-around number for African game, but it's not the best choice for the North American nimrod.

The key to versatility with any of the cartridges mentioned is to match the ammunition —specifically, the bullet type and weight—to the game being hunted. Select a heavy, solidly constructed bullet for big, dangerous game and ultralight projectiles designed to fragment al-

Cartridges like the 6mm Remington can be used with a variety of bullet weights to work well on both small varmints and deer-size game.

most instantly for varmint-size prey. Reverse this order, and you can find yourself in serious trouble.

If you handload, examine the specifications provided by each bulletmaker for the projectiles he offers. Nosler, Hornady, Sierra, Speer, Remington, Winchester and Federal all offer various weights, shapes and degrees of toughness in the bullets they manufacture. A look at their literature lets you pick the type and weight you need for the kind of hunting you have in mind. Bitterroot and Barnes are well known for their very heavily constructed projectiles for the largest, hardiest game, and they offer lightweight bullets for the smaller critters, too.

Another thing handloaders would do well to remember is that they can stretch the utility of any centerfire rifle cartridge by customizing the ammo they assemble to fit the game and the conditions. If you load down a .338 or .300 magnum when hunting deer or smaller game, you will enjoy much lighter recoil and noise levels. But be careful when trying to tame large-volume cartridges. A too-light load with the wrong kind of powder can result in something called a "pressure excursion," and this can destroy your gun and may cause serious injury to the shooter. This is most likely to happen when greatly reduced charges of slow-burning powder are used in a large-capacity case. Dupont's SR 4759, a specialized powder manufactured expressly for reduced rifle loads, is recommended. Always consult a good loading manual before experimenting. (Speer's Reloading Manual Number 10 offers reduced load data.) Remember, too, that a too-light load may leave the bullet stuck in the bore. If this happens and another round is fired while the bore remains plugged, you'll have a nasty accident on your hands.

The "all-around" hunting rifle is a reality. But any cartridge drafted for this kind of duty will represent some degree of compromise. Which is why most hunters serious about the sport eventually wind up with a multiple-rifle battery.

Estimating Range and Sighting-In 15

A few years ago I was temporarily suspending my deer-hunting activities for a leisurely lunch break when a flurry of shooting just over the ridge caught my attention. After four or five rapid shots were fired, the shooting continued at well-spaced intervals.

As any hunter knows, a single shot usually signals a clean kill, while several signify a missed target. I mentally chalked up a point for the deer, but when the firing continued with metronome regularity my curiosity was piqued. After wolfing down the last half of a ham-and-cheese sandwich, I wandered over the ridge to see what was going on.

I discovered an orange-clad rifleman kneeling behind a large stump, which he was resting his rifle on as he threw shot after carefully aimed shot at a hillside across the canyon. At first I couldn't imagine what he might be shooting at, but a few minutes' careful glassing with my 6x25mm binoculars eventually revealed a feeding deer. The distance was so great that even with binoculars I couldn't tell if the animal was a large doe or a small-antlered buck. It's almost impossible to judge range accurately when looking across an open space like a canyon, as there are no intervening reference marks to help keep things in perspective. I don't know exactly how far away that deer was, but I guessed it was well over 700 yards, perhaps farther than that.

I politely asked the hunter if he was actually shooting at the deer.

"Sure am!" he replied happily. "Can you see where I'm hitting?"

After locating the animal first with binoculars, I could barely see the deer with my naked eye, much less the strike of his bullets. "Don't you think the range is a little far?" I asked. "That deer's a third of a mile away."

"The hell it is!" he answered, growing belligerent. "He's maybe three, four hundred yards off. If I can just get the right holdover, I can pick him off. Easy!"

The fact that the ground around him was becoming littered with empty brass cases, coupled with the deer's apparent lack of alarm, didn't faze him. The animal wasn't even aware it was being shot at!

Optical aids for long-range hunting include binoculars, spotting scope and rangefinder.

I picked up an empty case and looked at the headstamp. My marksman was shooting a lever-action model 99 chambered (apparently) for the .300 Savage. I asked what kind of bullet he was shooting, and he replied "Hundred-and-eighty-grainers — they really reach out. Hey! I made him jump that time."

Sure enough, another check through the binoculars showed that the animal was either getting tired of all that racket from the far hillside, or a near miss had finally got the message of the unwanted attention across. Whatever the reason, the animal bounced to the edge of the clearing and disappeared.

"I almost had 'im!" the disappointed sniper cussed, slamming his lever shut in frustration. He was firmly convinced that the next shot or two would have driven home, anchoring his year's venison supply.

From past bitter experience, I knew better than to tell this clown what an idiot he was. Far too many once-a-year hunters have only the haziest idea of range estimation, and are even less informed about the trajectory of the rifle they're shooting. Just for fun I asked him how far he was holding over.

"I had the crosshairs right on his backbone," came the answer. "This rifle's a flat-shooting son-of-a-gun, and I should've got him. Do you think maybe I was shooting too high?"

I didn't have the heart to tell him that, with his particular load and rifle, if his 400-yard estimate had been anywhere close to being accurate, he would have had to hold a good 4 feet high. He was shooting a rounded soft-point bullet, and if his rifle had been sighted to print 1½ inches high at 100 yards, it would print nearly 9½ feet below point of aim at 500 yards. Out where the deer actually was, I have no idea of the holdover needed.

Of course shooting at that kind of range is ridiculous, even if trajectory and holdover are accurately known. The lever-action Savage likely gave no better than 1½- or 2-minute accuracy, which meant 1½- or 2-inch groups at 100 yards. At 700 or 800 yards, the same bullet could be as much as 16 inches either side of the intended target without considering the human factor at all. And the vertical dispersion at that distance would be an eye-opener if calculated.

As I watched the disappointed hunter gather up his empties and walk away, I only hoped he'd brought enough ammunition to last the weekend. I also hoped he'd make damn sure his distant targets were always deer and not some two-legged target he tried to grow antlers on. I vowed right then to hunt in the opposite direction he'd taken.

Rangefinders and Other Devices

Range estimation is a bugaboo riflemen have tried to solve in many different ways over the years. Military artillery spotters use expensive binocular rangefinders, and even they require a sighting round or two to check their calculations.

Compact versions of these rangefinders are available to sportsmen, but these are as bulky as the average spotting scope. They're just one more item for the hunter to carry, and most feel a good rifle with scope and a pair of binoculars constitute enough hardware to tote around.

While a good, portable rangefinder isn't a bad idea for sheep and goat hunters who will likely have some long shots offered, in my experience it often isn't very helpful under field conditions. In the first place, the hunter often doesn't have the leisure to haul out the rangefinder, then fiddle with the dials while he tries to get the twin target images to coincide in the eyepiece. And in the second place, the rangefinding devices I've tried simply weren't all that accurate. Because they rely on the operator's ability to precisely move one floating image atop the other—and those images are small, let me tell you—a certain amount of error is bound to creep in. I and three other experienced hunters once tried to find the distance to a band of pronghorn eyeing us from a patch of desert, and the rangefinder gave four different readings varying from 250 to 425 yards. What's more, the same man had trouble getting two consecutive readings to agree. Perhaps a well-trained operator could get the thing to work right, but country boys like us sure couldn't!

Various riflescope manufacturers have tried another approach. They produce a reticle with a pair of horizontal stadia hairs and some kind of printed range indicator within the shooter's field of vision. This reticle is attached to a variable-power scope, and as the magnification is increased or decreased, the image of the target animal grows larger or smaller until its body height just fills the gap between the stadia hairs. Once that is accomplished, the rifleman notes the distance registered on the reticle display, and makes his holdover calculations accordingly.

There are two basic problems with this system. The calibrations only work when the animal bracketed by the stadia hairs has a chest cavity just 18 inches deep. Many deer-size animals approach that back-to-brisket measurement, but many don't. There are big deer and little deer, and many hunters seek sheep, goats, pronghorn, elk or caribou. They all have differing body depths.

If you have a fair-to-good idea of the average body thickness of the particular game you're hunting, you can make some compensation as you bracket your beast in the reticle. But again, we're relying on the human ability to guesstimate. And manufacturing tolerances automatically cause some inaccuracy. In my opinion, if the shooter has to make a blind guess at animal body depth, he might just as well go ahead and eyeball the distance in the first place.

The other problem is one of time. It takes a patient animal to wait, posing, while the sportsman centers it in the stadia wires and then rotates the power knob back and forth until the necessary fine adjustment has been achieved. Then the shooter must either figure his holdover and adjust the sight picture, or twirl another dial (more on this in a moment), before he shoots. Sometimes the hunter has the time for all this, but more often he doesn't!

I mentioned yet another dial—this is what you get when your rangefinder riflescope is also equipped with a trajectory-compensating device. This piece of equipment uses interchangeable dial scales that are supposed to raise the crosshairs the appropriate amount to compensate for bullet drop at any given range. Thus, you don't have to figure your holdover—the scope does it for you. All you have to do is dial in the range, and the compensator does the rest.

These range-compensating accessories are offered all by themselves in several riflescope models or in combination with the aforementioned rangefinding equipment.

While range-compensating devices are subject to the same tolerance errors rangefinders are, some work reasonably well and they do have a purpose. Metallic silhouette target shooters, who know exactly the ranges they shoot over, find the ability to simply add or subtract a few clicks on the elevation dial a tremendous boon. Thus they can use their crosshairs to center every target and don't have to rely on "Kentucky elevation," or holdover.

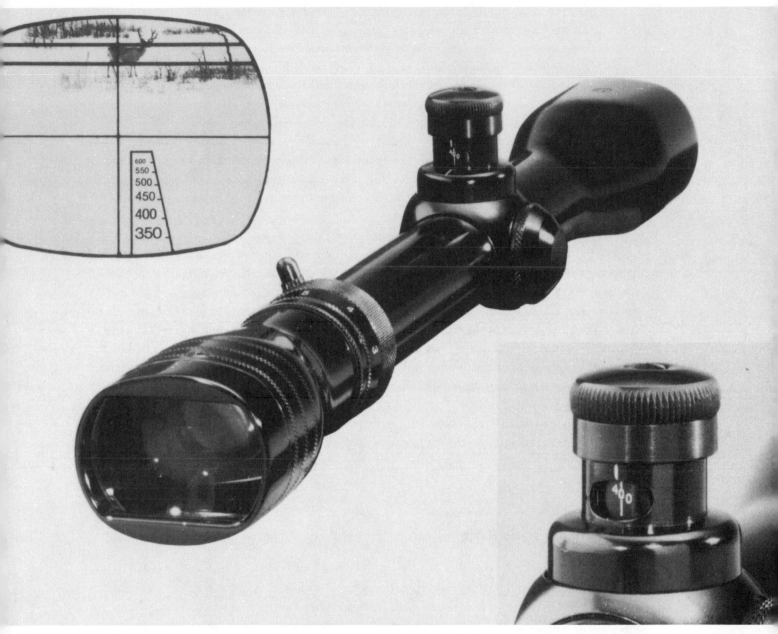

This range-estimating, trajectory-compensating scope is made by Redfield. When the animal is brack-eted by the stadia hairs (*left*), the range appears at the lower edge of the reticle. This distance is then dialed into the elevation turret (*right*), and the rifle theoretically shoots to point of aim at that range.

Since hunters don't know the ranges they shoot over with any degree of precision, any error made in estimating the distance will be continued in the elevation adjustment. And again, clicking in the estimated range takes precious time the hunter may not have.

235

Matching the Gun to the Game

It's ironic that the highly conservative, tradition-minded American rifleman almost rigidly resists change and innovation when it comes to the firearms he uses—but goes absolutely bonkers over the assorted gadgetry the scopemakers advertise. Rangefinding and range-compensating systems sell like crazy, and the big 3–9X variable is the most popular scope in the marketplace today. One manufacturer offers a small camera that can be attached to the riflescope to give the nimrod magnified portraits of his game before he shoots it. It seems the more bells and whistles a scopemaker can add, the better his product sells.

We're all in love with technology today, and the hunting sportsman is no exception. Unfortunately, the faith we place in this technology is often greater than its performance warrants. Because many rangefinding and trajectory-compensating scopes calibrate distance out to 600 yards, naive riflemen sometimes attempt marksmanship feats no veteran would ever consider trying.

The wise sportsman knows the limitations of both himself and his equipment. An honest 300-yard shot is a long one, and most riflemen would be well advised to limit their shooting to shorter distances. The thrill of the hunt doesn't come from seeing how far away you can drop an animal, but from testing your stalking and woodsmanship skills. If you can't get close enough to be assured of a clean kill, there's always tomorrow. Play the game, and you can be justly proud of the trophies you take. Since the hunt ends when you pull the trigger, the experienced sportsman tries to delay that moment until the time is right. The hunting experience should be prolonged, not cut short at the first possible opportunity. Find the patience to stalk within range, or somehow outmaneuver your quarry, rather than attempt a too-long shot.

I have shot a few animals beyond the 300-yard mark, but only when there was no way to stalk closer, and I had a dead rest to steady my rifle. Even at that, the longest game shot I've ever taken was no more than 350 yards. Most deer-size game has been harvested at less than 200 yards.

Sighting-In Your Rifle

If you're willing to limit your shots to 300 yards or less—and try to be conservative when estimating distance—you don't really need fancy rangefinding gadgets or trajectory-compensating sights. Strange as it may sound, you don't even need more than a rudimentary idea of your rifle's trajectory. Any modern medium- to large-game cartridge shoots flat enough to let you shoot at a deer-size animal out to 275 or even 300 yards without using any holdover, as long as you properly sight in your rifle.

I'm not talking about old-timers such as the .45-70, .30-40 Krag, .300 Savage, or .30-30 Winchester. These aging numbers sport looping, rainbow trajectories that preclude anything but relatively short-range marksmanship (to maybe 200 yards) unless the sights are raised a significant amount.

But with modern, high-intensity loads such as the .243 Winchester, 6mm Remington, the .25-06, the .270 Winchester, 7mm Mauser, 7mm-08 Remington, 7mm Express Remington,

Sighting your high-velocity hunting rifle to print 2½ to 3 inches high at 100 yards should allow you to kill deer-size game at 275-plus yards without holdover.

7mm Remington Magnum, .308 Winchester, .30-06, .300 Winchester Magnum, 8mm Remington Magnum, .338 Winchester Magnum and .375 Holland & Holland, a rifle can be sighted in to allow point-blank kills on any decent-size animal out to 275 yards, and often to the 300-yard mark. Some bullet styles and weights shoot flatter than others in these loads, and a look at any ballistics chart shows which are the most desirable for long-distance gunning.

Once your rifle is sighted-in, shoot at extended ranges from a solid rest to see how it actually performs at those distances.

But all these cartridges shoot flat enough to do what I've promised with almost any of the projectile weights appropriate to the medium-size game being hunted.

The trick is an easy one: simply sight in your rifle to print from 2½ to 3½ inches high at 100 yards, depending on the individual trajectory of the load you intend to use. If you can't

238

be bothered with checking this out, simply set the sight to print an even 3 inches above point of aim at that distance.

At 275 yards, most of the loads you shoot with that zero should drop no more than 4 to 6 inches under the point of aim. The bullet will print right "on" zero at around 225 yards, and at shorter ranges will be an inch or two high. The vitals of a deer or pronghorn are large enough that missing dead center a few inches either way won't make much difference.

A good, solid shooting position is needed to kill game reliably beyond 150 yards.

Some loads shoot flat enough to let you hold dead on target out to 300 yards and still drop your game cleanly. Again, a quick look at a bullet-drop table shows you which bullet-cartridge combinations do this.

While I've used this "3-inches high at 100 yards" sight-in trick with good success in a number of different rifles over the years, I advise any rifleman contemplating 250- to 300-yard game shots to first actually try a few shots at targets placed that distance away. Seeing the results on paper gives both confidence in your rifle and in your own shooting ability, and an appreciation of how far away those targets actually are. And if for some reason your bullets aren't printing where they're supposed to, it gives you a chance to figure out what's wrong and correct the problem. The time to do that is before hunting season begins, not after you've wounded or missed a distant trophy.

Doing a fair amount of target shooting at known, long range provides excellent practice in both shooting discipline and estimating range. Once you've fired at a number of 200- and 300-yard targets at the rifle range, you begin to get a feel for what those distances look like. The next time you watch a football game (from the stands, not on your television screen), take several good looks at the distance between the end zones. A good many experienced hunters estimate yardage by "one football field, two football fields..." (On the very remote chance that non-football fans may be reading this, a football field is just 100 yards long.)

With the kind of sight-in picture I've recommended, it won't matter very much if you miscalculate an animal's distance by 50 or 75 yards, as long as he's no farther than 275 or 300 yards downrange. The critical point here is to know when a target begins to look too far away, and this means passing up shots that appear questionable until you can stalk closer.

One thing to remember when shooting in mountainous country is that range can be particularly deceiving when firing uphill or down. The tendency is to shoot *over* targets standing on a steep slope, whether the rifleman is above or beneath the animal. The reason? On a very steep slope, a trophy mule deer or mountain goat may be 300 yards or more from the hunter measured along the slope. But measured in a straight, horizontal line (or "as the crow flies") the two may be less than 150 yards apart. If the marksman allows for a 300-plus-yard bullet drop, he could miss altogether. Gravity acts on the bullet only in relation to its *horizontal* path. In other words, the *effective* range as it affects trajectory would be just 150 yards.

Hunting handgunners have a more serious trajectory problem than centerfire riflemen do and must have a clear idea of bullet drop if they intend to shoot a .357 or .44 magnum at targets more than 100 yards off. However, since most pistoleers try to stalk to within that range or closer, it isn't usually much of a problem. Handgunners who scope their firearms and try for more distance should get in lots of practice before venturing afield after game.

BULLET TRAJECTORIES

(Courtesy Remington Arms Co., Inc., Federal Cartridge Corp., and Winchester-Western)

TRAJECTORY† 0.0 Indicates yardage at which rifle was sighted in.

CALIBERS	Wt.-Grs.	Style	SHORT RANGE 50 Yds.	100 Yds.	150 Yds.	200 Yds.	250 Yds.	300 Yds.	LONG RANGE 100 Yds	150 Yds.	200 Yds.	250 Yds.	300 Yds.	400 Yds.	500 Yds.	BARREL LENGTH
17 REM.	25	Hollow Point	0.1	0.5	0.0	− 1.5	− 4.2	− 8.5	2.1	2.5	1.9	− 0.0	− 3.4	− 17.0	− 44.3	24"
22 HORNET	45	Pointed Soft Point	0.3	0.0	− 2.4	− 7.7	−16.9	−31.3	1.6	0.0	− 4.5	−12.8	−26.4	− 75.6	−163.4	24"
	45	Hollow Point	0.3	0.0	− 2.4	− 7.7	−16.9	−31.3	1.6	0.0	− 4.5	−12.8	−26.4	− 75.6	−163.4	
222 REM.	50	Pointed Soft Point	0.5	0.9	0.0	− 2.5	− 6.9	−13.7	2.2	1.9	0.0	− 3.8	−10.0	− 32.3	− 73.8	24"
	50	Hollow Point	0.5	0.9	0.0	− 2.4	− 6.6	−13.1	2.1	1.8	0.0	− 3.6	− 9.5	− 30.2	− 68.1	
	55	Metal Case	0.6	1.0	0.0	− 2.5	− 7.0	−13.7	2.2	1.9	0.0	− 3.8	− 9.9	− 31.0	− 68.7	
222 REM. MAG	55	Pointed Soft Point	0.4	0.8	0.0	− 2.2	− 6.0	−11.8	1.9	1.6	0.0	− 3.3	− 8.5	− 26.7	− 59.5	24"
	55	Hollow Point	0.4	0.8	0.0	− 2.1	− 5.8	−11.4	1.8	1.6	0.0	− 3.2	− 8.2	− 25.5	− 56.0	
223 REM.	55	Pointed Soft Point	0.4	0.8	0.0	− 2.2	− 6.0	−11.8	1.9	1.6	0.0	− 3.3	− 8.5	− 26.7	− 59.6	24"
	55	Hollow Point	0.4	0.8	0.0	− 2.1	− 5.8	−11.4	1.8	1.6	0.0	− 3.2	− 8.2	− 25.5	− 56.0	
	55	Metal Case	0.4	0.8	0.0	− 2.1	− 5.9	−11.6	1.9	1.6	0.0	− 3.2	− 8.4	− 26.2	− 57.9	
22-250 REM.	55	Pointed Soft Point	0.2	0.5	0.0	− 1.5	− 4.3	− 8.4	2.2	2.6	1.9	0.0	− 3.3	− 15.4	− 37.7	24"
	55	Hollow Point	0.2	0.5	0.0	− 1.4	− 4.0	− 7.7	2.1	2.4	1.7	0.0	− 3.0	− 13.6	− 32.4	
243 WIN.	80	Pointed Soft Point	0.3	0.7	0.0	− 1.8	− 4.9	− 9.4	2.6	2.9	2.1	0.0	− 3.6	− 16.2	− 37.9	24"
	80	Hollow Point	0.3	0.7	0.0	− 1.8	− 4.9	− 9.4	2.6	2.9	2.1	0.0	− 3.6	− 16.2	− 37.9	
	100	Pointed Soft Point	0.5	0.9	0.0	− 2.2	− 5.8	−11.0	1.9	1.6	0.0	− 3.1	− 7.8	− 22.6	− 46.3	
6mm REM.	80	Pointed Soft Point	0.3	0.6	0.0	− 1.6	− 4.5	− 8.7	2.4	2.7	1.9	0.0	− 3.3	− 14.9	− 35.0	24"
	80	Hollow Point	0.3	0.6	0.0	− 1.6	− 4.5	− 8.7	2.4	2.7	1.9	0.0	− 3.3	− 14.9	− 35.0	
	100	Pointed Soft Point	0.4	0.7	0.0	− 1.9	− 5.1	− 9.7	1.7	1.4	0.0	− 2.7	− 6.8	− 20.0	− 40.8	
250 SAVAGE	87	Pointed Soft Point	0.5	0.9	0.0	− 2.3	− 6.1	−11.8	2.0	1.7	0.0	− 3.3	− 8.4	− 25.2	− 53.4	24"
	100	Pointed	0.2	0.0	− 1.6	− 4.9	−10.0	−17.4	2.4	2.0	0.0	− 3.9	−10.1	− 30.5	− 65.2	
256 WIN. MAG.	60	Hollow Point	0.3	0.0	− 2.3	− 7.3	−15.9	−29.6	1.5	0.0	− 4.2	−12.1	−25.0	− 72.1	−157.2	24"
257 ROBERTS	87	Pointed Soft Point	0.4	0.8	0.0	− 2.0	− 5.5	−10.6	1.8	1.5	0.0	− 3.0	− 7.5	− 22.7	− 48.0	24"
	100	Pointed	0.6	1.0	0.0	− 2.5	− 6.9	−13.2	2.3	1.9	0.0	− 3.7	− 9.4	− 28.6	− 60.9	24"
	117	Pointed Soft Point	0.3	0.0	− 1.9	− 5.8	−11.9	−20.7	2.9	2.4	0.0	− 4.7	−12.0	− 36.7	− 79.2	

SHORT RANGE — Bullet does not rise more than one inch above line of sight from muzzle to sighting in range.

LONG RANGE — Bullet does not rise more than three inches above line of sight from muzzle to sighting in range.

TRAJECTORY† 0.0 Indicates yardage at which rifle was sighted in.

†**SHORT RANGE** — Bullet does not rise more than one inch above line of sight from muzzle to sighting in range.

LONG RANGE — Bullet does not rise more than three inches above line of sight from muzzle to sighting in range.

CALIBERS	BULLET Style	Wt-Grs.	SHORT RANGE 50 Yds.	100 Yds.	150 Yds.	200 Yds.	250 Yds.	300 Yds.	LONG RANGE 100 Yds.	150 Yds.	200 Yds.	250 Yds.	300 Yds.	400 Yds.	500 Yds.	BARREL LENGTH
25-06 REM.	Hollow Point	87	0.3	0.6	0.0	-1.7	-4.8	-9.3	2.5	2.9	2.1	0.0	-3.6	-16.4	-39.1	24"
	Pointed Soft Point	100	0.4	0.7	0.0	-1.9	-5.0	-9.7	1.6	1.4	0.0	-2.7	-6.9	-20.5	-42.7	
	Pointed Soft Point	120	0.5	0.8	0.0	-2.1	-5.5	-10.5	1.9	1.6	0.0	-2.9	-7.4	-21.6	-44.2	
6.5mm REM. MAG.	Pointed Soft Point	120	0.4	0.7	0.0	-1.8	-4.9	-9.5	2.7	3.0	2.1	0.0	-3.5	-15.5	-35.3	24"
264 WIN. MAG.	Pointed Soft Point	140	0.5	0.8	0.0	-2.0	-5.4	-10.2	1.8	1.5	0.0	-2.9	-7.2	-20.8	-42.2	24"
270 WIN.	Pointed Soft Point	100	0.3	0.6	0.0	-1.6	-4.5	-8.7	2.4	2.7	1.9	0.0	-3.3	-15.0	-35.2	24"
	Pointed Soft Point	130	0.4	0.8	0.0	-2.0	-5.3	-10.0	1.7	1.5	0.0	-2.8	-7.1	-20.8	-42.7	
	Pointed	130	0.4	0.7	0.0	-1.9	-5.1	-9.7	1.7	1.4	0.0	-2.7	-6.8	-19.9	-40.5	
	Soft Point	150	0.6	1.0	0.0	-2.5	-6.8	-13.1	2.2	1.9	0.0	-3.6	-9.3	-28.1	-59.7	
7mm MAUSER	Pointed Soft Point	140	0.2	0.0	-1.7	-5.0	-10.0	-17.0	2.5	2.0	0.0	-3.8	-9.6	-27.7	-56.3	24"
7mm-08 REM.	Pointed Soft Point	140	0.6	0.9	0.0	-2.3	-6.11	-11.6	2.1	1.7	0.0	-3.2	-8.1	-23.5	-47.7	24"
280 REM.	Soft Point	165	0.2	0.0	-1.5	-4.6	-9.5	-16.4	2.3	1.9	0.0	-3.7	-9.4	-28.1	-58.8	24"
7mm EXPRESS REM.	Pointed Soft Point	150	0.5	0.9	0.0	-2.2	-5.8	-11.0	1.9	1.6	0.0	-3.1	-7.8	-22.8	-46.7	24"
284 WIN.	Pointed Soft Point	125	0.4	0.8	0.0	-2.0	-5.3	-10.1	1.7	1.5	0.0	-2.8	-7.2	-21.1	-43.7	24"
	Pointed Soft Point	150	0.6	1.0	0.0	-2.4	-6.3	-12.1	2.1	1.8	0.0	-3.4	-8.5	-24.8	-51.0	
7mm REM. MAG.	Pointed Soft Point	125	0.3	0.6	0.0	-1.7	-4.7	-9.1	2.5	2.8	2.0	0.0	-3.4	-15.0	-34.5	24"
	Pointed Soft Point	150	0.4	0.8	0.0	-1.9	-5.2	-9.9	1.7	1.5	0.0	-2.8	-7.0	-20.5	-42.1	
	Pointed Soft Point	175	0.6	0.9	0.0	-2.3	-6.0	-11.3	2.0	1.7	0.0	-3.2	-7.9	-22.7	-45.8	
30 CARBINE	Soft Point	110	0.9	0.0	-4.5	-13.5	-28.3	-49.9	0.0	-4.5	-13.5	-28.3	-49.9	-118.6	-228.2	20"
30 REM.	Soft Point	170	0.7	0.0	-3.3	-9.7	-19.6	-33.8	2.2	0.0	-5.3	-14.1	-27.2	-69.0	-136.9	24"
30-30 WIN. ACCELERATOR	Soft Point	55	0.4	0.8	0.0	-2.4	-6.7	-13.8	2.0	1.8	0.0	-3.8	-10.2	-35.0	-84.4	24"
30-30 WIN.	Soft Point	150	0.5	0.0	-2.7	-8.2	-17.0	-30.0	1.8	0.0	-4.6	-12.5	-24.6	-65.3	-134.9	24"
	Soft Point	170	0.6	0.0	-3.0	-8.9	-18.0	-31.1	2.0	0.0	-4.8	-13.0	-25.1	-63.6	-126.7	
	Hollow Point	170	0.6	0.0	-3.0	-8.9	-18.0	-31.1	2.0	0.0	-4.8	-13.0	-25.1	-63.6	-126.7	
30-06 ACCELERATOR	Pointed Soft Point	55	0.4	1.0	0.9	0.0	-1.9	-5.0	1.8	2.1	1.5	0.0	-2.7	-12.5	-30.5	24"
30-06 SPRINGFIELD	Pointed Soft Point	110	0.4	0.7	0.0	-2.0	-5.6	-11.1	1.7	1.5	0.0	-3.1	-8.0	-25.5	-57.4	24"
	Pointed Soft Point	125	0.4	0.8	0.0	-2.1	-5.6	-10.7	1.8	1.5	0.0	-3.0	-7.7	-23.0	-48.5	
	Pointed Soft Point	150	0.6	0.9	0.0	-2.3	-6.3	-12.0	2.1	1.8	0.0	-3.3	-8.5	-25.0	-51.8	
	Pointed	150	0.6	0.9	0.0	-2.2	-6.0	-11.4	2.0	1.7	0.0	-3.2	-8.0	-23.3	-47.5	
	Pointed Soft Point	165	0.7	1.0	0.0	-2.5	-6.7	-12.7	2.3	1.9	0.0	-3.6	-9.0	-26.3	-54.1	
	Soft Point	180	0.2	0.0	-1.8	-5.5	-11.2	-19.5	2.7	2.3	0.0	-4.4	-11.3	-34.4	-73.7	
	Pointed Soft Point	180	0.2	0.0	-1.6	-4.8	-9.7	-16.5	2.4	2.0	0.0	-3.7	-9.3	-27.0	-54.9	
	Bronze Point	180	0.2	0.0	-1.6	-4.7	-9.6	-16.2	2.4	2.0	0.0	-3.6	-9.1	-26.2	-53.0	
	Boat-tail Soft Point	200	0.6	0.0	-2.7	-6.0	-12.4	-18.8	2.3	1.8	0.0	-4.1	-9.0	-25.8	-51.3	
	Soft Point	220	0.4	0.0	-2.3	-6.8	-13.8	-23.6	1.5	0.0	-3.7	-9.9	-19.0	-47.4	-93.1	

Cartridge	Wt. (grs.)	Bullet Style														Barrel
30-40 KRAG	180	Pointed Soft Point	0.4	0.0	-2.4	-7.1	-14.5	-25.0	1.6	0.0	-3.9	-10.5	-20.3	-51.7	-103.9	24"
	180	Pointed	0.4	0.0	-2.1	-6.2	-12.5	-21.1	1.4	0.0	-3.4	-8.9	-16.8	-40.9	-78.1	
	220	Pointed	0.6	0.0	-2.9	-8.2	-16.4	-27.6	1.9	0.0	-4.4	-11.6	-21.9	-53.3	-101.8	
300 WIN. MAG.	150	Pointed Soft Point	0.3	0.7	0.0	-1.8	-4.8	-9.3	2.6	2.9	2.1	0.0	-3.5	-15.4	-35.5	24"
	180	Pointed Soft Point	0.5	0.8	0.0	-2.2	-5.5	-10.4	1.9	1.6	0.0	-2.9	-7.3	-20.9	-41.9	
	220	Pointed	0.2	0.0	-1.7	-4.9	-9.9	-16.9	2.5	2.0	0.0	-3.8	-9.5	-27.5	-56.1	
300 H.&H. MAG.	150	Pointed	0.4	0.8	0.0	-2.0	-5.3	-10.1	1.7	1.5	0.0	-2.8	-7.2	-21.2	-43.8	24"
	180	Pointed	0.6	0.9	0.0	-2.3	-6.0	-11.5	2.1	1.7	0.0	-3.2	-8.0	-23.3	-47.4	24"
	220	Pointed	0.3	0.0	-1.9	-5.5	-11.0	-18.7	2.7	2.2	0.0	-4.2	-10.5	-30.7	-63.0	
300 SAVAGE	150	Pointed Soft Point	0.3	0.0	-1.9	-5.7	-11.6	-19.9	2.8	2.3	0.0	-4.5	-11.5	-34.4	-73.0	24"
	150	Pointed	0.3	0.0	-1.8	-5.4	-11.0	-18.8	2.7	2.2	0.0	-4.2	-10.7	-31.5	-65.5	
	180	Pointed Soft Point	0.5	0.0	-2.6	-7.7	-15.6	-27.1	1.7	0.0	-4.2	-11.3	-21.9	-55.8	-112.0	
	180	Pointed	0.4	0.0	-2.3	-6.7	-13.5	-22.8	1.5	0.0	-3.6	-9.6	-18.2	-44.1	-84.2	
303 SAVAGE	190	Pointed	0.9	0.0	-4.1	-11.9	-24.1	-41.4	2.7	0.0	-6.4	-17.3	-33.2	-83.7	-164.4	24"
303 BRITISH	180	Pointed Soft Point	0.3	0.0	-2.1	-6.1	-12.2	-20.8	1.4	0.0	-3.3	-8.8	-16.6	-40.4	-77.4	24"
308 WIN. ACCELERATOR	55	Pointed Soft Point	0.2	0.5	0.0	-1.5	-4.2	-8.2	2.2	2.5	1.8	-0.0	3.2	-15.0	-36.7	24"
308 WIN.	110	Pointed Soft Point	0.5	0.9	0.0	-2.3	-6.5	-12.8	2.0	1.8	0.0	-3.5	-9.3	-29.5	-66.7	24"
	125	Pointed Soft Point	0.5	0.8	0.0	-2.2	-6.0	-11.5	2.0	1.7	0.0	-3.2	-8.2	-24.6	-51.9	24"
	150	Pointed Soft Point	0.2	0.0	-1.5	-4.5	-9.3	-15.9	2.3	1.9	0.0	-3.6	-9.1	-26.9	-55.7	
	180	Soft Point	0.3	0.0	-2.0	-5.9	-12.1	-20.9	2.9	2.4	0.0	-4.7	-12.1	-36.9	-79.1	
	180	Pointed Soft Point	0.2	0.0	-1.8	-5.2	-10.4	-17.7	2.6	2.1	0.0	-4.0	-9.9	-28.9	-58.8	
	165	Boat-tail Soft Point	1.3	0.0	-1.3	-4.0	-8.4	-14.4	2.0	1.7	0.0	-3.3	-8.4	-24.3	-48.9	24"
32-20 WIN.	100	Lead	0.0	-6.3	-20.9	-44.9	-79.3	-125.1	0.0	-11.5	-32.3	-63.8	-106.3	-230.3	-413.3	
	100	Soft Point	0.0	-6.3	-20.9	-44.9	-79.3	-125.1	0.0	-11.5	32.3	-63.6	-106.3	-230.3	-413.3	
32 WIN. SPECIAL	170	Soft Point	0.6	0.0	-2.9	-8.6	-17.6	-30.5	1.9	0.0	-4.7	-12.7	-24.7	-63.2	-126.9	24"
8mm MAUSER	170	Soft Point	0.5	0.0	-2.7	-8.2	-17.0	-29.8	1.8	0.0	-4.5	-12.4	-24.3	-63.8	-130.7	24"
8mm REM. MAG.	185	Pointed Soft Point	0.5	0.8	0.0	-2.1	-5.6	-10.7	1.8	1.6	0.0	-3.0	-7.6	-22.5	-46.8	24"
	220	Pointed Soft Point	0.6	1.0	0.0	-2.4	-6.4	-12.1	2.2	1.8	0.0	-3.4	-8.5	-24.7	-50.5	
338 WIN. MAG.	200	Pointed Soft Point	0.5	0.9	0.0	-2.3	-6.1	-11.6	2.0	1.7	0.0	-3.2	-8.2	-24.3	-50.4	24"
	225	Pointed Soft Point	1.2	1.3	0.0	-2.7	-7.1	-12.9	2.7	2.1	0.0	-3.6	-9.4	-25.0	-49.9	
	250	Pointed	0.2	0.0	-1.7	-5.2	-10.5	-18.0	2.6	2.1	0.0	-4.0	-10.2	-30.0	-61.9	
348 WIN.	200	Pointed	0.3	0.0	-2.1	-6.2	-12.7	-21.9	1.4	0.0	-3.4	-9.2	-17.7	-44.4	-87.9	24"
35 REM.	150	Pointed Soft Point	0.6	0.0	-3.0	-9.2	-19.1	-33.9	2.0	0.0	-5.1	-14.1	-27.8	-74.0	-152.3	24"
	200	Soft Point	0.8	0.0	-3.8	-11.3	-23.5	-41.2	2.5	0.0	-6.3	-17.1	-33.6	-87.7	-176.4	
350 REM MAG.	200	Pointed Soft Point	0.2	0.0	-1.7	-5.1	-10.4	-17.9	2.6	2.1	0.0	-4.0	-10.3	-30.5	-64.0	20"
358 WIN.	200	Pointed	0.4	0.0	-2.2	-6.5	-13.3	-23.0	1.5	0.0	-3.6	-9.7	-18.6	-47.2	-94.1	24"
	250	Pointed	0.5	0.0	-2.7	-7.9	-16.0	-27.1	1.8	0.0	-4.3	-11.4	-21.7	-53.5	-103.7	
375 WIN.	200	Pointed Soft Point	0.6	0.0	-3.2	-9.5	-19.5	-33.8	2.1	0.0	-5.2	-14.1	-27.4	-70.1	-138.1	24"
	250	Pointed Soft Point	0.9	0.0	-4.1	-12.0	-24.0	-40.9	2.7	0.0	-6.5	-17.2	-32.7	-80.6	-154.1	
375 H.&H. MAG.	270	Soft Point	0.2	0.0	-1.7	-5.1	-10.3	-17.6	2.5	2.1	0.0	-3.9	-10.0	-29.4	-60.7	24"
	300	Metal Case	0.3	0.0	-2.2	-6.5	-13.5	-23.4	1.5	0.0	-3.6	-9.8	-19.1	-49.1	-99.5	

TRAJECTORY† 0.0 Indicates yardage at which rifle was sighted in.

Bullet does not rise more than one inch above line of sight from muzzle to sighting in range. (SHORT RANGE)

Bullet does not rise more than three inches above line of sight from muzzle to sighting in range. (LONG RANGE)

CALIBERS	BULLET Wt.-Grs.	BULLET Style	SHORT RANGE 50 Yds.	100 Yds.	150 Yds.	200 Yds.	250 Yds.	300 Yds.	LONG RANGE 100 Yds.	150 Yds.	200 Yds.	250 Yds.	300 Yds.	400 Yds.	500 Yds.	BARREL LENGTH
44-40 WIN.	200	Soft Point	0.0	-6.5	-21.6	-46.3	-81.8	-129.1	0.0	-11.8	-33.3	-65.5	-109.5	-237.4	-426.2	24"
44 REM MAG.	240	Soft Point	0.0	-2.7	-10.0	-23.0	-43.0	-71.2	0.0	- 5.9	-17.6	-36.3	- 63.1	-145.5	-273.0	20"
	240	Semi-Jacketed Hollow Point	0.0	-2.7	-10.0	-23.0	-43.0	-71.2	0.0	- 5.9	-17.6	-36.3	- 63.1	-145.5	-273.0	
444 MAR.	240	Soft Point	0.6	0.0	- 3.2	- 9.9	-21.3	-38.5	2.1	0.0	- 5.6	-15.9	- 32.1	- 87.8	-182.7	24"
	265	Soft Point	0.7	0.0	- 3.6	-10.8	-22.5	-39.5	2.4	0.0	6.0	-16.4	- 32.2	- 84.3	-170.2	
45-70 GOVERNMENT	405	Soft Point	0.0	-4.7	-15.8	-34.0	-60.0	-94.5	0.0	- 8.7	-24.6	-48.2	- 80.3	-172.4	-305.9	24"
	500	Metal Case	0.7	0.0	- 3.3	- 9.6	-19.2	-32.5	2.2	0.0	- 5.2	-13.6	- 25.8	- 63.2	-121.7	24"
458 WIN. MAG.	510	Soft Point	0.8	0.0	- 3.5	-10.3	-20.8	-35.6	2.4	0.0	- 5.6	-14.9	- 28.5	- 71.5	-140.4	24"

Which Shotgun Type For You? 16

Which shotgun is the one for you? That's a question every upland gunner and wildfowler must decide. If you intend to hunt everything with a one-shotgun battery, the question has greater significance than it does to the lucky sportsman with a whole gun rack to fill.

Selection of gauge is relatively easy, particularly when you're considering the purchase of an all-around scattergun. If a single smoothbore is to handle all small game and bird-gunning chores, the obvious choice is the workhorse 12. The wide variety of loads available for this popular gauge makes it right for everything from grouse to geese, ducks to doves. Standard-length 2¾-inch 12-gauge shotshells are available to throw everything from 1⅛ to a full 1½ ounces of lead skyward, with shot sizes ranging from No. 9 "dust" to ooo Buck. And if your gun sports 3-inch chambers, you can add 1⅝- and 1⅞-ounce magnum loads to the list.

Most 20 bores are added as second-gun purchases, although a 20 makes a reasonably good all-around gauge for most upland work and does a fair job on decoyed ducks. The 16, which lacks a 3-inch magnum load, is a bit less versatile but is adequate for most gunning chores.

The big 10 and the small-bore 28 and .410 are specialized gauges with a narrow range of real utility.

But what about shotgun type? Today's sportsman can choose from a variety of action types, ranging from the gas-operated autoloader to the inexpensive break-top single shot. Pumpguns enjoy wide popularity, while the bolt-action smoothbore boasts far fewer fans. Twin-tube aficionados can select a classic side-by-side or a stackbarrel double with its single sighting plane.

The selection is bewildering, and asking another's opinion may not help matters much. Every shotgunner firmly believes *his* pet smoothbore is the best possible choice and can be counted on to defend his selection with missionary fervor.

The fact is, though, every shotgun type has its good and bad points, and shines best for a particular brand of gunning. Too, personal preference plays a large part, and it's hard to argue against subjective thinking.

Let's take a look at the attributes and shortcomings of each basic action type.

Side-by-side double carried with the action open can't fire accidentally.

Semi-Automatic Shotguns

The autoloader is a good example of a shotgun type that shooters tend to be strongly biased either for or against. Early self-loaders not surprisingly earned reputations for contrariness and unreliability. Some blame can be laid at the feet of the paper-hull shotshells used at the time, as these had a tendency to swell when wet. Too, these shells were comparatively fragile compared to modern plastic-bodied hulls, and this caused occasional feeding or extraction problems.

Some owners neglected their recoil-operated autos, and when a certain amount of grit and dirt accumulated, the guns simply quit operating. The fact that these guns were often more expensive than a good slide-action smoothbore made owners of balky models even more unhappy.

If some early autoloaders were unreliable, that era has long since passed. Nearly all the self-loaders on the market today are marvels of engineering perfection, and they can be counted on to function day after day without a hitch. In a shotgun torture test a few years ago, I had the chance to use a new gas-operated auto during a week-long dove hunt in Mexico. I was using Mexican-made ammunition that left a heavy, dirty residue in the gas system of the gun. I and the other writers participating in the endurance test purposely refrained from cleaning our guns for the duration of the hunt. This in spite of the fact that dry, Mexican dust was everywhere and settled in the gun actions along with the powder residue.

Each shotgun digested more than 2,000 rounds of the relatively dirty 12-gauge ammo before any functioning problems appeared. Even then, only an occasional round would fail to fully chamber, and a blow on the operating rod would usually set things right. When we finally did strip the guns down for a thorough cleaning, I was amazed at the accumulation of carbonized gunk. We had to soak the gas system in gasoline and spend an entire evening scrubbing things clean.

While the Browning-designed long-recoil-operated action, still in production after the better part of a century, remains a classic, most self-loading smoothbores sold today feature gas operation. Combustion gasses are bled from the barrel through one or more ports located near the front part of the fore end. These gases force a short-stroke piston back and then exit through a relief valve. The piston, in turn, activates an action rod that transmits this force to a reciprocating breechbolt. The breechbolt travels back, compressing a return spring and cocking the action. As the breechbolt moves rearward, it extracts the empty hull from the chamber, and an ejector stop kicks it clear through the ejection port. Once the action is cocked, the compressed return spring starts the bolt forward once again. The bolt strips a fresh round from the magazine carrier arms and chambers it as the locking bolt cams upward into place. The gun is then ready to fire once again.

The use of modern, lightweight alloys has made today's autoloader much lighter and handier than auto shotguns of an earlier age. Still, many autoloaders sport relatively long barrels, and this in combination with the action length and under-the-barrel magazine often gives them a characteristic muzzle-heavy feel. Pass shooters like this, as they feel it helps smooth the swing when tracking an overhead goose.

In an earlier chapter I mentioned that autoloading shotguns produce less apparent recoil than fixed-breech types. This can be attributed to the fact that the brief span of time needed to cycle the action serves to delay the final jolt to the shooter's shoulder. This spreads the recoil force over several milliseconds, so that the shooter feels a firm push rather than a violent blow. Believe it or not, this makes a big difference in shooter comfort and is one of the primary reasons so many scattergunners swear by the self-loader.

Autoloading shotguns like this Ithaca model 51 help cushion recoil without reducing shot velocity significantly. Today's autoloaders are highly dependable.

Trap and skeet gunners, who may burn up 50 to 100 rounds in the course of a single shoot, find auto shotguns a real aid to higher scores. The recoil from even light target loads has a cumulative effect on a shooter's shoulder, and the auto's lighter recoil helps minimize this effect. Magnum-shooting wildfowlers find this feature even more appealing.

With interchangeable barrels or a variable choke device to give the shooter a variety of choke constrictions, the auto shotgun exhibits a high degree of versatility. It isn't as well balanced or as fast handling as a short-coupled double gun, but it has a lot to offer.

Pump Shotguns

The slide-action or trombone gun shares the versatility of the self-loader and appeals to those who feel more secure with a manually operated firearm. It can be operated almost as fast as the auto, and digests an even wider range of ammunition without adjustment. Magnum-chamber autoloaders usually require a different barrel (with more or larger gas ports) to digest non-magnum fodder efficiently.

In addition, pumpguns are typically less expensive than autoloaders, making them a more affordable choice for budget-minded nimrods. This undoubtedly helps account for the pump's overwhelming popularity in this country. It's a wholly reliable, fast-firing, exceedingly durable firearm that places multiple shots at the hunter's disposal. And it's priced right!

While the pump beats the auto in price comparison, it fails to offer the same shoulder-saving, recoil-buffering action. A 12-gauge magnum pump shooting full-house 3-inch loads tends to kick! That's particularly true with lightweight models, although such guns can be made heavier when magnums are on the menu by adding weights to the hollowed-out channel beneath the buttplate. A recoil pad would be another excellent addition if the gun isn't already so equipped.

Bolt-Action Shotguns

While the trombone gun rates a "best buy" label when compared in price to most other repeaters, the least costly magazine gun on the market is the bolt-action type. While bolt-action rifles make excellent firearms, the same can't be said about bolt-operated scatterguns. These guns are unattractive, ungainly and slow to operate. Bolt-action scatterguns are mostly purchased by young, economy-minded shooters who want a repeater and can afford no other type.

Gas action of this autoloader shows carbon accumulated during a heavy day of firing. Autoloaders must be kept relatively clean to work dependably, although some models survive surprising neglect and keep right on firing.

Single-Shot Shotguns

Of course the least expensive shotgun type is the break-top single shot. While these simple guns offer a lone shot before reloading is necessary, most are streamlined and have at least a degree of appeal. As a matter of fact some of the most costly and sought-after trap guns in the world are high-grade single shots. However, most break-top singles are made to be sold at a very affordable price, and they provide reliability and safe operation. These guns are available in the full range of gauges, and some models are fitted with sized-down stocks for the younger nimrod.

The main drawback of most single-shot field guns is a lack of sufficient weight to help tame recoil. A light 12-gauge single shot can be punishing to shoot, and a recoil pad is a wise investment. Single-barrel one-shooters are also frustrating when two or more birds flush before the gunner, or when that first shot misses!

Double-Barrel Shotguns

That brings us to the double-barrel guns, of which there are two basic varieties: the traditional side-by-side and the stackbarrel, or superposed, shotgun. The term "superposed" has long been associated with Browning's Belgium-made over-under classic shotgun, but it can be applied to any double with the barrels vertically aligned.

All twin-tube shotguns have several features in common. Because they lack a reciprocating bolt action, the double's receiver is several inches shorter, and that makes the entire gun shorter. A double-barrel break-top with 28-inch barrels will measure from 4 to 5 inches shorter overall than a magazine gun in the same gauge and featuring the same tube length.

Shorter length translates into better balance and faster handling. In a twin-tube shotgun, the weight is better distributed between the shooter's hands, which makes for a very lively, highly responsive smoothbore.

Too, nearly all double-barrel shotguns offer an almost instant choice of two different degrees of choke. This feature alone helps make the double one of the most versatile scatterguns around, as the same gun can fill a variety of hunting needs. Typically, the gun is carried with the more-open-choke tube ready to fire first. When one or more birds flush at the shooter's feet, the order of firing is to drop the first bird in close, and then reach out to take the second target at greater distance. If a lone single appears at long range, it takes just a moment to flick the selector and reverse the order of firing.

The more costly doubles feature automatic, selective ejectors which kick the fired hulls free, while merely raising unfired shotshells slightly from their chamber. If both barrels are fired, both empties are ejected when the gun is broken. On less expensive field guns and most target models, simple extractors are used. These lift the shells a half-inch or so from the chambers for removal by hand.

Gunners who prefer classic side-by-side models cite the shallow, graceful profile these guns offer. They also claim that the broad, double-barrel sighting plane helps them get on target faster. Too, the side-by-side double strikes a much shorter arc when the action is opened than do stackbarrel guns.

The side-by-side is *the* choice of the traditionalist, and in some European and English driven-bird shoots may be the only gun that's fully acceptable. At least those guests who show up with cased pairs of high-grade side-mounted double guns are socially one-up on those who bring the newer superposed models. At such affairs, magazine guns are definitely out of place.

Over-under fans find they shoot better with the narrower, single-barrel sighting plane stackbarrel guns provide. A shooter used to a single-barrel pump or autoloader usually prefers the over-under barrel arrangement to the side-by-side double, because he's used to the single-barrel sight picture.

The superposed models are much deeper through the frame, and the fore end is always fuller and provides greater gripping surface than the traditional "splinter" fore end found on many side-by-side guns. Some horizontally aligned doubles do sport full beavertail fore ends, which are exceptionally hand filling.

Stackbarrel smoothbores offer one mechanical advantage over side-by-sides. Because neither barrel rides directly over the centerline in a side-by-side double, as each one is fired there's a certain amount of "left-right" torque generated, which pulls the gun slightly to either side. This isn't a force that most consciously notice, but it's there.

With a stackbarrel double set to fire the more open tube first, the recoil of that first shot is not only centered on the stock, but is low and almost directly in line with that stock. This creates a "straight back" recoil force that is mostly absorbed by the shooter's shoulder without creating any significant muzzle jump to throw the gun off target. This is why the more-open-choke tube is always the lower one in an over-under shotgun.

While side-by-side and over-under adherents may offer numerous, pseudo-scientific arguments defending their choice, that choice is nearly always made on the basis of pure personal taste. Both types make highly versatile, delightful-handling hunting guns.

Barrel Length

As mentioned earlier, both choke and shot size play an important part in shotgun performance, regardless of the type of shotgun used. Contrary to popular opinion, barrel length doesn't significantly affect the velocity of the shot string or the efficiency of the pattern. A short barrel shoots just as hard and far as a longer one.

Barrel length affects shotgun performance by affecting the handling characteristics of the gun. A short-tube gun is faster in the hands than a long-barrel model, while the muzzle heaviness a 30- or 32-inch tube provides helps smooth the swing. A long barrel offers a longer sighting plane, which pass shooters and some other gunners find helpful. A long-barrel gun is also less noisy, but that is seldom a factor considered in the hunting field.

Most shotgun manufacturers offer 26-, 28-, and 30-inch barrel lengths, although all choke

The slide-action shotgun is totally reliable and offers repeat shots without reloading.

combinations may not be available in each. Typically the improved-cylinder barrels are the shortest, while the 30- or 32-inch tubes come in full choke only. The middle-ground 28-inch barrels are usually offered in either full or modified choke. Pumps and autoloaders with interchangeable barrels can usually be ordered with a 20-inch "slug" barrel designed for hunting deer. These tubes come with rifle-type sights and usually feature straight cylinder or improved-cylinder choke constrictions. These make dandy choices for upland hunting, as do police-model riot guns. Many gunners can't appreciate barrels quite that stubby, but they make for lightning-fast handling.

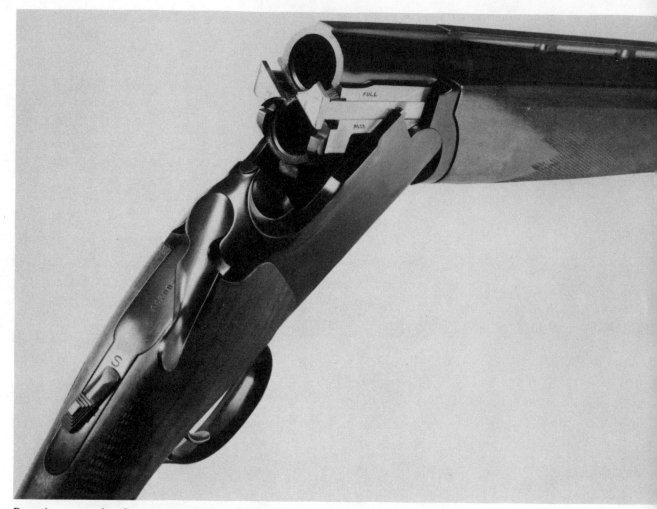

Ruger's over-under shotgun, available in 12 and 20 gauge and with two different chokes, is popular with upland gunners and waterfowlers.

Shotgun Chokes

Six basic choke choices are offered in today's scatterguns: full, which throws 65 to 75 percent patterns at 40 yards; improved modified, which averages 55 to 65 percent; modified—45 to 55 percent; improved cylinder—35 to 45 percent; skeet—30 to 35 percent; and straight cylinder—25 to 35 percent. Some adjustable chokes also offer an "extra full" setting for the absolute maximum in pattern density.

While these are the recognized choke choices, most hunting shotguns sold in America today are offered in only three basic choke configurations: improved cylinder, modified or full. Full choke is best from 35 to 50 yards or so, while modified gives optimum performance from perhaps 30 to 40 yards. Improved cylinder is a 20-to-35-yard proposition. As you can see, there's a certain amount of overlap.

The markings on the barrel may not provide a true indication of a gun's choke performance. With hard, high-antimony shot, plastic shot cups and pellet-protecting granulated-plastic fillers, today's modern ammunition is likely to throw denser patterns from your gun than you might expect. The only way to really know how your gun performs is to pattern it with a variety of shot sizes and loads.

To do this, tape a large (40-inch-square) piece of butcher paper to a large cardboard box (a refrigerator or television shipping container is usually large enough), step off 40 yards and shoot into the center of the paper. Then draw a 30-inch-diameter circle around the largest concentration of pellet holes on the paper. The easiest way to do this is to tie a black marking

Break-top over-under shotgun offers fast handling and easy reloading.

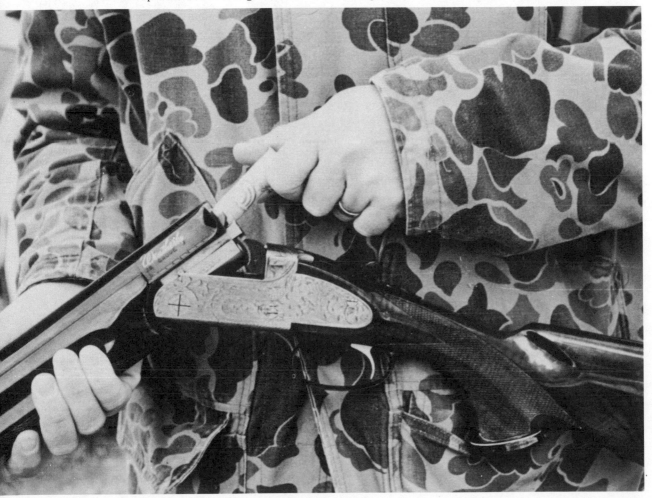

If an over-under or side-by-side double has auto ejectors, empty hulls are thrown clear but unfired shells remain chambered when the gun is broken.

Mossberg, Winchester and other scattergun makers offer interchangeable, built-in choke tubes on certain models.

pen to one end of a 15-inch-long piece of string, tie a thumb tack to the other end, and use this combination as a makeshift compass.

Next, count the pellet holes within the circle (using the felt-tip pen to mark off each hole as it's tallied). Finally, use the chart found in the next chapter to determine how many individual pellets are contained in the load you were using, and divide this number into the number of pellet holes you counted. That will give you the pattern percentage.

It also pays to note how evenly the pattern is distributed within that 30-inch circle. Guns can be very individual when it comes to shot size or load preference, and you may find 7½'s produce a more even pattern than a similar load of 6's, or vice versa.

Adjustable choke devices can be added to the muzzle of any single-barrel shotgun to make the gun more versatile. These gadgets let you turn a knob, or collet, to adjust the choke constriction to your liking. This means you can shoot close-flushing quail or high-flying honkers with the same gun, without bothering to switch barrels in the field.

Adding an adjustable choke device to your gun gives it a bulbous appearance at the muzzle. Some gunners don't care for this from an aesthetic viewpoint, while others feel it serves as a fast-sighting aid. Winchester, Mossberg and other makers offer changeable choke tubes built into the muzzles of some models, and these show no bulge at all. The choke is an integral part of the barrel and can be changed by simply screwing each short choke tube in or out of the muzzle, using a small wrench provided. This is a lot handier than toting extra barrels around with you, as you can carry an extra choke tube or two in your pocket.

Which shotgun is the right one for you? That's a question only you can answer. All shotgun types have their good and bad points, and a case can be made for owning autoloaders, pumps, break-top single shots and double-guns alike. Personal preference plays a large part when choosing a hunting scattergun, and most of us would have it no other way.

Gauges and Shot Sizes 17

A number of years ago I astonished some old bird-shooting buddies by uncasing a skeet-choke 28-gauge pump at the beginning of an Idaho pheasant hunt. The group of us had hunted the area several times before, and nearly everyone toted full- or modified-choke 12's.

November in Idaho is a wind-swept time, and once a big rooster was airborne it didn't take long for him to be carried out of range. Sometimes the wind blew so hard the cock didn't even have to flap his wings. As a result, many shots came at long range. Hence the predilection for tightly choked 12's.

I had been testing some tiny 28's and had a theory I wanted to try. I was willing to waste the first morning of the pheasant hunt testing it, although I had my 12-bore pump tucked away in the trunk in case things didn't work out. The little gun was loaded with Federal's ⅞-ounce fodder throwing No. 7½ shot (this ammunition is no longer manufactured, sad to say). It delivered fine, even patterns with these loads and could be counted on to kill out to maybe 30 yards. Beyond that, it would be hopelessly outclassed.

After all my companions had finished making fun of my armament, I quietly stacked the deck. "Since this little bitty gun is so puny," I said, "I hope you don't mind if I take the close shots as they're offered? I'll have to shoot fast before the birds are out of range."

"Sure, go ahead!" they chortled. "Don't wait for us to shoot, or you won't bring any birds home!"

The way things turned out, I had my limit before the first hour was up—and none of the other gunners had even fired a shot! As often happens early in the season, the birds were holding well, and even those few ringnecks the dogs missed in that heavy cover flushed right at our feet.

Since I had carte blanche to shoot at every bird as it got up, I did just that. The little 28 was so light and fast I was on each bird almost immediately, and each died within 20 yards of the gun. At that range the skeet-choke smallbore was deadly, and the birds never had a chance to gain much velocity. I've never enjoyed such an easy shoot.

By the time my friends caught on, I had my three birds hanging from my belt and was

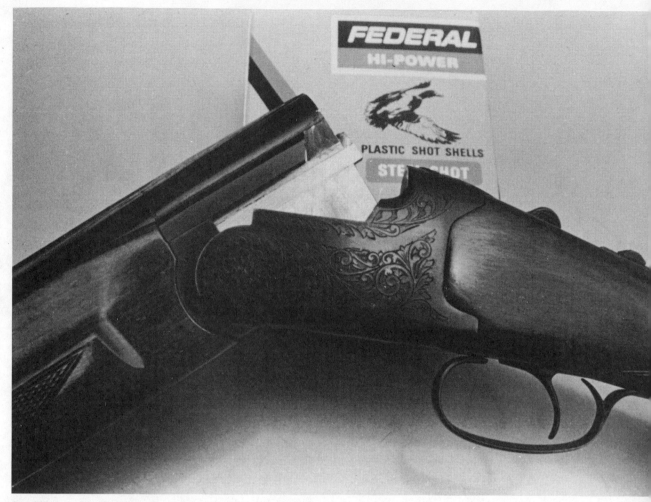

Steel shot will not damage modern, hard-chrome barrels, even in double guns.

carrying my gun unloaded. My grin told them they'd been had, and the next day they insisted I take my turn shooting like everyone else.

Under normal circumstances, a 28-gauge skeet gun isn't a very good choice for hunting the wily ringneck, particularly with the light ¾-ounce loads currently available. But for birds that flush at point-blank range, it certainly does the job.

Choosing the Best Load

The smart hunter does his best to match the loads he chooses to the conditions he expects to encounter. If long shots are expected, heavy loads of large-size shot are called for. For shorter range, lighter charges of smaller shot are a better choice. The same holds true with gauge and choke selection. Large-bore 10's and 12's are the only intelligent choice for super-long shots from a pass-shooting stand, while lighter gauges work fine at typical upland gunning ranges of 40 yards or less. Sub-bore 28's and .410's are strictly close-range propositions. As far as choke is concerned, the longer the distance to the target, the tighter the choke should be, and vice-versa.

Similarly, shot size should be governed by the size and hardiness of the game being hunted, and range should also be considered. While a duck over decoys 30 yards away will readily succumb to a well-placed spread of 6's or even 7½'s, shoot his twin at 45 or 50 yards and you need 4's to do the job right. The larger pellets offer less pattern density at that distance, but the lightweight 7½'s lack the momentum to penetrate and kill. This is why few waterfowlers bother with such small shot. They need a load that will reach out when required. Consequently, most duck hunters use nothing smaller than 6's when it comes to shot size.

Because steel (soft-iron) shot is less dense than lead, steel pellets are lighter than lead shot of the same size. Steel shot also loses momentum faster, and is therefore less effective at long range. For this reason, experienced wildfowlers use steel shot a size larger than they would employ when using lead pellets.

Since large pellets (of either lead or steel) are fewer to the ounce than smaller shot, patterns are thinner. To assure good killing patterns at long range, magnum loads are needed. A magnum shotshell doesn't shoot harder or farther than a standard express load (in fact the shot travels slightly slower to minimize pressure problems). What the magnum does is put a heavier load of pellets in the air. This helps bring pattern density to a more acceptable level when large shot is used.

For instance, a 12 gauge throwing patterns that average 67 percent puts 170 No. 6 shot pellets from a 1⅛-ounce field load into a 30-inch pattern at 40 yards. If the gunner switches to 4's in the same 1⅛-ounce load, only 102 pellets appear in the 30-inch circle at that range. That provides but 60 percent of the coverage the lighter shot gives, which reduces the chances of hitting a bird's vital area. The hunter is faced with a tradeoff. Does he stick with the smaller shot to improve pattern density, knowing that the tinier pellets may not give adequate penetration, or switch to 4's and hope the thinner pattern does the job?

If the shooter is using a gun with 3-inch chambers, he can use a 3-inch magnum load throwing 1⅞ ounces of 4's. Coincidentally, that particular magnum load also puts 170 individual pellets in the 30-inch target at 40 yards, providing the same pattern density the gunner would obtain with the field load of 6's. The hunter gets both adequate coverage and deadly penetration.

While magnums are specially designed for long-range shooting, the brush, or scatter, load is intended for ultra-short range. This specialty ammo lets a tight full- or modified-choke shotgun throw a more open pattern. Both Winchester and Remington once offered this fodder, but I don't see it listed in their latest ammo catalogs. Handloaders can make their own scatter loads by inserting an X-shaped cardboard separator inside the shotshell just before adding the shot to the load. Another approach is to insert a round, cardboard disc every ¼

When using steel shot, pellets a size larger than those used in comparable lead-shot loads should be selected.

inch or so in the shot column. These cardboard separators serve to scatter the shot, even from a full-choke bore. Patterns aren't anything to get excited about, as they tend to be splotchy and uneven. But these loads do spread the shot around in a hurry.

When you purchase factory-loaded shotgun ammo, you may be briefly puzzled by the series of numbers that appear on the box. Here's how to decipher these hieroglyphics. A typical example would be: 12 2¾ 1⅛ 8. The first number in the series refers to gauge; this box contains 12-gauge ammo. The second number refers to shotshell length *after the shell has been fired*. This is the *chamber length* the load was designed for, although as it comes from the box, the shell may measure but 2¼ inches. *Never* attempt to use a 3-inch magnum load in a gun with 2¾-inch chambers. Doing so causes severe pressure problems and is dangerous. Three-inch shotshells *will fit* the shorter chamber length, and it may not be apparent something is wrong until the gun is fired. By then, it may be too late. When the shell opens up, there's not sufficient room for the case mouth, or crimp, to open up. In other words, the 3-inch shell sim-

Shot Patterns and Choke

The amount of constriction in a gun's muzzle is referred to as the "choke." Different amounts of constriction give different sized patterns to a shot charge. For example, a "full choke" forces the shot charge closer together as it leaves the gun, delaying the tendency of the shot to spread. As a result, a "full choke" pattern is effective at greater distances. At close range, however, a "full choke" pattern may be too small to insure being on target, or so dense that the game is ruined.

FULL CHOKE:

Shot pattern effective at long range up to 50 to 55 yards, but too small and too dense at short range.

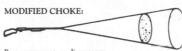

MODIFIED CHOKE:

Best patterns at medium range. 25 to 45 yards.

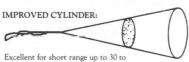

IMPROVED CYLINDER:

Excellent for short range up to 30 to 35 yards, but pattern may be too thin at long range to insure enough hits.

RANGE – Waterfowl hunting usually involves the longest distances for shotgun shooting. The practical range for taking ducks and geese is 35 to 50 yards.

Individual pellets, however, may travel great distances. For safety when hunting, consider these possible extreme ranges.

00 Buck	610 yds.
No. 2 Shot	337 yds.
No. 6 Shot	275 yds.
No. 9 Shot	225 yds.

The Shotshell Selector

Lead shot Unless Indicated "Steel"

	Type of Shell	Size
DUCKS	Magnum or Standard	4, 5, 6 Steel, 2, 4
GEESE	Magnum or Standard	BB, 2, 4 Steel BB, 1, 2
PHEASANTS	Magnum or Standard	5, 6, 7½
QUAIL	Standard or Field Load	7½, 8, 9
RUFFED GROUSE & HUNGARIAN PARTRIDGE	Standard or Field Load	6, 7½, 8
OTHER GROUSE CHUKAR PARTRIDGE	Standard or Field Load	5, 6, 7½
DOVES & PIGEONS	Standard or Field Load	6, 7½, 8, 9
RABBITS	Standard or Field Load	4, 5, 6, 7½
WOODCOCK, SNIPE, RAIL	Field Load	7½, 8, 9
SQUIRRELS	Standard or Field Load	4, 5, 6
WILD TURKEY	Magnum or Standard	2, 4, 5, 6
CROWS	Standard or Field Load	5, 6, 7½
FOX	Magnum or Standard	BB, 2, 4

NO.	9	8½	8	7½	6	5	4	2	1	BB
SHOT SIZES Diameter in inches	.08	.085	.09	.095	.11	.12	.13	.15	.16	.18

BUCKSHOT Diameter in inches	No. 4 .24	No. 3 .25	No. 2 .27	No. 1 .30	No. 0 .32	No. 00 .33	No. 000 .36

SHOT PELLETS PER OUNCE (Approximate)

LEAD		STEEL			
Size	Pellets	Size	Pellets	Size	Pellets
BB	50	6	225	BB	72
2	87	7½	350	1	103
4	135	8	410	2	125
5	170	9	585	4	192

Rifled Slugs Approximate Ballistics

	VELOCITY In Feet Per Second			ENERGY – In Foot/Lbs.			DROP – In Inches		Barrel*
Gauge	Muzzle	50 yds.	100 yds.	Muzzle	50 yds.	100 yds.	50 yds.	100 yds.	Length
12	1600	1175	950	2485	1340	875	2.1	10.4	30
16	1600	1175	950	1990	1070	700	2.1	10.4	28
20	1600	1175	950	1555	840	550	2.1	10.4	26
410	1830	1335	1025	650	345	205	1.6	8.2	26

Shot patterns should be examined for consistency and pellet percentages.

ply runs out of chamber, and the shot jams in the case mouth, raising pressures dangerously. It's okay to fire 2¾-inch loads in guns of the same gauge sporting 3-inch chambers, but not vice-versa.

Just to make things even more confusing, not all shotshell makers follow the same convention in labeling their boxes. If that 2¾ figure isn't followed by "inches" or the abbreviation for inches ("), but "dram eq." or "Dr. Eq.," it refers not to shell length, but to the amount of propellant powder used in the load. To further muddy the waters, this isn't an actual weight measurement, but "dram equivalents." Early black-powder shells were loaded by the dram (¹⁄₁₆ of an ounce), and when the more efficient smokeless powder was introduced the measurement was changed to reflect how much black powder the load was equivalent to!

The third number should have "ounces" or "Oz." printed somewhere near it, as this refers to the weight of the shot load. The final number identifies the size of shot used, in this case, 8's.

As mentioned in earlier chapters, shot size should be matched to the game being hunted. As a general rule, the larger the game, the larger the shot required to do the job. Everyone has his own tastes when it comes to selecting shot size, but there are certain accepted conventions most sportsmen follow in choosing game loads.

For geese, use high-base (high-velocity or "express") or magnum loads of either BB's, 2's or 4's. If steel shot is required, use BB's, 1's or 2's.

Ducks require high-velocity or magnum loads of 4's or 6's, or steel 2's and 4's.

Pheasants are best hunted with high-velocity or magnum 5's, 6's or 7½'s (steel shot is required only for waterfowl, unless you happen to be hunting ringnecks in a marsh where steel pellets are the only legal projectiles).

Rabbits take high-velocity or medium-velocity field loads of 4- to 7½-size shot. Ditto for squirrels.

Foxes and other large varmints hunted with scatterguns require BB's, 2's or 4's, in magnum or high-velocity loads. Wild turkeys are hunted with anything from 2's to 6's, again in magnum or high-velocity loads. When the smaller shot is used, shoot for the head.

Grouse of any species can be hunted with high-velocity or field loads of 5's, 6's or 7½'s.

Quail require high-velocity or field loads of relatively light shot—7½'s or 8's, although some gunners favor 9's in heavy cover.

Doves and pigeons can be hunted with everything from 6's to 9's. I favor 7½'s and 8's.

Woodcock and snipe don't need much killing, and light field loads of 7½'s, 8's or 9's do the job.

Gauges—Large and Small

I've discussed shotgun gauges in several earlier chapters, so let me simply reiterate that the 12 gauge is the most efficient choice available for all waterfowl and upland game. It throws the most shot, and therefore kills best at all ranges. It's the number-one choice, whatever game you hunt with a scattergun.

Gauges and Shot Sizes

An over-under 12 gauge bagged this mixed harvest of furred and feathered game.

The 16 was once America's sweetheart gauge, but when both the 20 and the 12 emerged with 3-inch chambers, the 16 was left out—and soon left behind. The 16 is still a fine choice, but both the standard 12 and the magnum 20 (with 3-inch loads) outperform it. In some scattered locations, particularly in the south and east, the 16 still enjoys enormous local popularity. When 16-gauge doubles were made on honest 16-gauge frames, the 16 made a nice compromise between the 12 and 20. But for many years now 16-gauge guns have been made only on 12-gauge frames, so the weight advantage that once existed (and that made for the fine handling the 16 was once famous for) has sadly disappeared.

The 20 is easily the second most popular scattergun gauge extant, primarily because most guns so chambered are significantly lighter and faster handling than a 12. The 20 throws less shot, but because you can theoretically "get on" a fleeing target faster, this disadvantage is partly nullified. Not for long-range pass shooting.

Skeet shooters have kept the 28 gauge alive. At one time Winchester offered a 1-ounce magnum 28-gauge load, while Federal produced a ⅞-ounce hunting load. No more. The ¾-ounce factory loads currently available are too light for anything but very close-range work. This is our least popular shotgun gauge, although why it ranks far under the .410 bore I'll never know.

The .410 has my nomination for "the most useless shotgun gauge," although the .410 designates bore size in inches and should more properly be called "caliber." The .410 would actually be a 67 gauge, which gives you a better idea of how it stacks up against the 28! It's possible to kill birds with a .410, and that's the kindest thing I can say about it. Only a practiced expert should use a .410 in the hunting field, and even then only if he wants to show off! Large birds like pheasants and ducks are more likely to be wounded than cleanly killed with the .410, which handles $^{11}/_{16}$-ounce shot loads poorly because of the long shot column required. The puny ½-ounce load is too light for serious sporting consideration.

The big 10 gauge is best reserved for geese, long-range ducks and wild turkey. When used with rifled slugs, it makes a formidable defense load against angry grizzlies and would be devastating on deer. Primary disadvantages are gun bulk and weight, and if fired in anything but a Mag-10 autoloader—recoil!

As with the choice of the shotgun itself, scattergun gauge selection is colored heavily by personal preference. But at least here you have some strong ballistic evidence to guide you. The most efficient all-around hunting gauge is the 12, while the 16 and 20 are also capable of turning in fine field performance. The smaller and larger gauges are for specialized shooting and aren't good choices for all-around gunning.

Matching the Gun to the Game

SHOTGUN HUNTING LOAD GUIDE
(Courtesy Federal Cartridge Corp.)

Magnum Shotshells

Gauge	Length Inches	Drams Equivalent	Ounces Shot	Shot Sizes
10	3½	4¼	2	BB, 2, 4
12	3	4	1⅞	BB, 2, 4
12	3	4	1⅝	2, 4, 6
12	2¾	3¾	1½	BB, 2, 4, 5, 6
16	2¾	3¼	1¼	2, 4, 6
20	3	3	1¼	2, 4, 6, 7½
20	2¾	2¾	1⅛	4, 6, 7½

Standard Shotshells

Gauge	Length Inches	Drams Equivalent	Ounces Shot	Shot Sizes
12	2¾	3¾	1¼	BB, 2, 4, 5, 6, 7½, 8, 9
16	2¾	3¼	1⅛	4, 5, 6, 7½
20	2¾	2¾	1	4, 5, 6, 7½, 8, 9
28	2¾	2¼	¾	6, 7½, 8
410	3	Max.	¹¹⁄₁₆	4, 5, 6, 7½, 8
410	2½	Max.	½	6, 7½

Field Load Shotshells

Gauge	Length Inches	Drams Equivalent	Ounces Shot	Shot Sizes
12	2¾	3¼	1¼	7½, 8, 9
12	2¾	3¼	1⅛	4, 5, 6, 7½, 8, 9
16	2¾	2¾	1⅛	4, 6, 7½, 8
20	2¾	2½	1	4, 5, 6, 7½, 8, 9

Steel Shotshells

Gauge	Length Inches	Drams Equivalent	Ounces Shot	Shot Sizes
10	3½	4¼	1⅝	BB, 2
12	3	3½	1⅜	BB, 1, 2, 4
12	2¾	3¾	1¼	BB, 1, 2, 4
12	2¾	3¾	1⅛	1, 2, 4
20	3	3¼	1	4

Gauges and Shot Sizes

Buckshot and Rifled Slugs

Gauge	Length Inches	Drams Equivalent	Shot Sizes
BUCKSHOT			
10	3½	Magnum	4 Buck-54 Pellets
12	3	Magnum	000 Buck-10 Pellets
12	3	Magnum	00 Buck-15 Pellets
12	3	Magnum	1 Buck-24 Pellets
12	3	Magnum	4 Buck-41 Pellets
12	2¾	Magnum	00 Buck-12 Pellets
12	2¾	Magnum	1 Buck-20 Pellets
12	2¾	Magnum	4 Buck-34 Pellets
12	2¾	Max.	000 Buck- 8 Pellets
12	2¾	Max.	00 Buck- 9 Pellets
12	2¾	Max.	00 Buck- 9 Pellets
12	2¾	Max.	0 Buck-12 Pellets
12	2¾	Max.	1 Buck-16 Pellets
12	2¾	Max.	4 Buck-27 Pellets
16	2¾	Max.	1 Buck-12 Pellets
20	3	Magnum	2 Buck-18 Pellets
20	2¾	Max.	3 Buck-20 Pellets
RIFLED SLUGS			
10	3½	Max.	1¾ oz. Rifled Slug
12	2¾	Max.	1¼ oz. Rifled Slug
12	2¾	Max.	1 oz. Rifled Slug
16	2¾	Max.	4/5 oz. Rifled Slug
20	2¾	Max.	5/8 oz. Rifled Slug
410	2½	Max.	1/5 oz. Rifled Slug

Hunting With Handguns 18

Anyone who chooses to hunt with a handgun is placing severe limitations on his game-getting ability. A rifle is much easier to shoot accurately and is effective over much longer range. Rifles are available with much greater killing power, and recoil is less noticeable with either light or magnum loads.

Until a few years ago, magnifying scope sights were available only for rifle use. That gave the rifleman yet another big advantage over his handgunning counterpart. A scope's optics not only help clarify distant targets but also allow the hunter to see well enough to shoot several minutes earlier and later in the day. What's more, a scope's narrow crosshairs obscure the target not at all, permitting the marksman to place his bullets precisely.

Now, several manufacturers offer long-eye-relief handgun scopes, and these are enjoying wide use among hunting handgunners. However, adding a scope to a pistol or revolver doesn't necessarily simplify matters for the sportsman. In the first place, the scope's viewing eyepiece isn't positioned just a few inches from the shooter's eye, but held at arm's length. Consequently, the sight picture is far from the same, and if anything more than 2.5X magnification is used it takes real practice to hold the scope (and gun) steady on target.

While handgun scopes can be highly helpful for 100-plus-yard shooting, these devices make a handgun twice as bulky and harder to carry. For relatively close-range shooting at deer-size game, a magnifying handgun sight can be more of a hindrance than a help. Tradition-minded pistoleers shun handgun scopes, while the new breed of hunting handgunner revels in their use.

Even when factory iron sights are used, the handgun comes off a poor second. Rifle sights are usually less coarse than those used on a pistol or revolver, and they're much farther apart. The longer sighting plane is a real aid to accuracy.

A rifle is braced, through the stock, to the shooter's shoulder, and can easily be steadied against another object, including a portable bipod that attaches directly to the fore end and folds up out of the way when not in use. Shooting a handgun—any handgun—is always less steady.

Leupold-scoped Smith & Wesson magnum is a 100-yard-plus combination in the right hands.

At the most, a hunting handgun is a 150- to 200-yard shooting tool, and most pistoleers must stalk within 75 yards to have a decent chance of dropping their game cleanly. A good rifleman can kill consistently at 300 yards or even farther.

So why do sportsmen elect to hunt with a handgun? For the same reason so many do their hunting with modern versions of the ancient longbow—by making the hunt more difficult and challenging, the experience becomes a lot more fun. Handgunners are very aware of the limitations their equipment places on them, and they are fully prepared to either stalk within good killing range or pass the animal by. If the stalk is unsuccessful, that's all part of the game.

Handguns for Big Game

Some hunters venture to take dangerous game with their handguns, and a few have killed such large, pugnacious carnivores as the Alaskan brown bear. While I admire the courage these nimrods display, I seriously question their intelligence. Most handgunners who tackle dangerous game use a .44 magnum revolver. While a full-house magnum .44 may buck and roar impressively, the ballistic figures put things in better perspective. From a 4-inch barrel, a .44 magnum factory load generates somewhere around 1,050 foot-pounds of muzzle energy.

Handguns make fine hunting firearms if you learn to use them properly and don't try to stretch the range too far.

.357 or .44 magnum revolvers are suitable for hunting deer-size game.

That's with a 180-grain bullet. The 240-grain fodder most hunters favor generates but 740 foot-pounds of point-blank punch.

Some hunters who can't wait to tackle a grizzly with their big .44 would never consider using a pipsqueak .30-30 carbine for the same task. Yet the 170-grain .30-30 factory load produces more than 1,800 foot-pounds of energy at the muzzle, and 1,360 foot-pounds at 100 yards. Out at that distance, the .44 magnum yields less than half as much oomph. You figure it out!

The reason so many handgunners of large bear-size game live to tell the tale is because their licensed guides have better sense than to let them brace a bruin solo with a six-gun. Allowing grizzlies to chew on their clients is bad for business. Generous tips are uncommon after such an experience, and the guide's license may be lifted if he doesn't bring most of his hunters back in one piece.

So the hunter happily totes his pet .44, while the guide backs him up with a .375 Holland & Holland or something of similar persuasive powers. The client will be allowed to get the first shot in (to "kill" the bear), but the guide's follow-up shot won't be far behind, I guarantee. The client is then reassured that his shot(s) would have ultimately proven fatal, but that things might have become a mite *too* interesting if the animal had been allowed to succumb at leisure.

I'm all for hunting any of the horned herbivores with a handgun, as long as the most potent cartridge available is used. Deer can be legally harvested with a .357 magnum in most states, and while not ideal, this will do the job. But for moose and elk, use nothing less potent than a .41 or .44 magnum. Flat-shooting, semi-wildcats such as the .357 and .30 Herrett loads may be even better, and more potent choices are available from custom pistolsmiths who specialize in developing small hand cannons.

While even big deer like elk can be killed with a well-placed .44 magnum slug fired at reasonable range, drilling a moose in not-quite-the-right spot can provide plenty of excitement. Once a moose's attention has been gained and his adrenaline is pumping, he can be dead a long time before the message sinks in. He can be very irksome in the meantime. And an irksome animal that scales three-quarters of a ton and wears sharp-tined antlers 60 inches across makes for lively entertainment, I know from experience.

For deer-size and larger game, the .357 magnum is the least powerful cartridge that should be considered. The .41 and .44 magnums are considerably better for use on trophy deer, and for elk or black bear should be considered minimum.

The single-shot Contender, Sterling X-Caliber and the Merrill Sportsman are all offered in a variety of chamberings suitable for serious hunting. I've already mentioned the .30 and .357 Herrett rounds, but the .45 Winchester Magnum, .35 Remington and .30-30 Winchester cartridges also deserve consideration. J. D. Jones offers Contender "Hand Cannon" conversions chambered for some truly potent bigbores, but these are custom guns unobtainable in most local sporting goods stores. Too, wildcat ammo is used in these guns, and this isn't readily available over the counter.

At the moment, no commercially produced auto pistols are chambered for rounds potent enough for hunting large game, although some prototypes are on the drawing boards and this could change at any time.

Handguns for Small Game

Most handgunning hunters wisely settle for much smaller game. More rabbits and squirrels are taken with a revolver or auto pistol than moose, elk or even whitetail deer. Sportsmen

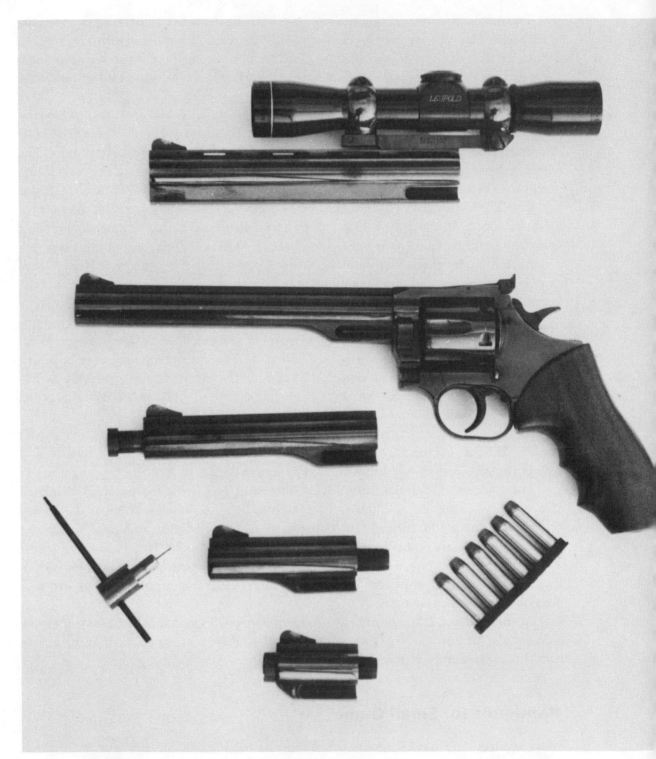

A feature of Dan Wesson's .357 magnum revolver is readily interchangeable barrels of different lengths.

Single-action Interarms Virginian Dragoon in .44 magnum can take deer and black bear.

who lure foxes, coyotes and bobcats to an expertly blown call often favor handguns, while bear and cougar hunters who follow the hounds like the light, handy compactness these guns offer. Long-range killers of ground squirrels, woodchucks and other verminous rodents find added challenge when a scoped handgun is used. Indeed, an ever-increasing number of sportsmen are toting handguns in the hunting field.

Plinkers and hunters of very small game are most likely to carry a .22 rimfire revolver or auto pistol. These are capable of doing a fine job out to 50 yards, and are relatively inexpensive to own and operate. Rimfire ammunition can't be reloaded, but it costs so little that you can shoot all afternoon without damaging the budget. Both recoil and report are very mild, although the noise can damage a shooter's hearing. For prolonged shooting or practice at the range, some form of approved hearing protection is advised.

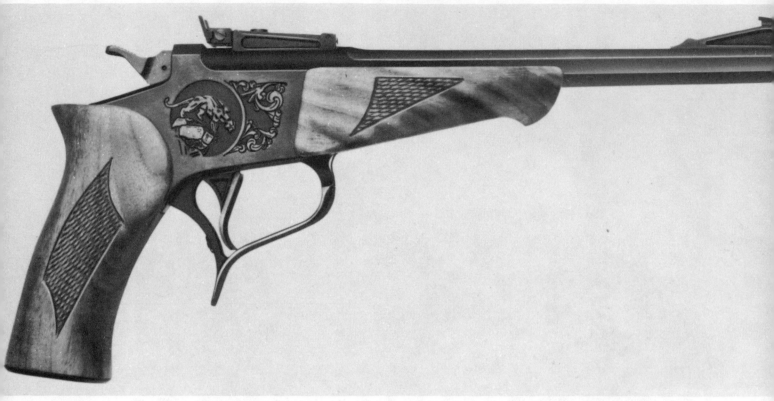

Thompson/Center Contender pistol handles many hunting chores. It's chambered for a variety of rifle and handgun cartridges and can be fitted with a long eye relief scope.

A .22 handgun used for small-game hunting should have a crisp, light trigger pull, and micro-adjustable sights. As a rule, the barrel should be no shorter than 4, or better yet 6, inches (although I own a 3-inch-barrel .22 Charter Arms Pathfinder that's accounted for a number of jackrabbits, cottontails and even squirrels). Lightweight handguns are okay (that Pathfinder weighs just 19 ounces), but heftier models are easier to shoot well. Although scope sights can be mounted on rimfire handguns, they are better suited to centerfire models.

For edible critters like squirrels and cottontails, a .22 works fine. You must get fairly close and place your shots carefully, but a long-rifle rimfire is plenty potent enough in the right hands. And it doesn't destroy much meat.

In jackrabbit country, a .38 Special, 9mm auto or .357 magnum is favored by many desert-bound nimrods. These same selections are good for foxes and other small carnivores when they respond to calling.

Again, a long-barrel handgun works best. Revolvers with barrels ranging from 6 to 8⅜ inches in length or 10-inch single shots offer the greatest accuracy. Long barrels are also easier on the eardrums, although ear plugs or muff-type protectors are required on the practice

Charter Arms' unique .22 auto pistol uses rifle action, accepts interchangeable barrels and can be fitted with a handgun scope.

range. Some gunners even wear such protection when hunting, although it reduces hearing ability in the field.

Autoloaders should likewise sport barrels of reasonable length, and the small pocket-size guns should be avoided. Short-tube models simply lack the needed accuracy for anything but point-blank range. Good, adjustable sights are also required to get the most from a revolver or auto pistol.

Where small game is to be hunted at ranges beyond 50 or 75 yards, a single-shot pistol like the Thompson/Center Contender or Remington XP-100 makes an excellent choice. The bolt-action XP-100 is chambered for the hot, .221 Remington Fire Ball, while the Contender digests a wide variety of varmint loads ranging from the .22 Hornet to the .256 Winchester Magnum.

Even .22 rimfire revolvers are being scoped, as this Harrington & Richardson handgun and scope combination shows.

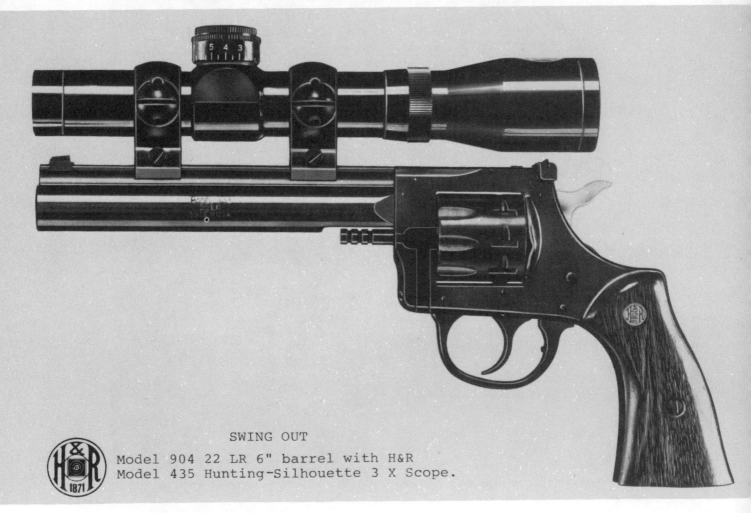

SWING OUT

Model 904 22 LR 6" barrel with H&R
Model 435 Hunting-Silhouette 3 X Scope.

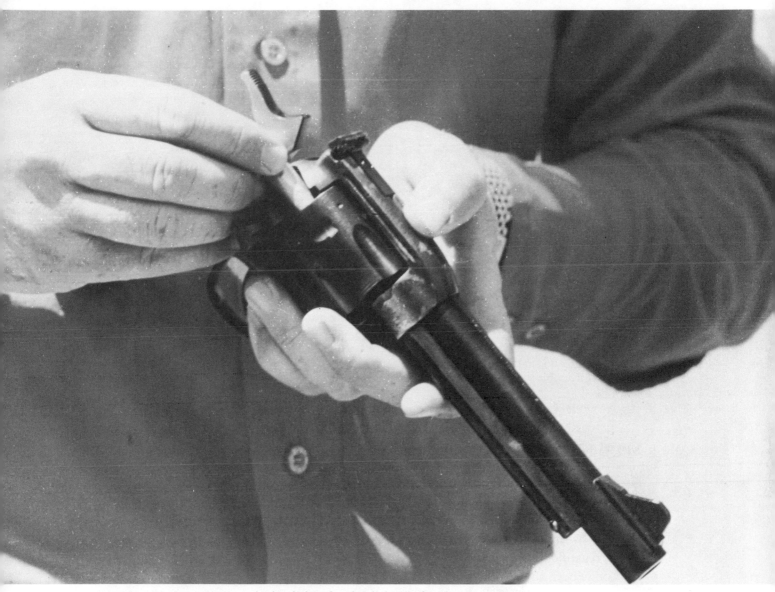

Single-action six-gun must be loaded and unloaded one chamber at a time.

Topped by a good long-eye-relief scope, these handguns are capable of surprising long-range accuracy. The centerfire .22's shoot flat and are plenty potent enough for most varmint-size critters.

Scoped centerfire revolvers can also be relied on to kill farther than iron-sighted wheel-guns, simply because the coarse, iron-sight handguns typically blot out most, if not all, of the target at much past 50 yards. The .357 magnum is probably the premier choice for this kind of varmint shooting, although the larger .41 and .44 magnums also work well.

Both double- and single-action handguns with 6-inch or longer barrels are suitable for hunting, although the double-action is faster to reload.

Single-Action or Double-Action

Both single-action and double-action revolvers are suitable for hunting, and both types have their dedicated fans. The single-action six-gun must be manually cocked by thumbing back the hammer with each shot, while double-action guns can be operated this way or fired repeatedly by simply pulling the trigger. Best accuracy is always obtained in the single-action mode, regardless of model used.

While both single- and double-action guns can be cocked by hand, most single-action revolvers feature a longer hammer fall than the double-action guns have. Because they sport a shorter "lock time," double-action revolvers are slightly more accurate, all other factors being equal, than single-action models. But both handgun types shoot well enough for hunting game of all sizes.

The single-action "thumbbuster" is slower to load and empty than double-action models are, as each cartridge must be poked one at a time from its chamber. All six chambers are emptied with a single stroke of the ejection rod in double-action models, which feature swing-out cylinders. Perhaps the fastest loading-unloading revolver of all is the Harrington & Richardson model 999 break-top .22, a handy 9-shot rimfire that empties by simply breaking the action open.

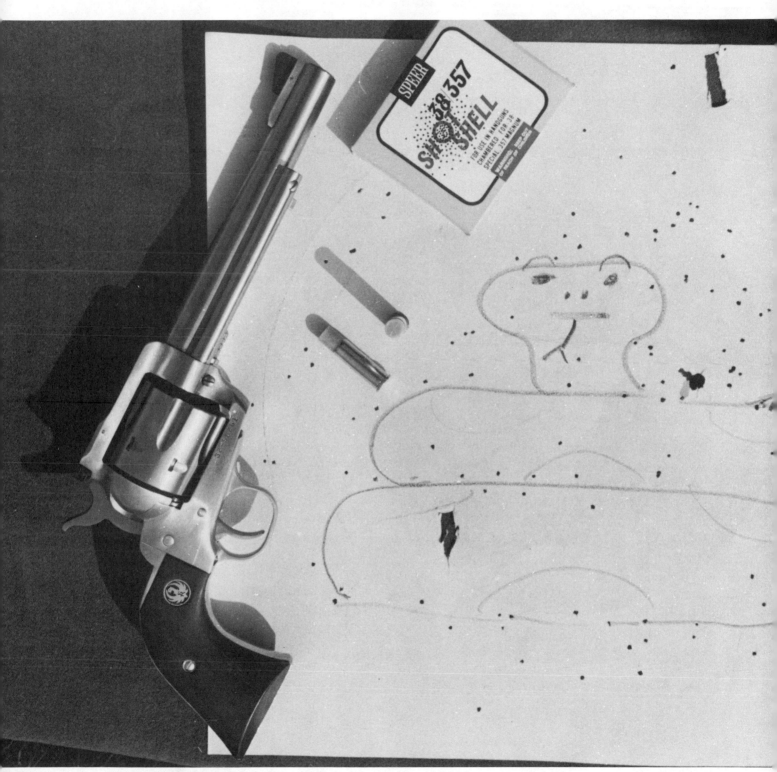

Shot cartridges, for use on snakes and other pests, are available for use in revolvers.

When not in use, a handgun should always be carried in a holster that has a flap, thong, or other device to hold the gun securely in place.

Holsters for Handguns

Hunting handguns should be carried in some kind of protective holster when not in actual use. Hip holsters work fine for guns with barrels up to 6 inches long. For longer tubes, a cross-draw belt rig or shoulder holster is the best choice. A shoulder holster may be the best all-around carrying gear for hunting use, as it keeps the gun high and out of the way.

Tucked under the arm in a shoulder holster, a long-barrel pistol or revolver is less likely to be snagged on branches or brush you pass through. It can be strapped on either over or under a hunting coat, although concealment laws almost make the former mandatory. Finally, a shoulder-slung holster makes the only logical choice for packing a scoped handgun. Specially designed rigs that accommodate scoped pistols or revolvers are available from several manufacturers.

If a scope isn't used, the full-flap holster designs are well worth considering. These completely enclose the handgun, offering valuable protection from the elements until you've located and stalked your game.

HANDGUN BALLISTICS

(Courtesy Remington Arms Co., Inc.)

Caliber	Bullet Wt. Grs.	Bullet Type	Velocity-fps Muzzle	Velocity-fps 50 Yds.	Velocity-fps 100 Yds.	Energy ft-lbs Muzzle	Energy ft-lbs 50 Yds.	Energy ft-lbs 100 Yds.	Mid Range Trajectory Inches 50 Yds.	Mid Range Trajectory Inches 100 Yds.	BARREL LENGTH
22 REM. JET MAG.	40	SP	2100	1790	1510	390	285	200	0.3	1.4	8⅜
221 REM. FIRE BALL	50	PSP	2650	2380	2130	780	630	505	0.2	0.8	10½
25 (6.35mm) AUTO. PISTOL	50	MC	810	755	700	73	63	54	1.8	7.7	2
30 (7.65mm) LUGER AUTO. PISTOL	93	MC	1220	1110	1040	305	255	225	0.9	3.5	4½
32 S.&W.	88	Lead	680	645	610	90	81	73	2.5	10.5	3
32 S.&W. LONG	98	Lead	705	670	635	115	98	88	2.3	10.5	4
32 SHORT COLT	82	Lead	745	665	590	100	79	62	2.2	9.9	4
32 LONG COLT	82	Lead	755	715	675	100	93	83	2.0	8.7	4
32 (7.65mm) AUTO. PISTOL	71	MC	905	855	810	129	115	97	1.4	5.8	4
357 MAG. (Vented Barrel)	110	SJHP	1295	1094	975	410	292	232	0.8	3.5	4
	125	SJHP	1450	1240	1090	583	427	330	0.6	2.8	4

HANDGUN BALLISTICS

(Courtesy Remington Arms Co., Inc.)

Caliber	Bullet Wt. Grs.	Bullet Type	Velocity-fps Muzzle	50 Yds.	100 Yds.	Energy ft-lbs Muzzle	50 Yds.	100 Yds.	Mid Range Trajectory Inches 50 Yds.	100 Yds.	BARREL LENGTH
357 MAG. (Vented Barrel)	158	SJHP	1235	1104	1015	535	428	361	0.8	3.5	4
	158	SP	1235	1104	1015	535	428	361	0.8	3.5	4
	158	MP	1235	1104	1015	535	428	361	0.8	3.5	4
	158	SJHP	1235	1104	1015	535	428	361	0.8	3.5	4
	158	Lead-BC	1235	1104	1015	535	428	361	0.8	3.5	4
9mm LUGER AUTO. PISTOL	115	JHP	1110	1030	971	339	292	259	1.0	4.1	4
	124	MC	1115	1047	971	341	280	241	0.9	3.9	4
380 AUTO. PISTOL	95	MC	955	865	785	190	160	130	1.4	5.9	4
	88	JHP	990	920	868	191	165	146	1.2	5.1	4
38 AUTO. COLT PISTOL	130	MC	1040	980	925	310	275	245	1.0	4.7	4½
38 SUPER AUTO. COLT PISTOL	115	JHP (+P)	1300	1147	1041	431	336	277	0.7	3.3	5
	130	MC (+P)	1280	1140	1050	475	375	320	0.8	3.4	5
38 S.&W.	146	Lead	685	650	620	150	135	125	2.4	10.0	4
	95	SJHP (+P)	1175	1044	959	291	230	194	0.9	3.9	4
	110	SJHP (+P)	1020	945	887	254	218	192	1.1	4.9	4
	125	SJHP (+P)	945	898	858	248	224	204	1.3	5.4	4
	148	TLWC	710	634	566	166	132	105	2.4	10.8	4
38 SPECIAL (Vented Barrel)	158	TLRN	755	723	692	200	183	168	2.0	8.3	4
	158	Lead	755	723	692	200	183	168	2.0	8.3	4
	158	SWC	755	723	692	200	183	168	2.0	8.3	4
	158	MP	755	723	692	200	183	168	2.0	8.3	4
	158	Lead (+P)	915	878	844	294	270	250	1.4	5.6	4
	158	LHP (+P)	915	878	844	294	270	250	1.4	5.6	4
	200	Lead	635	614	594	179	168	157	2.8	11.5	4
38 SHORT COLT	125	Lead	730	685	645	150	130	115	2.2	9.4	6
41 REM. MAG. (Vented Barrel)	210	SP	1300	1162	1062	788	630	526	0.7	3.2	4
	210	Lead	965	898	842	434	376	331	1.3	5.4	4
44 REM. MAG. (Vented Barrel)	240	LGC	1350	1186	1069	971	749	608	0.7	3.1	4
	240	SP	1180	1081	1010	741	623	543	0.9	3.7	4
	240	SJHP	1180	1081	1010	741	623	543	0.9	3.7	4
44 REM. MAG. (Conventional Barrel)	240	Lead-MV	1000	947	902	533	477	433	1.1	4.8	6½
44 S.&W. SPECIAL	246	Lead	755	725	695	310	285	265	2.0	8.3	6½
45 COLT	250	Lead	860	820	780	410	375	340	1.6	6.6	5½
	185	MCWC	770	707	650	244	205	174	2.0	8.7	5
	185	JHP	940	890	846	363	325	294	1.3	5.5	5
45 AUTO.	230	MC-Target	810	776	745	335	308	284	1.7	7.2	5
	230	MC	810	776	745	335	308	284	1.7	7.2	5
45 AUTO. RIM	230	Lead	810	770	730	335	305	270	1.8	7.4	5½

SP-Soft Point   PSP-Pointed Soft Point   MC-Metal Case   JHP-Jacketed Hollow Point   SJHP-Semi-Jacketed Hollow Point
BC-Brass Case   TLWC-Target Lead Wad Cutter   RN-Round Nose   GC-Gas Check   MV-Medium Velocity   MP-Metal Point
WC-Wad Cutter   SWC-Semi-Wad Cutter

Specifications are nominal. Test barrels are used to determine ballistics figures. Individual firearms may differ from these test barrel statistics.

+P Ammunition with (+P) on the case head stamp is loaded to higher pressure. Use only firearms designated for this cartridge and so recommended by the gun manufacturer.

Black-Powder 19 Hunting Guns

It was a frosty September morning, and the sun was still struggling to clear the horizon. The desert sage had a gray-blue cast in the morning light, obscuring half the world in shadow.

There were five of us extending in a loose skirmish line, perhaps 10 yards apart. Our destination was a watering pond a half-mile below us in the shallow, sagebrush-dotted valley. Our quarry? We were "chicken" hunting, which is the name applied locally to sage grouse, those big, 8-pound birds that can boom skyward literally at your feet with no advance warning at all.

Once airborne, the sage grouse makes a large, relatively easy target—if you're not too unnerved to shoot by its sudden, usually unexpected appearance. "Chickens" fly deceptively fast, and if you're slow to mount your gun you may garner only tailfeathers for your trouble.

I'd hunted sage grouse many times before, but this time I wasn't armed with a slick-shucking 12-bore pump or fast-firing auto. Instead, I cradled a 16-gauge black-powder double in my arms loaded with 1⅛ ounces of No. 6 shot and 3 drams of FFg black powder. Percussion caps rested under half-cock hammers on the twin firing nipples. I only had to haul back the hammers to their full-cock position, and the gun was ready to go.

My good friend Ken Turner was toting a single-barrel 12, again a modern replica of a century-old front stuffer. The rest of our party carried up-to-date scatterguns.

Sage grouse are funny birds to hunt. Until you locate a flock, you can comb mile upon fruitless mile of empty desert in search of the elusive birds. Literally walk your legs off. The tyro hunter often does just that, and may never see a sage hen in a full weekend of hard hunting.

But once you find a flock—which may number anywhere from a dozen upwards, sometimes way upwards—it's money in the bank. Mark your discovery well, and you'll be able to return year after year and find birds in almost the very same spot. As long as you hunt during the same time of day, the grouse, which are creatures of habit, are bound to be nearby. Of course there's always the chance of having a flock wiped out by too-severe weather, heavy predation or disease, but this is unlikely. The desert-dwelling grouse are very hardy birds, and generally enough survive each year to guarantee the flock's continued existence.

Percussion muzzleloaders are effective for hunting both large and small game.

The trick is finding a flock in the first place, which seems like an awesome task when hunting strange territory for the first time. But a few calls to local wildlife officers who know the area should put you on the right track. Keeping a few ice-beaded cans of beverage handy in a cooler then guarantees pinpoint information from the inevitable sheepherder once you're in the general vicinity.

We'd hunted these birds before, and knew they came to water at first light. Unless they happened to be in the sage at the other side of the small, 3-acre reservoir, the birds should be close by.

Sure enough, we hadn't walked 200 yards from the trucks before the big, mottled-gray birds exploded from the sage around us. As often happens, we'd walked almost into the center of the flock before any took wing, and I heard one boom up behind me as I thumbed back the hammers and trained my double on a big hen flying straightaway.

I pulled the front trigger, and the bird disappeared in a cloud of white smoke. I took a quick step windward to see the bird falling, its wings collapsed. Then I swung on a second target. This time when the smoke cleared, the bird was still going strong, by now safely out of range. Not that I could have done much about it even if the escaping fowl had been fleeing on foot rather than flapping away at 40 miles an hour. Reloading a front-stuffing scattergun takes a good minute, even if you hurry.

That doesn't make hunting with a muzzleloader any less fun. Whether you're hunting Chinese ringnecks or pintails with a shot-loaded smoothbore or stalking a trophy buck with a powder-and-ball Hawken rifle, using a black-powder percussion arm adds a new dimension to the sport.

A surprising number of sportsmen use a variety of black-powder rifles, pistols and shotguns to hunt both large and small game, and with much greater success than you might imagine. The fact is, these primitive firearms are highly effective when properly used, and if the range is reasonable a muzzle-loading rifleman can make the biggest deer or elk every bit as dead — and as quickly — as the nimrod shooting the latest in high-velocity centerfire rifles. Because the big, lead balls describe a rainbow trajectory and drift readily in the wind, shooting is best done at no more than 100 or 125 yards. But at that distance, a black-powder rifle is deadly!

This muzzle-loading rifle features set triggers for improved accuracy and control.

Calibers for Black-Powder Hunters

For deer-size game, a .45-caliber muzzleloader is adequate, although a .50- or .54-caliber arm is likely a better choice. The heavier projectiles have a lot more punch and offer better penetration. Either a patched, round ball or a heavily lubed Maxi-Ball does the trick.

The .50-plus calibers should also be chosen for hunting elk, moose and the like, for the reasons just mentioned. Some really large animals have been hunted successfully with muzzleloaders, including most African game and big bears.

Lightweight .36-caliber rifles are best for squirrel and rabbit hunting, although some use a .45 or a .44 muzzleloader for such game. Small-bore handguns are also suitable here, with .31 or .36 revolvers heavy favorites. The larger .44 and .45 wheelguns can be similarly employed, but destroy more meat when you're hunting for the pot.

Loading a Muzzleloader

Muzzle-loading revolvers aren't actually loaded from the muzzle, but through the front, open end of the revolving cylinder. First, measure in the powder charge (FFFg or FFFFg black powder, or "P" Pyrodex) and then insert a lead ball of the proper size. Rotate the cylinder until the chamber lines up with the rammer arm, and seat the ball firmly with the rammer. Finally, seal over the ball with commercial bullet lubricant, Crisco or some other vegetable shortening. Fill the front of the chamber *completely* to make sure no sparks can leak through to ignite the charge when one of the other chambers is fired.

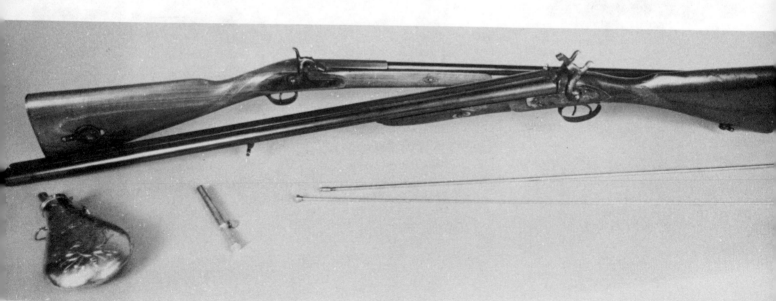

Muzzle-loading scatterguns are fun to use and can be deadly on upland game.

In a like way, load each of the other chambers, leaving one empty to ride under the lowered hammer when the gun is holstered. Add a fresh percussion cap to each nipple, and the revolver is fully loaded and ready to go.

With the exception of the revolver, all black-powder muzzleloaders are fed in pretty much the same way. First the powder charge is emptied down the barrel while the firearm is held with the muzzle up. (Be sure to double check that there's no percussion cap on the firing nipple before you begin the loading process.) This charge varies according to the caliber of the gun and the velocity desired—and a heavy charge may weigh two or even three times as much as a light load. It's possible to overload a muzzleloader, even dangerously, but as a rule black-powder firearms are much more forgiving than breech-loading smokeless-powder rifles are.

Most percussion-gun manufacturers print suggested loads and include this information with the operating instructions. In the field, both black powder and Pyrodex are loaded by volume rather than weight, so once a powder measure is set to throw the desired load you needn't worry about weighing charges. A few grains either way certainly won't affect safety, and may not even be critical to accuracy.

Once the charge has settled to the breech end of the barrel, the lead projectile is inserted in the bore. If a round ball is used, it should be sized slightly smaller than the bore. A cloth patch is then cut and placed beneath the ball as it's introduced to the bore. The patch should be heavy enough to make for a tight fit and large enough to almost completely enclose the ball, leaving only a little lead showing at the top. The patch must be well lubricated with commercial lubricant sold by black-powder suppliers.

If a Maxi-Ball or elongated projectile is used, no cloth patch is needed. Instead, the ball, which is first heavily coated with bullet lubricant, is inserted directly into the bore.

Both patched ball and Maxi-Ball are then seated firmly in the bore with a short, stiff ramrod called a "short starter." This allows the rifling to grip the cloth patch or form the greased lead to its contours. Next, a full-length ramrod is used to push the projectile home. The leaden sphere or slug must rest directly against the powder charge. If a space is left between these components, pressures may build dangerously when the arm is fired. Check the seating by measuring ball depth against barrel length with the ramrod.

Finally, a fresh percussion cap is placed on the nipple, and the rifle is ready to fire. Single-shot percussion pistols are loaded in exactly the same manner.

Some black-powder firearms use an even earlier method of ignition—the flintlock. The same procedure is used for loading, except that a charge of fine priming powder is placed in the pan rather than attaching a percussion cap to the firing nipple.

Loading a black-powder shotgun follows the same basic steps, except a cardboard card or wad is ramrodded down the bore before the shot charge is poured in. A second cardboard disc is seated over the shot to hold the loose pellets in.

When loading a black-powder scattergun, you can use the same, fixed measure to dole out both powder and shot. These components work well when loaded in equal volumes (not equal weight). Good, recommended loads consist of 1¼ ounces of shot for 12-bore guns, 1⅛ ounces for 16 gauges and 1 ounce for 20-gauge smoothbores. Simply load the same amount (again, by *volume*, not weight) of powder down the barrel first. Remember the over-shot wad, or you'll find the pellets rolling down and out the bore when you tip the gun forward.

Since most black-powder shotguns feature wide-open cylinder (or sometimes improved cylinder) chokes, they throw a wide pattern useful to around 30 yards, seldom more. As long as you confine your shooting to that distance or less, muzzle-loading bird guns work fine. Otherwise, these old-time fowling pieces perform every bit as well as their modern, smokeless-powder counterparts. They're slower to reload, but in this day of one- and two-bird limits that's not a serious consideration.

Charcoal-burning scatterguns are a lot of fun for upland gunning use, but a wet-weather duck hunter may have trouble keeping his powder dry on extra-stormy days. If a bit of moisture finds its way inside the firing nipple or under the percussion cap, you end up with a dud load. Water can also run down the barrels, eventually seeping past the shot load and wads. Wet powder doesn't work very well, and a misfire means several minutes of frustrating work with a worm-fitted ramrod to "pull" the useless charge. Then several caps should be snapped on each nipple to dry the interior before the gun is loaded again.

Every muzzleloader owner experiments with several component combinations to find the best load, and each gun may respond differently. As a general rule, a black-powder rifle

This imported Beretta black-powder double is a percussion muzzleloader.

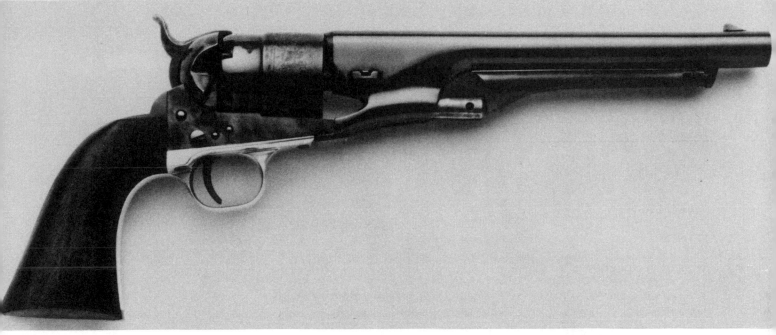

Colt's Model 1860 Army is a modern replica of the classic cap-and-ball revolver. It's suitable for hunting rabbits and other small game.

Military-style musket with adjustable sights is a good game-getter if the range isn't too long.

with a relatively slow rifling twist, one turn in 66 or 72 inches, is best for shooting patched balls, while a faster twist (1:48 or so) is better suited to conical projectiles such as the Maxi-Ball.

The sportsman who hunts with primitive black-powder firearms, or their modern replicas, adds a fresh challenge to an already challenging sport. At the same time, many who first sample this brand of shooting are surprised at how deadly and effective muzzle-loading firearms can be.

BALLISTICS TABLE

(Courtesy Remington Arms Co., Inc., Federal Cartridge Corp., and Winchester-Western)

CALIBERS	BULLET		VELOCITY FEET PER SECOND						ENERGY		
	Wt.-Grs.	Style	Muzzle	100 Yds.	200 Yds.	300 Yds.	400 Yds.	500 Yds.	Muzzle	100 Yds.	200 Yds.
17 REM.	25	Hollow Point	4040	3284	2644	2086	1606	1235	906	599	388
22 HORNET	45	Pointed Soft Point	2690	2042	1502	1128	948	840	723	417	225
	45	Hollow Point	2690	2042	1502	1128	948	840	723	417	225
222 REM.	50	Pointed Soft Point	3140	2602	2123	1700	1350	1107	1094	752	500
	50	Hollow Point	3140	2635	2182	1777	1432	1172	1094	771	529
	55	Metal Case	3020	2562	2147	1773	1451	1201	1114	801	563
222 REM. MAG.	55	Pointed Soft Point	3240	2748	2305	1906	1556	1272	1282	922	649
	55	Hollow Point	3240	2773	2352	1969	1627	1341	1282	939	675
223 REM.	55	Pointed Soft Point	3240	2747	2304	1905	1554	1270	1282	921	648
	55	Hollow Point	3240	2773	2352	1969	1627	1341	1282	939	675
	55	Metal Case	3240	2759	2326	1933	1587	1301	1282	929	660
22-250 REM.	55	Pointed Soft Point	3730	3180	2695	2257	1863	1519	1699	1235	887
	55	Hollow Point	3730	3253	2826	2436	2079	1755	1699	1292	975
243 WIN.	80	Pointed Soft Point	3350	2955	2593	2259	1951	1670	1993	1551	1194
	80	Hollow Point	3350	2955	2593	2259	1951	1670	1993	1551	1194
	100	Pointed Soft Point	2960	2697	2449	2215	1993	1786	1945	1615	1332
6mm REM.	80	Pointed Soft Point	3470	3064	2694	2352	2036	1747	2139	1667	1289
	80	Hollow Point	3470	3064	2694	2352	2036	1747	2139	1667	1289
	100	Pointed Soft Point	3130	2857	2600	2357	2127	1911	2175	1812	1501
250 SAVAGE	87	Pointed Soft Point	3030	2673	2342	2036	1755	1504	1773	1380	1059
	100	Pointed	2820	2467	2140	1839	1569	1339	1765	1351	1017
	60	Hollow Point	2760	2097	1542	1149	957	846	1015	586	317
256 WIN. MAG.	87	Pointed Soft Point	3170	2802	2462	2147	1857	1594	1941	1516	1171
257 ROBERTS	100	Pointed	2900	2541	2210	1904	1627	1387	1867	1433	1084
	117	Pointed Soft Point	2650	2291	1961	1663	1404	1199	1824	1363	999
25-06 REM.	87	Hollow Point	3440	2995	2591	2222	1884	1583	2286	1733	1297
	100	Pointed Soft Point	3230	2893	2580	2287	2014	1762	2316	1858	1478
	120	Pointed Soft Point	3010	2749	2502	2269	2048	1840	2414	2013	1668
6.5mm. REM. MAG.	120	Pointed Soft Point	3210	2905	2621	2353	2102	1867	2745	2248	1830
264 WIN. MAG.	140	Pointed Soft Point	3030	2782	2548	2326	2114	1914	2854	2406	2018
270 WIN.	100	Pointed Soft Point	3480	3067	2690	2343	2023	1730	2689	2088	1606
	130	Pointed Soft Point	3110	2823	2554	2300	2061	1837	2791	2300	1883
	130	Pointed	3110	2849	2604	2371	2150	1941	2791	2343	1957
	150	Soft Point	2900	2550	2225	1926	1653	1415	2801	2165	1649
7mm MAUSER	140	Pointed Soft Point	2660	2435	2221	2018	1827	1648	2199	1843	1533
7mm-08 REM.	140	Pointed Soft Point	2860	2625	2402	2189	1988	1798	2542	2142	1793
280 REM.	165	Soft Point	2820	2510	2220	1950	1701	1479	2913	2308	1805
7mm EXPRESS REM.	150	Pointed Soft Point	2970	2699	2444	2203	1975	1763	2937	2426	1989
284 WIN.	125	Pointed Soft Point	3140	2829	2538	2265	2010	1772	2736	2221	1788
	150	Pointed Soft Point	2860	2595	2344	2108	1886	1680	2724	2243	1830
7mm REM. MAG.	125	Pointed Soft Point	3310	2976	2666	2376	2105	1852	3040	2458	1972
	150	Pointed Soft Point	3110	2830	2568	2320	2085	1866	3221	2667	2196
	175	Pointed Soft Point	2860	2645	2440	2244	2057	1879	3178	2718	2313
30 CARBINE	110	Soft Point	1990	1567	1236	1035	923	842	967	600	373
30 REM.	170	Soft Point	2120	1822	1555	1328	1153	1036	1696	1253	913

FOOT-POUNDS			TRAJECTORY† 0.0 Indicates yardage at which rifle was sighted in. SHORT RANGE — Bullet does not rise more than one inch above line of sight from muzzle to sighting in range.						LONG RANGE — Bullet does not rise more than three inches above line of sight from muzzle to sighting in range.							BARREL LENGTH
300 Yds.	400 Yds.	500 Yds.	50 Yds.	100 Yds.	150 Yds.	200 Yds.	250 Yds.	300 Yds.	100 Yds	150 Yds.	200 Yds.	250 Yds.	300 Yds.	400 Yds.	500 Yds.	
242	143	85	0.1	0.5	0.0	− 1.5	− 4.2	− 8.5	2.1	2.5	1.9	− 0.0	− 3.4	− 17.0	− 44.3	24"
127	90	70	0.3	0.0	− 2.4	− 7.7	−16.9	−31.3	1.6	0.0	− 4.5	−12.8	−26.4	− 75.6	−163.4	24"
127	90	70	0.3	0.0	− 2.4	− 7.7	−16.9	−31.3	1.6	0.0	− 4.5	−12.8	−26.4	− 75.6	−163.4	
321	202	136	0.5	0.9	0.0	− 2.5	− 6.9	−13.7	2.2	1.9	0.0	− 3.8	−10.0	− 32.3	− 73.8	
351	228	152	0.5	0.9	0.0	− 2.4	− 6.6	−13.1	2.1	1.8	0.0	− 3.6	− 9.5	− 30.2	− 68.1	24"
384	257	176	0.6	1.0	0.0	− 2.5	− 7.0	−13.7	2.2	1.9	0.0	− 3.8	− 9.9	− 31.0	− 68.7	
444	296	198	0.4	0.8	0.0	− 2.2	− 6.0	−11.8	1.9	1.6	0.0	− 3.3	− 8.5	− 26.7	− 59.5	24"
473	323	220	0.4	0.8	0.0	− 2.1	− 5.8	−11.4	1.8	1.6	0.0	− 3.2	− 8.2	− 25.5	− 56.0	
443	295	197	0.4	0.8	0.0	− 2.2	− 6.0	−11.8	1.9	1.6	0.0	− 3.3	− 8.5	− 26.7	− 59.6	
473	323	220	0.4	0.8	0.0	− 2.1	− 5.8	−11.4	1.8	1.6	0.0	− 3.2	− 8.2	− 25.5	− 56.0	24"
456	307	207	0.4	0.8	0.0	− 2.1	− 5.9	−11.6	1.9	1.6	0.0	− 3.2	− 8.4	− 26.2	− 57.9	
622	424	282	0.2	0.5	0.0	− 1.5	− 4.3	− 8.4	2.2	2.6	1.9	0.0	− 3.3	− 15.4	− 37.7	24"
725	528	376	0.2	0.5	0.0	− 1.4	− 4.0	− 7.7	2.1	2.4	1.7	0.0	− 3.0	− 13.6	− 32.4	
906	676	495	0.3	0.7	0.0	− 1.8	− 4.9	− 9.4	2.6	2.9	2.1	0.0	− 3.6	− 16.2	− 37.9	
906	676	495	0.3	0.7	0.0	− 1.8	− 4.9	− 9.4	2.6	2.9	2.1	0.0	− 3.6	− 16.2	− 37.9	24"
1089	882	708	0.5	0.9	0.0	− 2.2	− 5.8	−11.0	1.9	1.6	0.0	− 3.1	− 7.8	− 22.6	− 46.3	
982	736	542	0.3	0.6	0.0	− 1.6	− 4.5	− 8.7	2.4	2.7	1.9	0.0	− 3.3	− 14.9	− 35.0	
982	736	542	0.3	0.6	0.0	− 1.6	− 4.5	− 8.7	2.4	2.7	1.9	0.0	− 3.3	− 14.9	− 35.0	24"
1233	1004	811	0.4	0.7	0.0	− 1.9	− 5.1	− 9.7	1.7	1.4	0.0	− 2.7	− 6.8	− 20.0	− 40.8	
801	595	437	0.5	0.9	0.0	− 2.3	− 6.1	−11.8	2.0	1.7	0.0	− 3.3	− 8.4	− 25.2	− 53.4	24"
751	547	398	0.2	0.0	− 1.6	− 4.9	−10.0	−17.4	2.4	2.0	0.0	− 3.9	−10.1	− 30.5	− 65.2	24"
176	122	95	0.3	0.0	− 2.3	− 7.3	−15.9	−29.6	1.5	0.0	− 4.2	−12.1	−25.0	− 72.1	−157.2	24"
890	666	491	0.4	0.8	0.0	− 2.0	− 5.5	−10.6	1.8	1.5	0.0	− 3.0	− 7.5	− 22.7	− 48.0	24"
805	588	427	0.6	1.0	0.0	− 2.5	− 6.9	−13.2	2.3	1.9	0.0	− 3.7	− 9.4	− 28.6	− 60.9	24"
718	512	373	0.3	0.0	− 1.9	− 5.8	−11.9	−20.7	2.9	2.4	0.0	− 4.7	−12.0	− 36.7	− 79.2	24"
954	686	484	0.3	0.6	0.0	− 1.7	− 4.8	− 9.3	2.5	2.9	2.1	0.0	− 3.6	− 16.4	− 39.1	
1161	901	689	0.4	0.7	0.0	− 1.9	− 5.0	− 9.7	1.6	1.4	0.0	− 2.7	− 6.9	− 20.5	− 42.7	24"
1372	1117	902	0.5	0.8	0.0	− 2.1	− 5.5	−10.5	1.9	1.6	0.0	− 2.9	− 7.4	− 21.6	− 44.2	
1475	1177	929	0.4	0.7	0.0	− 1.8	− 4.9	− 9.5	2.7	3.0	2.1	0.0	− 3.5	− 15.5	− 35.3	24"
1682	1389	1139	0.5	0.8	0.0	− 2.0	− 5.4	−10.2	1.8	1.5	0.0	− 2.9	− 7.2	− 20.8	− 42.2	24"
1219	909	664	0.3	0.6	0.0	− 1.6	− 4.5	− 8.7	2.4	2.7	1.9	0.0	− 3.3	− 15.0	− 35.2	
1527	1226	974	0.4	0.8	0.0	− 2.0	− 5.3	−10.0	1.7	1.5	0.0	− 2.8	− 7.1	− 20.8	− 42.7	24"
1622	1334	1087	0.4	0.7	0.0	− 1.9	− 5.1	− 9.7	1.7	1.4	0.0	− 2.7	− 6.8	− 19.9	− 40.5	
1235	910	667	0.6	1.0	0.0	− 2.5	− 6.8	−13.1	2.2	1.9	0.0	− 3.6	− 9.3	− 28.1	− 59.7	
1266	1037	844	0.2	0.0	− 1.7	− 5.0	−10.0	−17.0	2.5	2.0	0.0	− 3.8	− 9.6	− 27.7	− 56.3	24"
1490	1228	1005	0.6	0.9	0.0	− 2.3	−6.11	−11.6	2.1	1.7	0.0	− 3.2	− 8.1	− 23.5	− 47.7	24"
1393	1060	801	0.2	0.0	− 1.5	− 4.6	− 9.5	−16.4	2.3	1.9	0.0	− 3.7	− 9.4	− 28.1	− 58.8	24"
1616	1299	1035	0.5	0.9	0.0	− 2.2	− 5.8	−11.0	1.9	1.6	0.0	− 3.1	− 7.8	− 22.8	− 46.7	24"
1424	1121	871	0.4	0.8	0.0	− 2.0	− 6.3	−10.1	1.7	1.5	0.0	− 2.8	− 7.2	− 21.1	− 43.7	24"
1480	1185	940	0.6	1.0	0.0	− 2.4	− 6.3	−12.1	2.1	1.8	0.0	− 3.4	− 8.5	− 24.8	− 51.0	24"
1567	1230	952	0.3	0.6	0.0	− 1.7	− 4.7	− 9.1	2.5	2.8	2.0	0.0	− 3.4	− 15.0	− 34.5	24"
1792	1448	1160	0.4	0.8	0.0	− 1.9	− 5.2	− 9.9	1.7	1.5	0.0	− 2.8	− 7.0	− 20.5	− 42.1	24"
1956	1644	1372	0.6	0.9	0.0	− 2.3	− 6.0	−11.3	2.0	1.7	0.0	− 3.2	− 7.9	− 22.7	− 45.8	24"
262	208	173	0.9	0.0	− 4.5	−13.5	−28.3	−49.9	0.0	−4.5	−13.5	−28.3	−49.9	−118.6	−228.2	20"
666	502	405	0.7	0.0	− 3.3	− 9.7	−19.6	−33.8	2.2	0.0	− 5.3	−14.1	−27.2	− 69.0	−136.9	24"

CALIBERS	BULLET		VELOCITY FEET PER SECOND						ENERGY		
	Wt.-Grs.	Style	Muzzle	100 Yds.	200 Yds.	300 Yds.	400 Yds.	500 Yds.	Muzzle	100 Yds.	200 Yds.
30-30 WIN. ACCELERATOR	55	Soft Point	3400	2693	2085	1570	1187	986	1412	886	521
30-30 WIN.	150	Soft Point	2390	1973	1605	1303	1095	974	1902	1296	858
	170	Soft Point	2200	1895	1619	1381	1191	1061	1827	1355	989
	170	Hollow Point	2200	1895	1619	1381	1191	1061	1827	1355	989
30-06 SPRINGFIELD ACCELERATOR	55	Pointed Soft Point	4080	3485	2965	2502	2083	1709	2033	1483	1074
30-06 SPRINGFIELD	110	Pointed Soft Point	3380	2843	2365	1936	1561	1261	2790	1974	1366
	125	Pointed Soft Point	3140	2780	2447	2138	1853	1595	2736	2145	1662
	150	Pointed Soft Point	2910	2617	2342	2083	1843	1622	2820	2281	1827
	150	Pointed	2910	2656	2416	2189	1974	1773	2820	2349	1944
	165	Pointed Soft Point	2800	2534	2283	2047	1825	1621	2872	2352	1909
	180	Soft Point	2700	2348	2023	1727	1466	1251	2913	2203	1635
	180	Pointed Soft Point	2700	2469	2250	2042	1846	1663	2913	2436	2023
	180	Bronze Point	2700	2485	2280	2084	1899	1725	2913	2468	2077
	200	Boat-tail Soft Point	2550	2400	2260	2120	1990	1860	2890	2560	2270
	220	Soft Point	2410	2130	1870	1632	1422	1246	2837	2216	1708
30-40 KRAG	180	Pointed Soft Point	2430	2099	1795	1525	1298	1128	2360	1761	1288
	180	Pointed	2430	2213	2007	1813	1632	1468	2360	1957	1610
	220	Pointed	2160	1956	1765	1587	1427	1287	2279	1869	1522
300 WIN. MAG.	150	Pointed Soft Point	3290	2951	2636	2342	2068	1813	3605	2900	2314
	180	Pointed Soft Point	2960	2745	2540	2344	2157	1979	3501	3011	2578
	220	Pointed	2680	2448	2228	2020	1823	1640	3508	2927	2424
300 H.&H. MAG.	150	Pointed	3130	2822	2534	2264	2011	1776	3262	2652	2138
	180	Pointed	2880	2640	2412	2196	1991	1798	3315	2785	2325
	220	Pointed	2580	2341	2114	1901	1702	1520	3251	2677	2183
300 SAVAGE	150	Pointed Soft Point	2630	2311	2015	1743	1500	1295	2303	1779	1352
	150	Pointed	2630	2354	2095	1853	1631	1484	2303	1845	1462
	180	Pointed Soft Point	2350	2025	1728	1467	1252	1098	2207	1639	1193
	180	Pointed	2350	2137	1935	1745	1570	1413	2207	1825	1496
303 SAVAGE	190	Pointed	1940	1657	1410	1211	1073	982	1588	1158	839
303 BRITISH	180	Pointed Soft Point	2460	2233	2018	1816	1629	1459	2418	1993	1627
308 WIN. ACCELERATOR	55	Pointed Soft Point	3770	3215	2726	2286	1888	1541	1735	1262	907
308 WIN.	110	Pointed Soft Point	3180	2666	2206	1795	1444	1178	2470	1736	1188
	125	Pointed Soft Point	3050	2697	2370	2067	1788	1537	2582	2019	1559
	150	Pointed Soft Point	2820	2533	2263	2009	1774	1560	2648	2137	1705
	180	Soft Point	2620	2274	1955	1666	1414	1212	2743	2066	1527
	180	Pointed Soft Point	2620	2393	2178	1974	1782	1604	2743	2288	1896
	165	Boat-tail Soft Point	2700	2520	2330	2160	1990	1830	2670	2310	1990
32-20 WIN.	100	Lead	1210	1021	913	834	769	712	325	231	185
	100	Soft Point	1210	1021	913	834	769	712	325	231	185
32 WIN. SPECIAL	170	Soft Point	2250	1921	1626	1372	1175	1044	1911	1393	998
8mm MAUSER	170	Soft Point	2360	1969	1622	1333	1123	997	2102	1463	993

FOOT-POUNDS			SHORT RANGE Bullet does not rise more than one inch above line of sight from muzzle to sighting in range.						LONG RANGE Bullet does not rise more than three inches above line of sight from muzzle to sighting in range.							BARREL LENGTH
300 Yds.	400 Yds.	500 Yds.	50 Yds.	100 Yds.	150 Yds.	200 Yds.	250 Yds.	300 Yds.	100 Yds	150 Yds.	200 Yds.	250 Yds.	300 Yds.	400 Yds.	500 Yds.	
301	172	119	0.1	0.8	0.0	− 2.4	− 6.7	−13.8	2.0	1.8	0.0	− 3.8	−10.2	− 35.0	− 84.4	24"
565	399	316	0.5	0.0	− 2.7	− 8.2	−17.0	−30.0	1.8	0.0	− 4.6	−12.5	−24.6	− 65.3	−134.9	
720	535	425	0.6	0.0	− 3.0	− 8.9	−18.0	−31.1	2.0	0.0	− 4.8	−13.0	−25.1	− 63.6	−126.7	24"
720	535	425	0.6	0.0	− 3.0	− 8.9	−18.0	−31.1	2.0	0.0	− 4.8	−13.0	−25.1	− 63.6	−126.7	
754	550	356	0.4	1.0	0.9	0.0	− 1.9	− 5.0	1.8	2.1	1.5	− 0.0	− 2.7	− 12.5	− 30.5	24"
915	595	388	0.4	0.7	0.0	− 2.0	− 5.6	−11.1	1.7	1.5	0.0	− 3.1	− 8.0	− 25.5	− 57.4	24"
1269	953	706	0.4	0.8	0.0	− 2.1	− 5.6	−10.7	1.8	1.5	0.0	− 3.0	− 7.7	− 23.0	− 48.5	
1445	1131	876	0.6	0.9	0.0	− 2.3	− 6.3	−12.0	2.1	1.8	0.0	− 3.3	− 8.5	− 25.0	− 51.8	
1596	1298	1047	0.6	0.9	0.0	− 2.2	− 6.0	−11.4	2.0	1.7	0.0	− 3.2	− 8.0	− 23.3	− 47.5	
1534	1220	963	0.7	1.0	0.0	− 2.5	− 6.7	−12.7	2.3	1.9	0.0	− 3.6	− 9.0	− 26.3	− 54.1	24"
1192	859	625	0.2	0.0	− 1.8	− 5.5	−11.2	−19.5	2.7	2.3	0.0	− 4.4	−11.3	− 34.4	− 73.7	
1666	1362	1105	0.2	0.0	− 1.6	− 4.8	− 9.7	−16.5	2.4	2.0	0.0	− 3.7	− 9.3	− 27.0	− 54.9	
1736	1441	1189	0.2	0.0	− 1.6	− 4.7	− 9.6	−16.2	2.4	2.0	0.0	− 3.6	− 9.1	− 26.2	− 53.0	
2000	1760	1540	0.6	0.0	− 2.7	− 6.0	−12.4	−18.8	2.3	1.8	0.0	− 4.1	− 9.0	− 25.8	− 51.3	
1301	988	758	0.4	0.0	− 2.3	− 6.8	−13.8	−23.6	1.5	0.0	− 3.7	− 9.9	−19.0	− 47.4	− 93.1	
929	673	508	0.4	0.0	− 2.4	− 7.1	−14.5	−25.0	1.6	0.0	− 3.9	−10.5	−20.3	− 51.7	−103.9	
1314	1064	861	0.4	0.0	− 2.1	− 6.2	−12.5	−21.1	1.4	0.0	− 3.4	− 8.9	−16.8	− 40.9	− 78.1	
1230	995	809	0.6	0.0	− 2.9	− 8.2	−16.4	−27.6	1.9	0.0	− 4.4	−11.6	−21.9	− 53.3	−101.8	
1827	1424	1095	0.3	0.7	0.0	− 1.8	− 4.8	− 9.3	2.6	2.9	2.1	0.0	− 3.5	− 15.4	− 35.5	
2196	1859	1565	0.5	0.8	0.0	− 2.2	− 5.5	−10.4	1.9	1.6	0.0	− 2.9	− 7.3	− 20.9	− 41.9	
1993	1623	1314	0.2	0.0	− 1.7	− 4.9	− 9.9	−16.9	2.5	2.0	0.0	− 3.8	− 9.5	− 27.5	− 56.1	
1707	1347	1050	0.4	0.8	0.0	− 2.0	− 5.3	−10.1	1.7	1.5	0.0	− 2.8	− 7.2	− 21.2	− 43.8	
1927	1584	1292	0.6	0.9	0.0	− 2.3	− 6.0	−11.5	2.1	1.7	0.0	− 3.2	− 8.0	− 23.3	− 47.4	
1765	1415	1128	0.3	0.0	− 1.9	− 5.5	−11.0	−18.7	2.7	2.2	0.0	− 4.2	−10.5	− 30.7	− 63.0	
1012	749	558	0.3	0.0	− 1.9	− 5.7	−11.6	−19.9	2.8	2.3	0.0	− 4.5	−11.5	− 34.4	− 73.0	
1143	886	685	0.3	0.0	− 1.8	− 5.4	−11.0	−18.8	2.7	2.2	0.0	− 4.2	−10.7	− 31.5	− 65.5	
860	626	482	0.5	0.0	− 2.6	− 7.7	−15.6	−27.1	1.7	0.0	− 4.2	−11.3	−21.9	− 55.8	−112.0	
1217	985	798	0.4	0.0	− 2.3	− 6.7	−13.5	−22.8	1.5	0.0	− 3.6	− 9.6	−18.2	− 44.1	− 84.2	
619	486	407	0.9	0.0	− 4.1	−11.9	−24.1	−41.4	2.7	0.0	− 6.4	−17.3	−33.2	− 83.7	−164.4	
1318	1060	851	0.3	0.0	− 2.1	− 6.1	−12.2	−20.8	1.4	0.0	− 3.3	− 8.8	−16.6	− 40.4	− 77.4	
638	435	290	0.2	0.5	0.0	− 1.5	− 4.2	− 8.2	2.2	2.5	1.8	− 0.0	− 3.2	− 15.0	− 36.7	24"
787	509	339	0.5	0.9	0.0	− 2.3	− 6.5	−12.8	2.0	1.8	0.0	− 3.5	− 9.3	− 29.5	− 66.7	
1186	887	656	0.5	0.8	0.0	− 2.2	− 6.0	−11.5	2.0	1.7	0.0	− 3.2	− 8.2	− 24.6	− 51.9	
1344	1048	810	0.2	0.0	− 1.5	− 4.5	− 9.3	−15.9	2.3	1.9	0.0	− 3.6	− 9.1	− 26.9	− 55.7	
1109	799	587	0.3	0.0	− 2.0	− 5.9	−12.1	−20.9	2.9	2.4	0.0	− 4.7	−12.1	− 36.9	− 79.1	24"
1557	1269	1028	0.2	0.0	− 1.8	− 5.2	−10.4	−17.7	2.6	2.1	0.0	− 4.0	− 9.9	− 28.9	− 58.8	
1700	1450	1230	1.3	0.0	− 1.3	− 4.0	− 8.4	−14.4	2.0	1.7	0.0	− 3.3	− 8.4	− 24.8	− 48.9	
154	131	113	0.0	−6.3	−20.9	−44.9	−79.3	−125.1	0.0	−11.5	−32.3	−63.8	−106.3	−230.3	−413.3	24"
154	131	113	0.0	−6.3	−20.9	−44.9	−79.3	−125.1	0.0	−11.5	−32.3	−63.6	−106.3	−230.3	−413.3	
710	521	411	0.6	0.0	− 2.9	− 8.6	−17.6	−30.5	1.9	0.0	− 4.7	−12.7	−24.7	− 63.2	−126.9	24"
671	476	375	0.5	0.0	− 2.7	− 8.2	−17.0	−29.8	1.8	0.0	− 4.5	−12.4	−24.3	− 63.8	−130.7	24"

CALIBERS	BULLET		VELOCITY FEET PER SECOND						ENERGY		
	Wt.-Grs.	Style	Muzzle	100 Yds.	200 Yds.	300 Yds.	400 Yds.	500 Yds.	Muzzle	100 Yds.	200 Yds.
8mm REM. MAG.	185	Pointed Soft Point	3080	2761	2464	2186	1927	1688	3896	3131	2494
	220	Pointed Soft Point	2830	2581	2346	2123	1913	1716	3912	3254	2688
338 WIN. MAG.	200	Pointed Soft Point	2960	2658	2375	2110	1862	1635	3890	3137	2505
	225	Pointed Soft Point	2780	2572	2374	2184	2003	1832	3862	3306	2816
	250	Pointed	2660	2395	2145	1910	1693	1497	3927	3184	2554
348 WIN.	200	Pointed	2520	2215	1931	1672	1443	1253	2820	2178	1656
35 REM.	150	Pointed Soft Point	2300	1874	1506	1218	1039	934	1762	1169	755
	200	Soft Point	2080	1698	1376	1140	1001	911	1921	1280	841
350 REM. MAG.	200	Pointed Soft Point	2710	2410	2130	1870	1631	1421	3261	2579	2014
358 WIN.	200	Pointed	2490	2171	1876	1610	1379	1194	2753	2093	1563
	250	Pointed	2230	1988	1762	1557	1375	1224	2760	2194	1723
375 WIN.	200	Pointed Soft Point	2200	1841	1526	1268	1089	980	2150	1506	1034
	250	Pointed Soft Point	1900	1647	1424	1239	1103	1011	2005	1506	1126
375 H.&H. MAG.	270	Soft Point	2690	2420	2166	1928	1707	1507	4337	3510	2812
	300	Metal Case	2530	2171	1843	1551	1307	1126	4263	3139	2262
44-40 WIN.	200	Soft Point	1190	1006	900	822	756	699	629	449	360
44 REM. MAG.	240	Soft Point	1760	1380	1114	970	878	806	1650	1015	661
	240	Semi-Jacketed Hollow Point	1760	1380	1114	970	878	806	1650	1015	661
444 MAR.	240	Soft Point	2350	1815	1377	1087	941	846	2942	1755	1010
	265	Soft Point	2120	1733	1405	1160	1012	920	2644	1768	1162
45-70 GOVERNMENT	405	Soft Point	1330	1168	1055	977	918	869	1590	1227	1001
458 WIN. MAG.	500	Metal Case	2040	1823	1623	1442	1237	1161	4628	3689	2924
	510	Soft Point	2040	1770	1527	1319	1157	1046	4712	3547	2640

| FOOT-POUNDS | | | TRAJECTORY† 0.0 Indicates yardage at which rifle was sighted in. | | | | | | | | | | | | | BARREL LENGTH |
| | | | SHORT RANGE Bullet does not rise more than one inch above line of sight from muzzle to sighting in range. | | | | | | LONG RANGE Bullet does not rise more than three inches above line of sight from muzzle to sighting in range. | | | | | | | |
300 Yds.	400 Yds.	500 Yds.	50 Yds.	100 Yds.	150 Yds.	200 Yds.	250 Yds.	300 Yds.	100 Yds	150 Yds.	200 Yds.	250 Yds.	300 Yds.	400 Yds.	500 Yds.	
1963	1525	1170	0.5	0.8	0.0	− 2.1	− 5.6	−10.7	1.8	1.6	0.0	− 3.0	− 7.6	− 22.5	− 46.8	24"
2201	1787	1438	0.6	1.0	0.0	− 2.4	− 6.4	−12.1	2.2	1.8	0.0	− 3.4	− 8.5	− 24.7	− 50.5	
1977	1539	1187	0.5	0.9	0.0	− 2.3	− 6.1	−11.6	2.0	1.7	0.0	− 3.2	− 8.2	− 24.3	− 50.4	
2384	2005	1677	1.2	1.3	0.0	− 2.7	− 7.1	−12.9	2.7	2.1	0.0	− 3.6	− 9.4	− 25.0	− 49.9	
2025	1591	1244	0.2	0.0	− 1.7	− 5.2	−10.5	−18.0	2.6	2.1	0.0	− 4.0	−10.2	− 30.0	− 61.9	
1241	925	697	0.3	0.0	− 2.1	− 6.2	−12.7	−21.9	1.4	0.0	− 3.4	− 9.2	−17.7	− 44.4	− 87.9	
494	359	291	0.6	0.0	− 3.0	− 9.2	−19.1	−33.9	2.0	0.0	− 5.1	−14.1	−27.8	− 74.0	−152.3	24"
577	445	369	0.8	0.0	− 3.8	−11.3	−23.5	−41.2	2.5	0.0	− 6.3	−17.1	−33.6	− 87.7	−176.4	
1553	1181	897	0.2	0.0	− 1.7	− 5.1	−10.4	−17.9	2.6	2.1	0.0	− 4.0	−10.3	− 30.5	− 64.0	20"
1151	844	633	0.4	0.0	− 2.2	− 6.5	−13.3	−23.0	1.5	0.0	− 3.6	− 9.7	−18.6	− 47.2	− 94.1	24"
1346	1049	832	0.5	0.0	− 2.7	− 7.9	−16.0	−27.1	1.8	0.0	− 4.3	−11.4	−21.7	− 53.5	−103.7	24"
714	527	427	0.6	0.0	− 3.2	− 9.5	−19.5	−33.8	2.1	0.0	− 5.2	−14.1	−27.4	− 70.1	−138.1	24"
852	676	568	0.9	0.0	− 4.1	−12.0	−24.0	−40.9	2.7	0.0	− 6.5	−17.2	−32.7	− 80.6	−154.1	24"
2228	1747	1361	0.2	0.0	− 1.7	− 5.1	−10.3	−17.6	2.5	2.1	0.0	− 3.9	−10.0	− 29.4	− 60.7	24"
1602	1138	844	0.3	0.0	− 2.2	− 6.5	−13.5	−23.4	1.5	0.0	− 3.6	− 9.8	−19.1	− 49.1	− 99.5	
300	254	217	0.0	−6.5	−21.6	−46.3	−81.8	−129.1	0.0	−11.8	−33.3	−65.5	−109.5	−237.4	−426.2	24"
501	411	346	0.0	−2.7	−10.0	−23.0	−43.0	−71.2	0.0	−5.9	−17.6	−36.3	−63.1	−145.5	−273.0	20"
501	411	346	0.0	−2.7	−10.0	−23.0	−43.0	−71.2	0.0	−5.9	−17.6	−36.3	−63.1	−145.5	−273.0	
630	472	381	0.6	0.0	− 3.2	− 9.9	−21.3	−38.5	2.1	0.0	− 5.6	−15.9	−32.1	− 87.8	−182.7	24"
791	603	498	0.7	0.0	− 3.6	−10.8	−22.5	−39.5	2.4	0.0	− 6.0	−16.4	−32.2	− 84.3	−170.2	
858	758	679	0.0	−4.7	−15.8	−34.0	−60.0	−94.5	0.0	−8.7	24.6	−48.2	−80.3	−172.4	−305.9	24"
2308	1839	1469	0.7	0.0	− 3.3	− 9.6	−19.2	−32.5	2.2	0.0	− 5.2	−13.6	−25.8	− 63.2	−121.7	24"
1970	1516	1239	0.8	0.0	− 3.5	−10.3	−20.8	−35.6	2.4	0.0	− 5.6	−14.9	−28.5	− 71.5	−140.4	

Index